David Brainerd

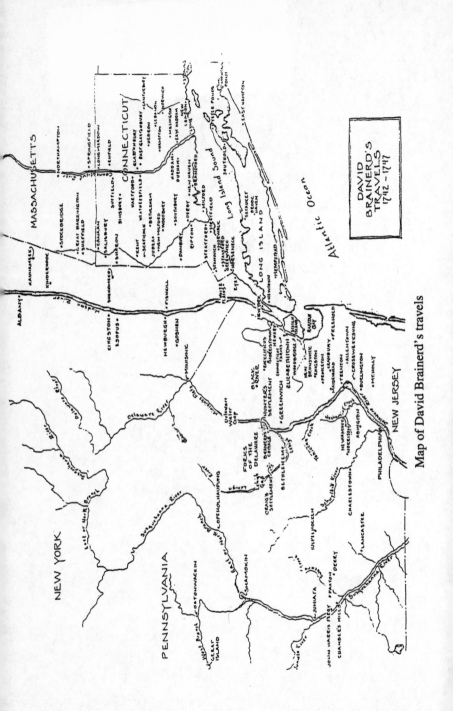

Map of David Brainerd's travels

David Brainerd
Pioneer Missionary to the American Indians

John Thornbury

 EVANGELICAL PRESS

EVANGELICAL PRESS
12 Wooler Street, Darlington, Co. Durham, DL1 1RQ, England

© Evangelical Press 1996
First published 1996

British Library Cataloguing in Publication Data available

ISBN 0 85234 348 5

Printed and bound in Great Britain at the Bath Press, Avon.

Contents

List of illustrations

Preface

'Both Brainerd himself and Edwards's *Life of Brainerd* need to be restored to their central place in American religious history.'

So wrote Joseph Conforti, a professor at Rhode Island College, one of the foremost authorities today on Jonathan Edwards and the school of theology he established. This book is a contribution in that direction.

In a peculiar way my own life has brushed frequently with the subject of this book. My first printed work was an essay on Brainerd, which won a prize and is included in a book on pioneer missionaries. Like him I had some difficulties in college and left prematurely. Unlike Brainerd, however, I did go back and finish. My earliest ambitions in Christian ministry were, like those of Brainerd, in the direction of missions, although this did not come to fruition in my case. I am convinced that my basic temperament is similar to that of the missionary.

When I took up my present place of ministry I was delighted that it was near the scenes of some of Brainerd's most memorable experiences. From my study window I can see Montour Ridge (named after the famous female Indian leader) which slopes down to the banks of the West Branch of the Susquehanna. Under its shadow David Brainerd frequently rode. About four miles east of my home one can stand on Shikellamy Overlook and see the town of Sunbury, site in the mid-eighteenth century of Shamokin, the ancient Indian capital. Here Brainerd preached to the 'drunken and ruffianlike' Delawares ruled over by the chief who has given his name to the bluff.

I am a confessed adherent of the theology and spiritual outlook of David Brainerd, in its leading elements. Like many far greater men before me, I have been inspired, challenged, encouraged and rebuked by his saintly example.

Recently I have been privileged to visit at last some of the places which have been immortalized by Brainerd's awakening ministry. Among these are Crosswicks, the modern corruption of Crossweeksung, where the mighty Indian revival took place; Cranbury, where there is a house in which once Brainerd slept; the Firestone Memorial Library at Princeton University, where the Hebrew lexicon which the Indians bound for Brainerd is housed; the Beinecke Rare Book and Manuscript Library at Yale, where I saw and examined the first portion of the original diary which Brainerd wrote and Jonathan Edwards published; and, last but not least, the little town of Haddam, Connecticut, the place where our hero was born and grew up. It was at Haddam in the Brainerd Memorial Library that I was able to examine the volumes dealing with the Brainerd family history. At all of these places many custodians and librarians, too numerous to mention, have been very courteous and helpful.

I am indebted to many others who have laboured before me for their invaluable research on our subject. Especially helpful, from a historical and critical standpoint, are *Beloved Yankee* by David Wynbeek (1964) and *The Life of David Brainerd* (1985), edited by Norman Pettit. The latter is a volume in the monumental Yale University project of the publication of the *Works* of Edwards. These books, along with the original *Life of Brainerd* by Edwards (my own copy is the 1830 edition edited by Sereno Dwight), have been my primary sources. Finally, I give here my due acknowledgements for copyright material which is cited in my book and listed in the notes.

John F. Thornbury

Introduction

On 28 May 1747 the colonial pastor Jonathan Edwards and his wife Sarah welcomed into their home at Northampton, Massachusetts, a solitary visitor who arrived on horseback. The young man who had come to stay with them looked pale and weak as he climbed down from his mount and ambled up to the door. His possessions were few. He carried with him a saddlebag, containing several books and a few clothes. Almost certainly the whole Edwards family was assembled there to greet the visitor. Not only were Jonathan Edwards and his wife glad to see him, but so were their children, including their seventeen-year-old daughter Jerusha.

The guest at the Edwards home was the twenty-nine-year-old Indian missionary David Brainerd. Worn out by long travels in the wilderness of the Susquehanna region of Pennsylvania, and his body wasted by tuberculosis in its final stages, he had come in the hope of recuperation. The possibility of recovery was slim, but still there was hope. As it turned out, David did not recover from his illness but died in the Edwards home and was buried in the Northampton cemetery. No place seemed as suitable for the frail guest than the Edwards homestead. His parents had been dead for many years. Although he had several brothers and sisters, who had cared for him during his childhood, a strong tie had been

established between Brainerd and the Edwards family. Here a
friendship bonded by several years of fellowship in the common faith of Christ would fill out its earthly course.

By the summer of 1747 Brainerd had already become
something of a celebrity, largely through his success in
preaching among the Indians. An endless stream of visitors,
including prominent people in the religious world, came to see
him at Northampton. Included among them was his brother
John, who had been assigned to replace him at his missionary
station in New Jersey. John brought with him David's personal
diary, which contained an account of his labours among the
Indians. The missionary had meticulously, almost on a daily
basis, detailed his experiences during his four-year appointment among Native American tribes in New York, Pennsylvania and New Jersey. With this document now in his custody, Jonathan Edwards had an opportunity to study it, a
circumstance which proved to be of considerable historical
importance.

The Northampton pastor had many reasons to be interested
in the material in the diary. For one thing, it gave a fascinating
first-hand description and evaluation of the Indian culture.
Also he was intrigued by the personal confessions and theological observations of its author. One of the most shrewd
judges of human character, as well as being a theologian of
considerable repute, Edwards recognized immediately the
biographical value of this material. He knew then, if he had
ever doubted it before, that this young man who was now a part
of his household was an extraordinary Christian. It was obvious to him that others could be instructed, encouraged and
motivated as he had been by reading this diary. Brainerd's
journal simply must be published.

Brainerd's diary was indeed published and the Christian
world has never been the same since. Of all the writings of
Edwards — and they included essays on science (composed

when he was young), sermons and theological treatises —
none has been printed more often than *The Account of the Life
of David Brainerd*. This volume very soon became a religious
classic and a kind of model for missionary enterprise. As
Thomas H. Johnson has stated, it was 'the first biography
written in America that achieved wide notice abroad as well as
at home'.[1] The fact that Yale University included an edited
version of this book in its monumental edition of the Works of
Edwards, which as I write is still in the process of publication,
shows how even the academic world regards the *Life of
Brainerd* as a significant literary work of this period in
American history.

The impact of Brainerd's life on the evangelical missionary
vision and Christian enterprise generally has been incalcu-
lable. Consider the galaxy of worthy names directly involved
in missions who have acknowledged a great debt to the reading
of Brainerd's life: John Wesley, Francis Asbury, William
Carey, Henry Martyn, Robert Morrison, Samuel Marsden,
Christian Frederick Schwartz, David Livingston, Robert
Murray M'Cheyne, Andrew Murray, Sheldon Jackson and
Jim Elliot, to name just a few. These people alone were
influential in spreading the gospel message to North America,
India, Australia, Africa, New Zealand, Palestine, Alaska and
South America.

The student of Brainerd's life must never forget, however,
that it was his mentor Jonathan Edwards who first saw its value
and made it available to the public. While acknowledging
minor flaws in the memoirs and the human frailties of the
young minister, he believed that in many ways the Indian
missionary was a model of devotion to God, theological
insight and personal commitment to evangelism. Also
Brainerd's *Journal* served Edwards' purpose of illustrating
the distinction between true religion and the many counterfeits
which had sprung up in the wake of the First Great Awakening.

Brainerd's memoirs were, of course, originally a very private piece of writing. He certainly never intended that eyes other than his own — Edwards himself excepted — should look upon them. Like any diary they contain confessions, attitudes and spontaneous outbursts which would surely have been restated, or withheld altogether, if the author had known the place history would afford them. Yet we can be grateful that, thanks to Edwards, Brainerd's thoughts were not consigned to oblivion. Not only do they give us valuable insights into the social and spiritual conditions of the times, but they reveal the depth of faith and commitment to which a sovereign God can bring one of his servants.

I take my place among the numerous biographers of Brainerd, believing that a modern study of this remarkable man, whose life was so short but so full, is in order. I fervently hope that the end sought so passionately by both Edwards and Brainerd, the glory of God, will be served by the following pages. I am sure that this will be the case if this life of Brainerd can be instrumental in the encouragement of God's people in their pilgrim walk, if it can effectively illustrate the power of the gospel upon human hearts, and if many believers, or even a few, are inspired by it to dedicate their lives to evangelism and missions.

1.
The contest for North America

The opening of the eighteenth century found three great European powers locked in a monumental struggle for territorial expansion. The prize was North America, the vast resources of which were only beginning to be appreciated by Europeans. When disputes about this coveted land could not be settled by debate and negotiation, open hostilities broke out on land and sea.

First to stake their rights to North America were the Spanish. It was under the sponsorship of the joint Spanish sovereigns Ferdinand and Isabella that Christopher Columbus sailed the Atlantic in 1492 and landed at an island in the Bahamas which he named San Salvador. By 1600 Spain had conquered almost the whole of coastal Southern America except Brazil. Their explorers travelled far into the interior of what is now the United States and were able actually to claim the whole of the Carolina coast for their homeland. They built forts and missions all up and down the Atlantic seaboard.

The French too were busy asserting their authority wherever possible. The initial explorers from France were fishermen and traders. Because of their interest in trading they were able to establish a good relationship with the Indians, especially in Nova Scotia and in the area of the Gulf of St

Lawrence. The first permanent settlement was Quebec, followed by a palisaded stronghold at Montreal. Most of the early French colonists were religious — secular priests and Jesuits, who helped to bring the Catholic religion and French culture to Canada.

English expeditions to the new world began with the voyage of John Cabot to the north-east coast of Newfoundland, five years after the initial discovery of Columbus. Under Queen Elizabeth I (1533-1603) the English Crown embarked on a spiritual and material expansion of enormous proportions, although these efforts did not result in any final territorial acquisitions. But in the early seventeenth century permanent settlements were established at Jamestown, Plymouth and Massachusetts Bay. These locations were originally trading posts which were owned by English merchants and settled by their employees.

The wars with Spain strengthened British economic and military prowess. Improved methods of navigation helped Britain to inaugurate its long reign as undisputed sovereign of the high seas. At the Treaty of Utrecht, which was negotiated in 1714, Britain measurably improved her influence as a power broker in the political struggles of Europe. This treaty ended the wars of Louis XIV and had important ramifications across the Atlantic. Through it Britain not only gained control of the valuable naval bases in the Balearic Isles and Gibraltar in the Mediterranean, but also obtained Nova Scotia, Newfoundland and the Hudson's Bay territory from France and Spain.

But despite their losses at the Peace of Utrecht, the French were hardly immobilized. They were able to build a mighty defensive fort at Louisbourg on Cape Breton Island which served as a check to British ambitions against Quebec. Even more importantly, French explorers penetrated unhindered throughout the fertile valleys of the Mississippi and Ohio.

There they engaged in a brisk fur trade and erected defensive forts. In 1718 they built New Orleans to control the traffic on what would become known later as the 'father of waters'. Up to this point the French had resisted all attempts to throw them out of the New World. They continued to expand their settlements and, in many cases, outcompete their rivals.

The King of England during the second quarter of the eighteenth century, the period in which David Brainerd lived, was George II, the only son of George I. He was meticulous and scrupulous in petty details of his court but relatively weak in political and international affairs. It is said that he made war in the spirit of a drill-sergeant, and he economized his income with the minute regularity of a clerk. More forceful was his wife Caroline, to whose wise but unobtrusive counsels he often yielded. Two powerful leaders during his reign were Robert Walpole, the leader of the Whig party, and the fiery orator William Pitt.

Several factors combined to propel Britain towards war in the 1730s. The radical patriots, the 'Francophobes', and the king himself were looking for any cause of aggression in order to secure more territory. There had been also long-standing manœuvres by leading London merchants to acquire a monopoly of the West Indian slave trade. (Disputes about trade rights had been at the bottom of the war against France and Spain in Queen Anne's reign a generation earlier.) Especially lucrative was the right to supply slaves to the Spanish colonies. When Philip V, the new King of Spain in 1700, awarded the coveted *assentio* (exclusive trade rights) to the French Guinea Company, the ire of the English merchants was aroused. The Peace of Utrecht had given the *assentio* back to Great Britain for thirty years. But when the South Sea Company, to which the British Government granted trade rights, carried out its business in a manner unacceptable to the Spanish government, they began to stop and search British ships in Spanish territorial waters. This once again caused open hostilities between Britain and Spain.

The pros and cons of war were debated for several years in the British Parliament. The war hawks were led by William Pitt, who was a forceful and influential speaker. Walpole pleaded eloquently for peace, but in vain. In October 1739 George II declared war against the Spanish government and another wave of deadly European conflicts had begun. When Walpole heard the bells ringing in celebration he warned, 'They are ringing their bells; they will be wringing their hands soon.'

George II quickly used the war as an occasion to attack St Augustine, the vital fort on the Southern Atlantic coast of America. So far as the New England colonies were concerned, the most important consequence of the conflict with Spain was the widening of the war to include hostilities against the French. In March 1745 an expeditionary force was organized to assault the vital French fortification on the Atlantic Coast of Cape Breton, Louisbourg.

Taking a leading interest in this expedition was the Governor of Massachusetts, William Shirley, who had been appointed to this office in 1741. He built up a lucrative patronage machine which created a powerful motive for raising money for a war. Provision contracts for favoured merchants, recruiting fees and naval expenditures were exceedingly profitable for Shirley and his friends. As is so often the case in such ventures, the cry of 'defence' proved to be an effective patriotic cloak for what in fact was based on pure greed.

Although this war against the French fortress has been described as 'one of the maddest schemes in the history of modern warfare', it worked. The Yankee force which pitched camp before the so-called 'impregnable' fortress refused to follow the customary rules of eighteenth-century warfare. In 1745 the French governor, worn out and frustrated by such antics, surrendered. Ironically the fort was returned three years later to France, with the British government agreeing to pay the expenses. A few months before the fortress of Louisbourg was returned to France, the colonial missionary David Brainerd died in the home of Jonathan Edwards.

2.
Puritanism

In order to understand David Brainerd it is necessary to understand his mentor and spiritual father, Jonathan Edwards. And in order to appreciate Jonathan Edwards one must have at least a rudimentary acquaintance with the vastly influential movement known as Puritanism. Who were the Puritans? Vindictive, witch-hunting bigots? Supersaints? Creators of the American Constitution? Militant religious warriors, bent on conquest like the Spanish conquistadors?

Unless one can dismiss those who take the Bible seriously as bigots, that epithet is not a proper designation for them. Saints they were, no doubt, though you would never have heard them claim this for themselves. The unique American system of government owes more to them than many are willing to admit, although they were dead by the time the revolutionary war was fought. They were warriors, of course, but their time and energy were spent primarily in theological and spiritual struggles, not the strife of arms.

The Pilgrims who settled New England in the 1620s and 1630s were first and foremost Christians seeking a place to worship in freedom. They believed that the Protestant Reformation was a mighty work of God and were in agreement with the teachings of its pioneer teachers, particularly Calvin. But they believed that the Church of England, while making a good start, had not gone far enough. They regarded the bishops, vestments and rituals of the Anglican Church as the leftovers of Catholicism. The Puritans wanted to restore the church to its primitive purity, as delineated in the New Testament.

Perhaps one of the chief excellences of Puritanism was its attempt to combine correct theology with real Christian godliness. They avoided a dead, doctrinaire intellectualism on the one hand and a formless subjective mysticism on the other. They strove to think right, believe right, speak right and live right. Dr D. Martyn Lloyd-Jones, who himself was once referred to as 'that formidable neo-puritan' says, '"Essential Puritanism" was not primarily a preference for one form of church government rather than another; but it was that outlook and teaching which put its emphasis upon a life of spiritual, personal religion, an intense realization of the presence of God, a devotion of the entire being to him.'[1]

It is easy, looking on the Puritan movement from the vantage-point of the twentieth century, to be critical. Their concepts of religious liberty were not matured. They were overly zealous in seeking to purge their communities of dissident groups. And yet these noble people brought with them a remarkably broad and progressive concept of the state, considering their European roots. The *Body of Liberties* adopted in 1641 and the *General Fundamentals* of Plymouth Colony embodied many of the safeguards that are cherished today. They defended and promoted such ideas as free elections, trial by jury, representative taxation and the right of due process of law. The Puritans admittedly did not envisage a land of unlimited religious pluralism such as the United States ultimately developed into. The state they set up was, however, an important step in that direction. As Samuel Eliot Morison says, 'Puritanism was a cutting edge which hewed liberty, democracy, humanitarianism, and universal education out of the black forest of feudal Europe and the American wilderness.'[2]

The Puritans were *a worshipping people*. The God of the

Hebrew prophets and the New Testament apostles was their God. They knew God as one who counts the stars and calls them all by name. Their God was one who has his way in the whirlwind and the storm and makes the clouds the dust of his feet. Theirs was the God of Paul — of whom, through whom and to whom are all things. They conceived of Jesus as the triumphant Saviour who appeared to the writer of Revelation in resplendent glory. They worshipped him as Creator, Redeemer and Preserver of his people. They trusted him as the God of holiness, providental oversight and infinite grace to the worst of sinners.

The Puritans were *a Bible-loving people*. They were not content to scan the Scriptures superficially but resolved instead to plumb their depths. They placed great value on both the Old and New Testaments, which they regarded as equally inspired. Were they right on every point of interpretation? Certainly not; indeed they often disagreed among themselves. But they were serious and intense seekers for truth. The rich imagery of Scripture was woven into the warp and woof of their common conversation, and the noble ethics of the New Testament were worked out in their daily lives.

The spiritual leaders of the Puritans were *men of learning*. Practically all their pastors were classical scholars and were thoroughly familiar with the original languages of Scripture. They were also versed in the philosophies of the ancient Greeks as well as the theologians of the early church and the Middle Ages. They had constantly before them the exegetical and theological writings of Luther, Calvin, Melanchthon and Knox, as well as those of such English reformers as Bradford, Foxe, Coverdale and Becon.

Contrary to popular prejudice, they were not haters of culture and pleasure. While making the Bible their standard of faith and practice, they *appreciated aesthetics*. They eschewed, of course, the ancient pageantry of Catholic worship, which they considered as incorporating sensual barriers to direct communication with God. But they achieved beauty in music, silverware, furniture and architecture. The Puritans believed that the harmonies of life were not divorced from, but were reflective of, the infinite skills of their Creator and Saviour.

For the Puritan *all life was sacred.* He believed that the mind was the greatest gift of God to humanity and sought to store it with all the information available. Unlike the Manichean ascetics he accepted the body as good, though it can become the instrument of sinful motives and desires. H. L. Mencken once described Puritanism as 'the haunting fear that someone, somewhere, may be happy'. There is not a shred of truth in this. It is not happiness which is wrong in the eyes of the Puritan, but the attempt to find it in carnal pleasure and ambition. It is when human desire and ambition go beyond the absolute boundaries of God's will that they need to be suppressed. J. I. Packer says, 'Seeing life whole, they integrated contemplation with action, worship with work, labour with rest, love of God with love of neighbour and of self, personal with social identity, and the wide spectrum of relational responsibilities with each other, in a thoroughly conscientious and thought-out way.'³

The Puritan work-ethic is famous. It was Hugh Peter of Salem who said that 'An hour's idleness is as bad as an hour's drunkenness.' The hunter, the woman who bears children, the merchant, the politician and the soldier are all employed in worthy occupations. Such an outlook would be a good model for the societies of our own 'post-modern' day which are drowning in debt, in part because of liberal welfare policies which often make people dependent rather than self-reliant. Of course, tilling of the soil absorbed the energies of most colonial families. Fully nine-tenths of the settlers of New England were farmers. Even those who were by occupation sailors, fishermen, fur traders, or merchants had to spend a good deal of their time cultivating farms or plantations.

The peculiar direction that Puritanism took in the settlements of North America can be ascribed primarily to the
limitless opportunities afforded by the New World freedoms
and the adaptations demanded by geography. Unrestricted by
a powerful state church, or indeed separated as they were from
the English crown itself, they caught a vision of building a
'holy commonwealth'. They strove to establish communities
where family ties were honoured, the Sabbath consecrated
and, above all, where God's sovereignty was practically
acknowledged. It took time, of course, and the efforts of
radicals like Roger Williams to teach the people of the New
World that religion cannot be forced. We can, however,
admire the vision and motives, if not the methods, of the
founders of New England.

Jonathan Edwards, who first pastored a Congregational
church at Northampton, Massachusetts, embodied the best of
the American Puritan spirit. He worked as a pastor among the
Indians for a brief time and served as the President of Princeton
University. A precocious youth, he mastered foreign languages, studied philosophy and wrote surprisingly abstruse
essays while still in his teens. The relative quiet of his rural
pastorate gave him the time to reflect on the meaning of life
and the nature of 'the Supreme Being'. In Edwards' philo-
sophical theology Puritanism flowered and matured. His studies on the nature of the human will and the meaning of
Christian experience remain classics in Reformed thought.
Edwards' concepts on the nature of faith and regeneration not
only made an impact on his immediate followers, like David
Brainerd and Joseph Bellamy, but inspired several generations.

It was into a Puritan home and a Puritan culture that David
Brainerd was born. The ideals of this movement challenged
him, its hopes nourished him and its spirit directed him.

3.
The Native Americans

The relationship of the Europeans who eventually dominated North America with the Indian tribes has been a major source of interest and investigation, not to mention entertainment, in the United States. For many years, largely through the influence of Hollywood films, a negative stereotype of these people prevailed. Today they are riding a crest of great popularity; in fact some sociologists have suggested that the beliefs of the North American Indians may even save decadent Western society. An article in *Parade* magazine (11 October 1992) opines, 'After years of urging Native Americans to take up our ways, however, we may have at last realized that it's time to take up theirs.'[1]

It is easy, of course, for modern Americans to forget how much they owe to the original inhabitants of their land. Unquestionably the Indians have played an important part in the nation's history. Since the land was once theirs, those of us who now live in it must say candidly that we owe our country itself to them. We need also to admit that the manner in which it was taken from them is not to the credit of the European settlers. Virtually every conceivable measure was used, at one time or another, to push them away from their homelands. The Indians were victims of deceit, theft, force of arms, treachery and murder, not to mention the corrupting influences of strong drink which the whites brought.

Few Americans realize when they sit down to a sumptuous meal how many of their essential food products were derived from the Indians. Among the foods unknown to the world before Columbus discovered America are corn, string beans, limas, peppers, potatoes, squash, tomatoes, peanuts and tapioca. We can also thank the Indians for methods of agriculture, turkeys, tobacco, rubber, root beer, lacrosse and sign language.

Without the help of friendly Indians the early colonists would never have survived. They taught the Europeans how to hunt and endure the hardships of the wilderness. Some of the ideas for the formation of the US federal government were derived from the Iroquois alliance. Their literature, music and art have enriched American culture. Hundreds of mountains, streams and cities have been named after them.

But from a spiritual standpoint the Native Americans were primitive and pagan. Although there were a great variety of distinctive beliefs and practices among the various tribes, they can all be classified under the general category of 'animism'. In animism there is a hierarchy of gods, although some animists believe that there is one god who is more powerful than the others. There were even traditions that this god was involved in creation. Some of the tribes worshipped living or dead human beings whom they regarded as gods or saviours. Others gave reverence to the sun and the other planets. One common idea was that the sun and the moon were brother and sister and lived in an incestuous relationship.

For the Native American the world was one inhabited by many spirits. Trees, rivers, animals, stones and men could be indwelt by the souls of spirits, some of whom were good and some were evil. It was, however, to the latter that the Indians primarily devoted their attention. Many of the elaborate and almost comical tribal rituals were designed to ward off, trick, or counteract in some way the demon spirits. One common practice was to don a grotesque mask and dance, shriek and gesture wildly, the intention being to scare away the feared spirits. Sometimes sacrifices were made to appease the gods. The concept of God as a loving and caring Father was unknown. The god is always to be feared, avoided and placated.

For the most part the Native American believed in life after death. A tribe which depended on securing wild game would naturally conceive of heaven as a place where there would be boundless wild life and fish available. Many, like the modern New Agers, believed in reincarnation. The ghosts of departed loved ones came back to earth, visited their old friends and tribesmen and, in certain situations, communicated with the living. During the death rituals the deceased were usually buried with their garments, ornaments, weapons and utensils, along with food and water to sustain them in their journey to the world beyond.

Practically every tribe had its medicine men, priests, shamans and witch doctors. These leaders were greatly feared and respected. They were for the most part of the higher intellectual order. Some of them evidently possessed hypnotic powers and claimed to be able to read minds. To the Indian the term 'medicine' did not refer merely to a remedy for disease. It implied an available cure, but also included magic, witchcraft, spiritualism, dreams, prophecies, visions, or anything suggestive of the mysterious or supernatural. Among the medicine man's resources were fetishes, charms, magic and all sorts of hocus-pocus. Drugs were also used, sometimes with actual curative properties but also simply for their hallucinogenic effects.

The Indians lived in a world of fantasy and superstition. They were wont to see in everything some occult or supernatural influence or meaning. In their unscientific world many things which are simple to us were attributed to spirits and devils, all of which had a profound influence on life. They made decisions based on myths, legends and folklore, some of which was incredibly far-fetched. No warrior would have gone to a battle or hunt without a talisman or charm. Often bits of hair, feather, beaks of birds, fingernails, seeds and bones were bound together into a ball and carried everywhere. This gave a hunter confidence in any enterprise.

From the earliest days of the European settlers hostilities with the Native Americans were an ever-present reality. This is hardly surprising, given the way some of them were treated. Columbus is alleged to have summoned hundreds of them to a feast at Santo Domingo. When the unsuspecting Indians were surrounded, in this defenceless and helpless situation, the Spaniards turned loose their half-starved, savage hounds on them. As Columbus and his men watched, the shrieking, terrified men and women were torn to pieces.[2]

In New England the natives naturally began to compete with the colonists for the land and game. Their sacred lands invaded, their friendships betrayed and their trust violated, the Indians fell with merciless vengeance on settlers whenever possible. To meet the Indian peril all the colonies made provision for a supply of arms and for the drilling of the citizen body into defensive militia.

But the flood of emigrants moved like a resistless tide against the natives, whose lands continued to shrink throughout the eighteenth and nineteenth centuries. In the Pequot War of 1637, carried on by Connecticut with a few men from Massachusetts and a number of Mohegan allies, the Pequot nation was overthrown. The most resourceful Indian of this period was the Wampanoang sachem, King Philip, who hated the white man as much as any and was superior to all in generalship. In 1675-1676 he headed up several Indian invasions during which not a few towns in Massachusetts were burned and their inhabitants were massacred. Such assaults kept the settlers in a state of terror. But in August 1676 the great chief Philip who had menaced New England for a year was slain by his own race and, effectively, the Indian uprising was crushed.

After the fall of Philip the Indians in Massachusetts, Rhode Island and Connecticut lingered for a century and a half as as a steadily dwindling remnant. Cut off from their natural culture and interests, they were unable to thrive simply as wards of the government and occupants of reservations. After a century and a half they ceased to exist as a people.

The more militant of the Indians had been driven west by the time of David Brainerd's ministry in the 1740s. The settlements in New York, New Jersey and Pennsylvania frontiers enjoyed, for the most part, peaceful relations with the colonial government. In fact the evangelistic efforts of the Christians had resulted in several communities of 'Praying Indians'. In 1675 they were estimated to be about four thousand. Unfortunately the subjugated Indians tended to decline culturally through their adoption of the customs of the whites. They typically became incurably slothful, idle, drunken and often hopelessly in debt. It was to such natives that David Brainerd was sent to minister.

4.
The Great Awakening

Notwithstanding the noble intentions of the first Pilgrims to establish a holy Christian commonwealth, sincere religious devotion was far from universal in the succeeding generations. Most of the early settlers came out of ambition and desire for material success rather than to serve God. They were, to be sure, an adventuresome breed: intelligent, determined and courageous. But they were not always godly by any means. It is estimated that in the early colonial days hardly a fifth of those in Massachusetts were professed Christians.

In the beginning of the eighteenth century the spiritual ideals of the Pilgrims had been largely forgotten and serious theological and moral decline had set in. The well-springs of piety that had flowed freely in an earlier generation had run nearly dry. Ardent devotion had given way to self-satisfaction and indifference. Historians generally acknowledge that pre-occupation with politics and personal security characterized this period. Drunkenness and debauchery were common. Even the ministers were not immune from the general apostasy. In the 1730s Governor Sharpe of Maryland cited cases among the clergy of 'scandalous behaviour', 'notorious badness,' 'immoral conduct' and 'abandoned and prostituted life and character'. Such epithets could easily have applied to the New England clergy.

Cotton Mather, whose opinions deserve great respect, gave a shockingly negative assessment of the religious situation in 1704: 'It is confessed by all who know anything of the matter … that there is a general and horrible decay of Christianity, among the professors of it… The modern Christianity is too generally but a very spectre, scarce a shadow of the ancient. Ah! sinful nation. Ah! children that are corrupters; what have your hands done? … So notorious is this decay of Christianity that whole books are even now and then written to inquire into it.'[1]

The churches seemed to be filled largely with nominal Christians who gave no evidence of regeneration. Part of the reason for this, no doubt, was the compromise of the biblical standards for participation in the church ordinances. The earlier Puritans required that those who were admitted to the Lord's Supper must give evidence of being genuinely converted. Later leaders receded from this standard and adopted the position that persons baptized in infancy who were not scandalous in life should not be excluded. The teachings of Solomon Stoddard on the 'Halfway Covenant' continued the corrupting influence. He taught that the sacraments should be taken by the unconverted and this would assist them in their pursuit of a relationship with God. This policy filled the churches with baptized pagans. Easy standards of church membership are always symptomatic of a backslidden church.

The moral corruption of the individuals who made up the rank and file of the churches was not the only problem. A liberal form of Arminianism was in vogue. It was thought that the unconverted could carry on a series of works preparatory to conversion which would more or less guarantee their acceptance with God. There was much self-satisfaction and security but little dependence upon God. The masses had no consciousness of the strict and holy requirements of the law of God and deluded themselves into thinking that as long as they did their best they had nothing to fear.

If a smug self-confidence characterized the churches, the educational institutions were plagued with arrogant scepticism. Joseph Tracy in his *History of the Great Awakening* said that 'The English universities at that time were little else than learned dens of infidelity and dissipation.'[2] Already the deism of the Continental 'Enlightenment' was beginning to infect the upper classes of New England, a trend which culminated in the French Revolution, with its violent reaction against all authority, especially religious. America was desperately in need of a spiritual awakening. Without such a movement a breakdown of the social order seemed likely. The dark clouds of divine wrath seemed to be hovering over the colonies, ready to burst forth with a torrent of judgement.

Then, suddenly, things began to change. Here and there the Spirit of God began to move mightily in the churches. It is generally acknowledged that the beginnings of the First Great Awakening were in the Dutch Reformed Churches in the semi-wilderness of the Raritan valley. The primary instrument was T. J. Frelinghuysen (1691-1747), who became pastor of the Dutch people in the vicinity of the present city of New Brunswick, New Jersey. He found the population in this newly and sparsely settled county to be formally religious but void of real spiritual life. Although he was often insulted, ridiculed and even attacked in the civil courts, he fearlessly preached the necessity of the new birth and the emptiness of mere nominal religion. Under his preaching large numbers were converted, including many prominent people and some notorious sinners. He once said, 'I would rather die a thousand deaths than not preach the truth.'

Another revivalist during this period was the fiery Irishman Gilbert Tennent (1703-1764). A graduate of his father's Log College at Neshaminy, Pennsylvania, he had been encouraged by the success of Frelinghuysen to embark on a course of evangelism. A silvery-tongued orator with long flowing hair, he burst upon such towns as New Haven and Boston with the fury of Elijah the Tishbite. His most famous sermon was 'The Danger of an Unconverted Ministry', which had been published by Benjamin Franklin in Philadelphia. Gilbert, like his less famous brother William (1673-1747), was convinced that many of the ministers were devoid of spiritual life. With devastating bluntness, he referred to the New England clergy as 'caterpillars who were laboring to devour every green thing'. Under such withering verbal fire many were angered but others came under conviction and were converted.

The two greatest human instruments in this revival, however, were the English evangelist George Whitefield (1714-1770) and the colonial pastor Jonathan Edwards (1703-1758). The former was, unquestionably, one of the premier evangelists in the history of the Christian church. D. M. Lloyd-Jones said that he was the greatest preacher that England has ever produced.[3] E. C. Dargan, in his *History of Preaching*, states, 'The history of preaching since the apostles does not contain a greater or worthier name than that of George Whitefield.'[4]

Whitefield was a man of entire devotedness to God, indomitable zeal and intense compassion for his fellow men. Along with these spiritual qualities he was blessed with magnificent talents as a public speaker. Benjamin Franklin, who considered him a personal friend, though unwilling to submit to the gospel he preached, often went to hear him simply for the pure pleasure of listening to his captivating oratory. He described Whitefield as having 'a loud and clear voice, and articulated his words so perfectly that he might be heard and understood at a great distance, especially as his auditors observed the most perfect silence'.[5] Once while listening to him speaking from the court-house steps in Philadelphia Franklin calculated by gradually stepping back away from the preacher that he could be heard by 30,000 in the open air.

George Whitefield

The Old Court-House, Philadelphia. When Whitefield preached from
the balcony of this building Benjamin Franklin estimated the size of the
crowd by walking as far away as the preacher's voice could be heard.

Whitefield preached the message of the Puritans uncompromisingly and passionately. His primary themes were the desperate depravity of human nature, the absolute necessity of regeneration and justification by faith. On the question of election he was a Calvinist, agreeing with a strict interpretation of the Thirty-Nine articles of the Church of England, to which he belonged all his life.

The English evangelist first came to America in 1738 in connection with the founding of an orphanage in Georgia. During his visit the next year he preached up and down the Eastern Seaboard to huge crowds of people. These meetings had a powerful moral impact on the community. Watson, in his *Annals of Philadelphia*, stated that after Whitefield preached to 15,000 people on Society Hill, 'The dancing school was discontinued and the ball and the concert rooms were shut up as inconsistent with the gospel.' The *Gazette* of the day said, 'The change to religion here is altogether surprising, through Whitefield's influence. No books sell but religious, and such is the general conversation.' Benjamin Franklin confirmed this appraisal of the power of the revival. He said, 'It was wonderful to see the change soon made in the manners of our inhabitants. From being thoughtless or indifferent about religion, it seemed as if all the world were growing religious, so that one could not walk through the town in an evening without hearing psalms sung in different families of every street.'[6]

Edwards experienced similar revival blessings while pastoring the Congregational Church in Northampton, Massachusetts. Shortly after he became pastor he began to protest against the prevailing ignorance of the people and preached on themes such as original sin, justification by faith and the sovereignty of God. These messages were not delivered with studied oratorial effect or flamboyance, but in simple and quiet dignity. In the winter of 1734-1735 many became very distressed about their spiritual condition.

In his *Narrative of Surprising Conversions* he describes what happened in his church: '... the Spirit of God began extraordinarily to set in and wonderfully to work among us... Presently ... a great and earnest concern about the great things of religion and the eternal world became *universal* in all parts of the town, and among persons of all degrees and of all ages. The noise among the *dry bones* waxed louder and louder; all other talk but about spiritual and eternal things was soon thrown by... The only thing in their view was to get the kingdom of heaven, and everyone appeared pressing into it. The engagedness of their hearts in this great concern could not *be hid*, it appeared in their very countenances. It was then a dreadful thing amongst us to lie out of Christ, in danger every day of dropping into hell . . . and the work of *conversion* was carried on in a most astonishing manner, and increased more and more. Souls did, as it were, come by flocks to Jesus Christ.'[7]

In a town of 1,400 inhabitants Edwards received about 100 into membership before one communion and sixty at another. A transformation took place in the appearance of the town: 'It was a time of joy in families on account of salvation being brought unto them; parents rejoicing over their children as new born, and husbands over their wives, and wives over their husbands. The goings of God were then seen in His sanctuary, God's day was a delight and his tabernacles were amiable. Our public assemblies were then beautiful; the congregation was alive in God's service ... every hearer eager to drink in the words of the minister ... the assembly in general were, from time to time, in tears while the Word was preached; some weeping with sorrow and distress, others with joy and love, others with pity and concern for the souls of their neighbors.'[8]

This flame of revival which was first ignited in Northampton spread to other towns.

As we shall see in time, the missionary to the Indians, David Brainerd, was a product, spiritually speaking, of this powerful movement which swept through New England, the Middle States and the colonies on the South-Eastern Seaboard. The strengths of this movement, as well as some of its weaknesses, permanently affected his life.

5.
Growing up in Haddam

Between 1634 and 1635 a group of Massachusetts Puritans, prompted partly by personal and partly by political motives, decided to move south and establish a new settlement in the fertile Connecticut valley. Among these were Thomas Hooker, the pastor of the Newtown church, and John Haynes, who had served as Governor of the Bay State. It was under summer skies in 1636 that about a hundred people, led by Hooker, made a famous pilgrimage through the woods that led to their destination. Bearing Mrs Hooker in a litter and driving their cattle before them, these courageous pioneers — men, women and children — after a journey of two weeks came to Hartford, the site of their future home. This was the beginning of a veritable floodtide which saw thousands of Puritans coming to establish what eventually became the state of Connecticut.

A few years after Hooker's original settlement, Daniel Brainerd, an English orphan who had come to the Massachusetts Bay Colony in 1649 when he was eight years old, also made his way south to the Connecticut River valley and established a little town named Haddam. Here, on a twelve-mile square tract of land, twenty miles south of Hartford and fifteen miles north of the river's mouth, Daniel Brainerd prospered and eventually became Haddam's chief landholder.

As a matter of fact, he also served as constable, surveyor, town assessor, collector, and a commissioner of the General Court. When the Congregational Church was gathered in Haddam in 1700 Daniel Brainerd was elected as a deacon.

This original Brainerd in America married Hannah Spenser and had a daughter and seven sons, the youngest of whom was Hezekiah, born in 1681. Daniel Brainerd's youngest son was evidently the most gifted, or at least the most fortunate, of the large family. He inherited most of the family estate and the homestead. He also became a powerful figure in the new Connecticut government. He was a representative to the General Assembly, Speaker of the House in 1721 and 1722 and a member of the Senate from 1723 to his death in 1727. Also he served on the council of the King of England. Hezekiah Brainerd was a country squire, a regimental commander and a Justice of the Peace in Haddam. He was also a Christian cut out of the authentic Puritan mould. One of his descendants described him as being a man 'of great personal dignity and self-restraint, of rigid notions of parental prerogative and authority, of the strictest puritanical views as to religious ordinances, of unbending integrity as a man and a public officer, and of extreme scrupulousness in his Christian life'.[1]

Hezekiah Brainerd married well. His chosen companion was Dorothy Hobart Mason, who had been married previously to Major John Mason, one of the heroes in the war with the Pequot Indians in 1637. Dorothy was the daughter of Jeremiah Hobart, who spent the last fifteen years of his remarkable life serving as pastor of the church at Haddam — the first pastor there in fact. Dorothy's maternal family tree included a whole host of notable Puritan preachers, among them the able and cultured Samuel Whiting who pastored congregations in England and Boston. Her great-uncle was Oliver St John, who was Chief Justice of England under Oliver Cromwell.

Sign at Haddam listing Daniel Brainerd among founders of the town

Old house in Haddam

As Hezekiah and Dorothy Brainerd's estate expanded and their influence in the social and political life of Connecticut increased, their family also grew. First there was Hezekiah, named after his father. Then came Dorothy, a namesake of her mother. Afterwards Nehemiah, Jerusha, and Martha arrived to gladden the family household. On a Sabbath day in the spring of 1718 a baby boy arrived whom they named David. Within seven years John, Elizabeth and Israel had also taken their places in the Brainerd homestead. Of all these children it was David who was destined to bring the Brainerd name imperishable fame.

God chose a charming setting in which the future Indian evangelist was to spend his childhood. From the country house a hundred feet above the west bank of the Connecticut River he could look eastward and see Mount Tom where the Salmon River emptied its sparking waters. As a boy David Brainerd climbed the rugged hills through which the beautiful Connecticut threaded its way to Long Island Sound. He also spent many a delightful hour resting under the stately trees which grew on its banks.

The Brainerd homestead, like most of the houses in interior Connecticut, was undoubtedly a large but simple wooden structure. Although in the larger towns good houses were built, generally of wood and sometimes of brick, in the more remote districts the buildings were crude, with rooms on one floor and a ladder to the chamber above where the corn was frequently stored. The simple lives of these hardy frontierspeople seemed, in their eyes, to be fitting for those who were obliged to count this world only a temporary dwelling.

There is no reason to believe that the early years of the young colonial David Brainerd were any different from those of other young people in similar circumstances. Since the Puritans were great hunters, he no doubt joined with his father and brother in pursuing the deer, wild turkeys, geese, pigeons, hares and squirrels in which the forests abounded. In the streams nearby there were fish such as perch, trout and salmon to be caught, and off the shores to the south there were lobsters and even oysters. He helped his mother plant and harvest the summer crops and prepare the smoked, salted and pickled foods which the family needed to sustain them before the onslaught of the long and rugged winters.

There were many diversions open for David Brainerd and his brothers and sisters, some of which were, to a very religiously inclined youth, also a source of temptation. Card-playing was common. A Boston invoice in the late seventeenth century listed 1,584 packs of cards and a single Pennsylvania importation was valued at £44 sterling. Along with the drinking and card-playing, gaming was prevalent among all companies, a vice that brought many families to bankruptcy. Colonial pastimes included horse-racing and cockfighting, although the latter prevailed primarily in the south. Although dancing was not encouraged, particularly if it was promiscuous, balls in both private and public houses were common among the aristocracy.

The education afforded David and the other Brainerd children would have been rudimentary. To most colonials popular education in the modern sense was as foreign as were purely democractic forms of government. The frontier communities, such as Haddam, had few schools of any kind, the best popular education being confined to the older towns along the coast. Governor Wolcott of Connecticut testified that he never went to school a day in his life, but was taught by his mother at home. Still the parents of each settlement recognized the need for providing local schools for their children. After 1715 tracts of land were frequently set aside for academies in Connecticut and Massachusetts. The town records of Haddam reveal that money was provided for a schoolhouse in 1728, so it is possible that David Brainerd was one of its first students.

The subjects taught in the log or clapboarded schoolhouses were reading, writing, arithmetic and the catechism. Some attention was given to spelling, though there was little uniformity or consistency. English grammar was not cultivated even in the larger cities until the seventh decade of the eighteenth century. The first aids to learning were the hornbook, the ABC book and the primer. Lists of imported books during this period reveal that Dilworth's speller was in general use. Grammar schools where Latin and Greek were taught were rare. David Brainerd eventually went to Yale, where he definitely became acquainted with the original languages of Scripture. This fact, along with the evident linguistic clarity which his diary demonstrated, shows that he received adequate instruction in the basics of learning, as judged by the standards of his day.

Cultural opportunities for the townsfolk of Haddam, Connecticut, in the early 1700s would have been limited, no doubt. Being removed from the larger population centres they would have had few opportunities for seeing plays, but the love of music was universal in Puritan households. Instruments such as the guitar, harpsichord, harmonica and violin were well known. How much interest the boy Brainerd took in aesthetic pleasures we can only speculate, although we do know that as he grew up he increasingly became grieved and even felt threatened by the frivolity and godlessness of many around him.

In every community in colonial New England religion was a dominant force. By far the most powerful denomination in Connecticut was Congregationalism. One of the first buildings built in each town was the Congregational meetinghouse, usually of wood, which was situated in the centre of the square. A visitor to one of the many picturesque towns of modern New England can still see how the church was the centrepiece of the community. The church which David attended was built in 1721. It was a simple structure, shingled, clapboarded and plastered inside with lime made from oyster shells. Like similar meeting-houses throughout New England it was a plain, unadorned structure. The English models with their graceful spires, characteristic of the work of Sir Christopher Wren, would come later.

Worship in these places would have been, by modern standards, a stern affair. The worship services were unadorned by organs, such as increasingly graced the Anglican churches of the period. The interior of the church building was bare and unattractive. The body of the sanctuary was filled with high, square pews, within which were movable seats capable of being turned back when the worshippers stood for the long prayers. In the winter these meeting-houses had neither fires nor lights. One can easily imagine the Brainerd family, along with many other hardy believers, huddled together Sunday after Sunday listening to sermons that often lasted for two hours. Their pastor may have even been like Mather Byles of Boston who measured his message very crisply by an hour-glass. He would preach for an hour and then, turning over the hourglass say, 'Now we shall take a second glass.' No wonder a fur-tipped rod was often needed to wake up the somnolent members of the congregation!

David Brainerd's weekly routine included not only faithful attendance at the Congregational Church at Haddam, but also regular Bible-reading and catechetical instruction. He was taught profound respect for the church elders and total allegiance to parental authority. He learned to look up in awe to the pastor of the church, for in those days the local minister was the most educated and influential leader in the community. He was, in fact, the chief citizen of the town. The deference shown to a pastor can be illustrated by a conversation between Parson Phillips of the South Church at Andover and a visitor to his town. When the stranger asked the minister if he were 'the parson who serves here', he received the reply, 'I am, Sir, the

Haddam Congregational Church.
This is not the original church, but is said to be modelled on it.

parson who rules here,' a retort that was backed up by his courtly bearing.[2] Since the ministry was such a prestigious and powerful position it is no wonder that this was the highest goal of the more religious young men in the community.

There is nothing really remarkable to report, as far as the authentic record goes, about David Brainerd as a youth. We can only say that God, who had marked him out for greatness, had laid a good foundation in his life through the devout family tradition he received at Haddam. While still in the tender years of childhood, however, a series of traumatic events began to unfold which helped to mould him into the serious pilgrim he became. Like a well-known citizen of Tarsus long ago, he was destined to suffer many things for the sake of his God. It was to be a life which knew the deepest sorrows but the highest joys. Great tragedy but also great triumph lay ahead for the son of Hezekiah and Dorothy Brainerd.

6.
The pilgrimage begins

It was impossible for a child brought up in a strict puritanical home like the family of Hezekiah Brainerd to be unaware of the reality of God and the need of a relationship with him. There was a continual emphasis on God's character, the authority of his Word, the duty of all men to worship him, the nature and consequences of sin, the awesomeness of eternity (to be spent either blissfully in heaven or miserably in hell) and the need for repentance.

The natural world, which a sceptic or materialist would accept simply as a development of natural processes, was regarded by the devout Puritan as reflective of the wisdom of an infinite Creator. The sun shining in its glory on the mountains, fields and rivers reminds one of his love and grace. Violent storms, with their rolling thunder and crashing lightning, illustrate his wrath and judgement against sinners. Dawn is like the beginning of life, with its hopes and dreams. Sunset is like death which draws its shadows around one and all and sends them to their eternal destiny.

In the home of Hezekiah and Dorothy, David was given daily lessons on the dangers of sinful conduct, abundant examples of which were all around. He was constantly directed to the Bible as the source of wisdom for preparing to meet God after death and given wise counsel for living. Religious books such as Janeway's *Token for Children*,

Bunyan's *Pilgrim's Progress* and Baxter's *Call to the Unconverted* were placed in his hands. Brainerd read these books and learned that the ultimate end of living is to know and glorify the Lord God Almighty. He heard day after day and week after week, both at home and at church, that personal redemption is the most important goal for living. For the Puritan this meant to undergo a radical, supernatural change, known as conversion. As this evangelical faith was taught to him it was contrasted with its many alternatives such as popery (Catholicism), legalism, antinomianism and, of course, the animism of the Indians.

Until he was seven or eight David, though 'somewhat sober and inclined to melancholy', had little or no conviction or concern about religion as such. But then, for reasons which he did not explain, he became 'concerned' about his soul and terrified with the thought of death. Such seriousness was no doubt increased when the first major trauma of his life took place. While away at Hartford attending to his duties as a senator, his father Hezekiah died. This was undoubtedly one

Hartford, Connecticut, in Brainerd's day

of the reasons why David was driven to the 'performance of religious duties' and also accounts for the fact that he was unable to enter into the frolics and pleasures that other children seemed to be enjoying. When he was fourteen the other major support of his life, his mother, died as well, leaving him an orphan. A kind of sadness then seemed to settle upon the Connecticut farmboy.

Brainerd's journal reflects his highly analytical, introspective nature. He describes in considerable detail the process his mind went through as he struggled to find peace with God. This part of his inner life, like the rest of his diary, reveals a young man who was very intelligent, deeply sincere, serious, self-judgemental and strongly inclined towards depression. The path to God was for him difficult, fraught with detours, pitfalls and at times reversals. He occasionally thought that he knew his way, but then he would almost routinely fall into a morass of theological confusion.

Unquestionably a person's spiritual pilgrimage will reflect his or her own psyche and the theological framework in which the individual's life is cast. Some regard entrance into the kingdom as a sort of natural development from the processes set in motion through early Christian training. One who is born into a Christian family is considered a 'covenant child' and all that is required to enter into the full blessing of salvation is to follow the commitments given at baptism and and accept the ordinary nurturing of the church. For others salvation comes through a specific crisis experience, but this is something that is relatively easy and is based on a personal 'decision'. A person can at any time 'accept Jesus as a personal Saviour'.

The tradition of which David Brainerd was a part differed drastically from both of these interpretations of conversion. The idea that the Christian life is a 'process' which, beginning at infant baptism, automatically incorporates a person into the kingdom of God is, according to Puritanism, essentially a ritualistic approach and leads to deception. Presbyterians and

Congregationalists baptized children, but conceived of the sacraments as a kind of promise, or 'seal', that places the child under the care of a gracious God.

The second view, that conversion originates in an individual 'decision' based on free will, is wrong because it takes too optimistic a view of human nature. There can be and will be many 'decisions', but such human efforts must be distinguished from authentic regeneration. This, in the Puritan view, is a supernatural work whereby God reveals himself to the heart of the sinner, who can do nothing to merit, or prepare himself for, this mercy. Not only the *will*, but also the *understanding* and the *heart*, or *affections*, are involved.

The conflict Brainerd endured before he arrived at the point of assurance of salvation illustrates, in a somewhat extreme and dramatic way, the tension that an unconverted person often experiences when he or she seeks God from a Calvinistic context. On the one hand, all mankind are *obligated* to serve the Creator and accept his gracious offers of mercy which come through the gospel. But at the same time all people lie under a fundamental *inability*, or disinclination, to yield to God. In other words, one should love God, but because of original sin cannot do so. God's holy and perfect law holds one and all in obligation to be righteous, but none is able to attain that standard. Even the command to repent embodies an impossibility, for how can a soul dead in sin do anything, including repent? Caught in between the two seemingly contradictory realities of obligation and inability, the sinner is often discouraged.

From the time he was fourteen David Brainerd struggled to bring his heart and life into harmony with what he knew the Christian standard to be. He knew that Bible-reading, religious conversation and church attendance were the 'means of grace' which one must ordinarily use if conversion is to come. Yet these things do not convey redemption automatically; in fact if they are relied on inherently an attitude of self-right-eousness will result. Between the ages of fourteen and twenty-one Brainerd did manage to convince himself that he was a truly religious person, based on his faithful performance of his duty. But then suddenly, through the enlightenment of the Holy Spirit no doubt, he realized that all his works were in vain and that he did not have a change of heart after all. It was his mature conclusion arived at later that during this period he was essentially a legalist, trusting in his own good deeds to recommend him to God.

Brainerd longed to be a Christian. He wanted to know God and have peace in his soul. But he simply could not break through. This led to times of confusion, discouragement and even anger. He could not understand why God would not give him peace. He actually found himself annoyed at times at what he knew the Bible taught about the way of life. He was irritated at the strictness of the law of God, for trying to live up to its demands was impossible. The fact that faith alone was the condition of salvation was troublesome because this made all his religious devotion of no account. He read in the Bible that he was to believe on Jesus Christ and come to him, but he was perplexed because he did not know what faith was or how to attain it. He was especially vexed by the truth of the sover-eignty of God, as taught in such passages as Romans 9:11-23: 'I could not bear, that it should be wholly at God's pleasure, to save or damn me, just as he would.'

These painful inner conflicts, based on weighty issues which sometimes baffle the greatest theologians, went on for several years. During this time he was living at home, although later, at the age of twenty-one, he took up his residence with Phineas Fiske, who was the pastor of the church at Haddam. Fiske knew the Brainerd family intimately, three of his six daughters having married Brainerds. The Haddam pastor tried to help David. He counselled him to abandon young company and to associate with grave elderly people, advice he heeded. David lived a strict religious life, attending not merely to outward duties such as church attendance, but also to private exercises such as prayer. On Sabbaths he repeated the discourses of the day and pondered their meaning even during the week. He even enjoyed being a devout person. He had a 'very good outside'. Yet, ever and anon, he would sink into despair again as he realized that all such external moral practices did not really touch his soul with saving grace. Thus, alternating between hope and despair, he staggered into his twenties.

Deliverance eventually came. The way it came is vastly important if we are to understand the power of Brainerd's life and testimony. If ever there was a quality conversion he had one. There was a profound depth in his encounter with God which laid the foundation for his future theology and missionary vision. Since this experience was recorded and then published throughout the world it has made a powerful impact on multitudes of people not only in his own day but in the lives of those who have studied his life since. It certainly moved Jonathan Edwards, who sought to interpret the meaning of conversion and true godliness in such classics as *The Religious Affections*. Brainerd's entrance into the realm of a personal acquaintance with God epitomized what it means for divine grace to touch the soul. Nothing short of Brainerd's own words can be adequate at this point:

> I continued, as I remember, in this state of mind, from Friday morning till the Sabbath evening following [12 July 1739], when I was walking again in the same solitary place, where I was brought to see myself lost and helpless, as before mentioned. Here, in a mournful melancholy state, I was attempting to pray, but found no heart to engage in that or any other duty; my former concern, exercise, and religious affections were now gone. I thought that the Spirit of God had *quite* left me;

but still was not distressed; yet disconsolate, as if there was nothing in heaven or earth could make me happy. Having been thus endeavoring to pray — though, as I thought, very stupid and senseless — for near half an hour; then, as I was walking in a dark thick grove, *unspeakable glory* seemed to open to the view and apprehension of my soul. I do not mean any *external* brightness, for I saw no such thing; nor do I intend any imagination of a body of light, somewhere in the third heavens, or any thing of that nature; but it was a new inward apprehension or view that I had of God, such as I never had before, nor any thing which had the least resemblance of it. I stood still, wondered, and admired. I knew that I never had seen before anything comparable to it for excellency and beauty; it was widely different from all the conceptions that ever I had of God, or things divine. I had no particular apprehension of any one person in the Trinity, either the Father, the Son, or the Holy Ghost; but it appeared to be *Divine glory.* My soul *rejoiced with joy unspeakable,* to see such a God, such a glorious Being; and I was inwardly pleased and satisfied, that he should be *God over all* and for ever and ever. My soul was so captivated and delighted with God, that I was even swallowed up in him; at least to that degree that I had no thought (as I remember) at *first,* about my own salvation, and scarce reflected that there was such a creature as myself.

Thus God, I trust, brought me to a hearty disposition to *exalt him*, and set him on the throne, and principally and ultimately to aim at his honour and glory, as King of the universe. I continued in this state of inward joy, peace and astonishment, till near dark, without any sensible abatement; and then began to think and examine what I had seen; and felt sweetly *composed* in my mind all the evening following. I felt myself in a new world, and every thing about me appeared with a different aspect from what it was wont to do. At this time the way of salvation opened to me with such infinite wisdom, suitableness, and excellency that I wondered I should ever think of any other way of salvation; was amazed that I had not dropped my own contrivances and complied with this lovely, blessed and excellent way before. If I could have been saved by my own duties, or any other way that I had formerly contrived, my whole soul would now have refused it. I wondered that all the world did not see and comply with this way of salvation, entirely by the *righteousness of Christ*.[1]

There are several things to note in this testimony. First of all, Brainerd's conversion came through a vision — not a physical vision of God, or even a mental picture of some visible representation of God, but a concept of the spiritual greatness of the triune God in his attributes. Second, in Brainerd's own perception at the time of this encounter he was focusing not on the *benefit* he was to receive from God but an objective appreciation of God's own inherent character. This is extremely important because a whole school of theology was rooted later in it. The third thing which is noteworthy is that Brainerd was delivered from his despair. Real joy, real hope, real peace did come to him. The clouds of doubt were dispelled as he for the first time delighted in the Puritan way of salvation (which before had annoyed him). The perplexity, irritations and confusion were permanently banished never to return.

Brainerd's vision of God has parallels in such Bible experiences as David's conceptions of God's transcendence in the Psalms, Isaiah's vision of God's holiness when he visited the temple and John's encounter with the sovereign Christ in Revelation chapter 1. Not all believers, apparently, are granted such experiences, which produce incredibly expanded views of God and emotional raptures. At the very time of his conversion Brainerd, through a special divine visitation, was introduced into the special circle of those who 'see the King in his beauty'. Unfortunately he had a tendency (people tend to make their own experiences a standard) of making this revelation a pattern for all conversions. Be that as it may, we must all stand in awe at the marvellous mercy and grace granted to the twenty-one-year-old man who now was ready to embark on a course of Christian service.

7.
Yale scholar

All the sons of Hezekiah Brainerd, David's father, devoted their lives to public service through professional careers. Hezekiah, the oldest son, succeeded his father as representative to the General Assembly. Nehemiah, who was in the Yale class of 1732, had entered the ministry. It seemed natural that David, the third son, would also prepare for Christian service, particularly in the light of his recent powerful religious experience. Two months after his conversion he went to New Haven and enrolled at Yale.

In 1739 Yale College consisted of a three-storied frame building 165 feet long and twenty-two feet wide. There was a hall, a library and a kitchen. There were forty-five resident students enrolled, most of whom were much younger than Brainerd. Two-thirds of the newly enrolled students were between thirteen and seventeen years of age. The pattern of social life among students, so much in evidence today, had been set even in colonial days. The freshmen had little privacy and were subjected to constant harassment and domination by the older students.

David's first year at college was not a happy one. Aside from the usual adjustment problems of a new student, he did not find the atmosphere at Yale conducive to his accustomed life of devotion. Even before becoming a Christian his daily

The Brainerd House in the Yale Divinity School Quadrangle. The oval plaque says, 'David Brainerd, Class of 1743'.

regime had included times of prayer, fasting and Bible-reading. Since inheriting a portion of his father's land, a farm at Durham, ten miles west of Haddam, he had lived in relative solitude. For David Brainerd life was serious. The raucous, frivolous ways of most youth were definitely not for him.

What Brainerd found at Yale was an environment exceedingly injurious to the quiet, contemplative life he was accustomed to. When Jonathan Edwards attended Yale two decades earlier he too had found the students to be wild and unruly. Pastimes included stealing livestock, playing cards and breaking out windows, all the while cursing and swearing as if there were no God. Ezra Clapp, who entered Yale two years before David, revealed graphically what life as a residential student was like in 1738. Several freshmen became intoxicated on rum and hard cider and engaged in midnight revelry. They sounded as if they were 'killing dogs' as they yelled, screamed and ran about. Such conduct was extremely distressing to the young mystic from Haddam.

David Brainerd's first winter in college was harsh in other respects. It was cold. The Delaware River had frozen as far south as Philadelphia from 15 December to March and a market was conducted on the ice. Long Island Sound was also frozen all winter from Connecticut to Long Island. Furthermore a measles epidemic broke out in January and Brainerd contracted the disease and had to go back to his farm at Haddam to recuperate. Already exhausted by his strenuous studies, and vexed too no doubt by what he calls the inconveniences of his 'freshmanship' (referring to the harsh treatment of the senior students), he was laid low by the disease. The combination of physical weakness and academic pressure exacerbated his proneness to depression. 'It seemed to me, that all comfort was forever gone.' But while walking alone in a retired place and engaged in meditation and prayer he enjoyed a 'sweet refreshing visit' from God which raised him from the fear of death.

He recovered from the measles and returned to college, but in the summer of 1740 symptoms of a worse disease appeared. After a time of particularly 'close application to my studies' he began to spit blood. His condition was so grave that his tutor advised him to go home again. We can only regard this as the first sign of tuberculosis, the 'plague of colonial New England', which most probably had brought both his parents to an untimely grave.

He came back to college in November and found that some significant changes had taken place in the student population. While he had been recuperating in the quiet of his farm at Haddam, the power of the Great Awakening had fallen with full force on Yale. George Whitefield had visited New Haven on 27 October on a preaching tour which had taken him through Georgia, South Carolina, Philadelphia and the Middle Colonies as well as New England. The young Anglican preacher, already famous, had gathered great crowds wherever he went. As he travelled from place to place he left behind him hundreds of converts and transformed towns. After visiting Boston one minister stated that 'The very face of the town seemed to be altered.'[1] David Wynbeek comments, 'Taverns were closed for lack of patrons and ministers of Boston were soon besieged by anxious inquirers of all ages and stations in life.'[2] Whitefield left Boston and spent several days with Edwards at Northampton and preached in his church.

Many of the students at Yale were caught up in the spirit of the awakening, which Edwards had called 'an extraordinary religious commotion'. Scholars at Yale were among those who heard Whitefield and obviously many became convicted of their godless living and showed intense interest in salvation. The campus was changing drastically. Prayer meetings replaced drunken parties and frivolities gave place to serious times of Bible study and conversation about the Christian faith.

The revival took a new direction when the thirty-eight-year-old Gilbert Tennent came to New Haven in March 1741 to take up and perpetuate the work of Whitefield. A somewhat sterner preacher than his English associate, he placed great emphasis on the strict demands of the law of God and warned of coming judgement. Whitefield gave his unqualified endorsement to Tennent. In November 1739 he said of Tennent, 'He went to the bottom indeed, and did not daub with untempered Mortar... Hypocrites must either soon be converted or enraged at his preaching. He is a son of thunder, and I find doth not fear the faces of men.'[3] Samuel Hopkins, who was a senior at Yale and destined to become a major figure in the theology of New England, was enthralled at the tall evangelist from New Jersey. He said, 'When I heard Mr Tennent, I thought he was the greatest and best man, and the best preacher, that I had ever seen or heard. His words were to me like "apples of gold in pictures of silver". And I thought that, when I should leave the college, as I was then in my last year, I would go and live with him, wherever I should find him.'[4]

At the time of the Great Awakening the pulpits of New England were, for the most part, occupied by leaders who were conservative in style and largely sedate in their approach to faith. For many of them the Christian life was one of formal adherence to the orthodox creed and avoidance of the grosser evils of human society. No one would have accused them of being particularly emotional or zealous. Excessive religious heat was, in their view, 'enthusiasm' — a description with largely negative overtones. The faculty and administrative leaders at Yale represented this moderate approach to Christian experience.

But the revivalists were different. In theological emphasis and style the leading lights of the awakening movement, such as Whitefield, Tennent, Ebenezer Pemberton (1704-1777), who pastored the Presbyterian Church in New York, and James Davenport (1716-1757) believed in and practised a more intense religion. They insisted on a powerful and conscious experience of conversion as an essential evidence of true religion. This led them to regard many of the pastors as hypocritical and spiritually dead. Inevitably their followers became censorious and critical of those who were cool towards the spreading revival fire. Even the leaders at Yale, such as the rector Thomas Clap (1703-1767), fell under their disapprobation. Students began to regard their own academic superiors as spiritually dead, even unsaved. A clash between the evangelists and the established leadership at Yale and in the churches became inevitable.

David Brainerd was from the very start sympathetic with the revivalists, and he became one of the leaders of the students who supported them. He may have been among the band of students who followed Tennent on foot when he went to preach at Milford. At any rate he joined the private gatherings of those who promoted the revival and the teachings of the evangelists. He visited other students, talked with them about spiritual matters and prayed with them. It was through a visit of Brainerd that Samuel Hopkins was first aroused to a concern about the state of his soul and converted.

The leaders at Yale soon became uncomfortable with the attitudes of the students who were following the evangelists. It was apparent that the new religion made their own leadership style, and even their relationship to God, appear in a bad light. They were not shy in denouncing the harsh attitudes of those sympathetic with the revivalists. They regarded the ministries of Whitefield and Tennent as divisive and disruptive of the harmony of the college. They were particularly antagonistic to James Davenport, who went even beyond Whitefield and Tennent in his intemperate judgements on others. Ezra Stiles referred to him as 'indecent, mad and blasphemous'.

Matters came to a head at Commencement Week in 1741 when Davenport was 'raging and fuming'. The Yale trustees voted on 9 September 'that if any student of this College shall directly or indirectly say, that the Rector, either of the Trustees or Tutors are hypocrites, carnal or unconverted men, he shall for the first offence make a public confession in the hall, and for the second offence be expelled'.[5] This powerful edict was to have a significant impact on David Brainerd personally and in fact determined the future course of his career.

In spite of his illness, exhaustion from hard study and bouts with melancholia, Brainerd reached the top of his class academically. His natural intellectual acumen, his intense interest in self-improvement and his personal ambition propelled him to excellence. But he fell in head over ears with the harsh and judgemental attitude of the revivalists. In the winter of 1741-1742 he broke the rule which had been laid down at Commencement and was heard to say that one of the tutors, Chauncey Whittelsey (1717-1787) 'had no more grace than a chair'. Allegedly he also said that he was surprised that Rector

Clap did not 'drop dead' for fining the students who followed Tennent to Milford. He denied the second offence, but he was arraigned before Clap for the remark against Whittelsey, which he could not deny. The rector demanded a public confession on Brainerd's part in the college hall for his remark.

The rector had been informed of Brainerd's harsh comment through a kind of hearsay. Reportedly a freshman had told a lady, perhaps his landlady, that Brainerd had said something or other against one of the leaders of the college. She told Clap who called in the informant and insisted that he divulge the whole story. The young student was of course embarrassed, but before the interview was over the full details were out. Brainerd's comment, which was made in private, was now made a public issue and the outraged head of the school demanded the ultimate humiliation — a formal apology.

Brainerd regarded Clap's demand as unreasonable. After all, he had not been guilty of some open or notorious crime. He had said what he did in a private conversation, annoyed no doubt by something he had observed in class. He was not willing to degrade himself before the whole student body for a private remark, particularly when, in his view, the leaders of the college were opposing what he believed to be a great work of God, namely the revival. So he refused to humble himself publicly. The rector was now out on a limb. He felt he had to enforce the rule and make an example of the miscreant student. So he expelled him. Brainerd's college career was over, free speech lost in the interest of a teacher's reputation.

Brainerd's negative evaluation of Whittelsey was doubtless undeserved. The latter was, evidently, a pious man whose faith expressed itself in different channels from those of the revivalists. Other contemporary associates regarded him as a gracious and mild-mannered teacher. His speciality was teaching the ancient languages: Latin, Greek and Hebrew. Actually he did not openly oppose the 'New Lights', as

Whitefield and his associates came to be called; he had merely tried to control their extremes and excesses.

Thomas Clap, the Harvard-trained rector, was a strict disciplinarian who was notorious for his unwillingness to bend rules. Wynbeek sums up his basic personality: 'Before his rectorship he had served Windham as a faithful but overbearing pastor for fourteen years. Although learned, pious and capable, Clap was unduly strict and set in his ways. He was especially opposed to every innovation in doctrine, itinerant preachers, lay exhorters, and the enthusiasm of which Brainerd was probably Yale's leading exponent.'[6] In short, the authoritarian leader of Yale College would not extend any tender mercies to the fervent, but still rash and immature scholar, David Brainerd. He brought down upon him the full fury of the law.

8.
Dealing with disgrace

David Brainerd's expulsion from Yale is one of the most famous disciplinary measures in the history of the American academic scene. Since it was related directly to the Great Awakening, a movement which from the start had been divisive, this event was guaranteed to polarize the pastors, students and other Christians who were acquainted with it. How far were the college officials justified? Was Brainerd's offence a serious crime, or a mistake that Christian charity should have overlooked? Should he have apologized publicly and settled the matter immediately? Succeeding generations of Brainerd scholars have endlessly debated these issues.

One thing is clear: Brainerd was devastated by his misfortune. On 12 April 1742 he referred in his diary to his 'great trial at college'.[1] There can be no doubt that the shame and disgrace which came upon him was to a great extent responsible for the shadow of gloom which seemed to hover over him so often during the rest of his life. In December 1743 he wrote to his brother John, then a student at Yale, 'The whole *world* appears to me like a huge *vacuum,* a vast empty space, whence nothing desirable, or at least satisfactory, can possibly be derived; and I long *daily* to *die* more and more to it; even though I obtain not that comfort from spiritual things which I earnestly desire. *Worldly* pleasures, such as flow from greatness, riches, honours and sensual gratifications, are infinitely *worse* than none. May the Lord deliver us more and more from these *vanities.*'[2]

Yet his personal humiliation seemed also to have a sancti-fying effect upon him. All was not darkness. During the months after leaving college the beauty of his spiritual life, which has thrilled the hearts of so many, began to flower. The rapturous visions of the glory of God and times of 'sweet' (one of his favourite words) fellowship with the Redeemer contin-ued. On 27 April he said, 'O my sweet Saviour! O my sweet Saviour! Whom have I in heaven but thee? And there is none upon earth that I desire beside thee. If I had a thousand lives, my soul would gladly have laid them all down at once, to have been with Christ. My soul never enjoyed so much of heaven before; it was the most refined and most spiritual season of communion with God, I ever yet felt.'

With so many of the normal comforts of life cut off he turned increasingly to a life of communion and service: 'I never seemed to be so unhinged from *myself*, and to be so wholly devoted to God. My heart was swallowed up in God most of the day' (15 June). Holiness and consecration to the Saviour were now his supreme passion. 'My soul seemed to breathe after holiness, a life of constant devotedness to God' (18 June).

Gradually he was able to submit totally to God's will for him, including resignation to the fact that he would not get his college degree. He speaks of being 'revived' in his mind at the thought of the 'infinite wisdom in all the dispensations toward me' (12 April). He felt 'a great degree of resignation' (27 April). All of this refers to his loss of his college status. He had dreaded the day of graduation when he would actually have appeared at the head of his class. But when the time for Commencement arrived (14 September) through 'divine goodness', his mind was calm, sedate and comfortable. The Lord enabled him to say, 'Thy will be done.'

But in spite of the great comfort his faith afforded him there is no doubt that Brainerd never fully recovered from this setback. Thomas Brainerd, the biographer of his brother John, stated candidly that his life was shortened 'by his college persecution'. Also a section of the diary which was in Thomas's possession, but which Edwards saw fit to exclude from the published version, revealed 'the most intense and overwhelming mental suffering from the stigma fastened on him'.[3] In short, the college officials 'broke his heart'.[4]

After Brainerd had been expelled from Yale and as time wore on, it became increasingly clear to him that, to a great extent, he had been wrong in the Whittelsey affair. A naturally sensitive and conscientious believer, when he reflected on his wrongdoing his sense of unworthiness became acute. The language he uses is shocking. Here are some examples of diary entries in which his self-deprecation appears:

> I was filled with amazement and shame, that God should stir up the hearts of any to show so much kindness to such a *dead dog* as I (22 July 1742).

> Just at night, underwent such a dreadful conflict as I have scarce ever felt. I saw myself vile and unworthy; so that I was guilty, and ashamed that anybody should bestow any favour on me, or show me any respect (21 August).

> I have been so crushed down sometimes with a sense of my meanness and infinite unworthiness, that I have been ashamed that any, even the meanest of my fellow-creatures, should so much as spend a thought about me; and have wished sometimes, while travelling among the thick brakes, to drop, as one of them, into everlasting oblivion (2 July 1743).

Such feelings of regret followed him into the wilderness where he ministered to the Indians; indeed it is doubtful whether they ever wholly departed.

Jonathan Edwards pondered such statements and came to the conclusion that they were directly related to a sense of shame and guilt over his former intolerant attitude: 'It is apparent, that one main occasion of that distressing gloominess of mind ... was reflection on his past errors and misguided zeal at *college* in the beginning of the late religious commotions.'[5]

The greatest of saints, as their biographies abundantly show, have been conscious of their own unworthiness. There is a sort of morbidity, however, in Brainerd's self-deprecation which went beyond the normal. Edwards disapproved of this excessive introspection on the part of his young friend and felt that it was unhealthy either mentally or spiritually. After all, the Christian life should be primarily one of joy.

The circumstances of Brainerd's life, however, provide considerable extenuation, or at least explanation, for his fits of depression. In the first place, this was a constitutional trait which all of his family exhibited over the course of many years. In the second place, we must not forget that he had already gone through several severe shocks, including the death of both his parents. Thirdly, the feeling of total rejection which the college officials produced can easily throw any person, even the most sanguine, into despondency. Finally, there is evidence that even from this early point in his life he was not physically well, for, as we have seen, the signs of tuberculosis had already appeared. As any psychologist can testify, the body, mind and soul are bound up together and what affects one part of the personality affects all.

The life of this devout man, just barely into his twenties, becomes more pathetic in the light of his diligent, but unsuccessful attempts, to right the wrongs he had done. Convicted as he was that he was blameworthy in the offence which had caused him to lose his college status, he tried desperately to make amends. In early June he rode to New Haven and attempted a reconciliation with the college officials, at which time he submitted a complete apology. Clap was still unbending, however. David even made another special trip to New Haven in July seeking to correct the situation, but still in vain.

In succeeding months he continued to try to clear his name and if possible be reinstated. With the help of Jedediah Mills (1697-1776), a pastor with whom he took up residence after leaving college, he asked a council of ministers at Hartford to intercede for him with Clap and the trustees. But everything seemed to be working against him. A law was passed condemning lay preachers and providing that only men who had been educated at Yale, Harvard, or some other accredited foreign college or university be allowed to function as ministers of the government. Another law, passed in the spring of 1742, outlawed itinerant preachers. Such decisions were obviously an attempt to deal as severely as possible with such preachers as Whitefield and Tennent. These provisions forced Brainerd either to be silent or to break the law. Therefore all attempts at intervention at this point, even by reputable pastors, were ineffectual to reinstate him to Yale.

Finally, in September 1743, actually after Brainerd had already begun to explore a career as an Indian evangelist, he composed a poignant confession which seems to go as far as was humanly possible in admitting blame and seeking forgiveness. It is worthy of particular attention:

> Whereas I have said before several persons, concerning Mr Whittelsey, one of the tutors of Yale College, that I did not believe he had any more grace than the chair I then leaned upon; I humbly confess, that herein I have sinned against God, and acted contrary to the rules of his

word, and have injured Mr Whittelsey. I had no right to
make thus free with his character; and had not just
reason to say as I did concerning him. My fault herein
was the more aggravated, in that I said this concerning
one who was so much my superior, and one whom I was
obliged to treat with special respect and honor, by
reason of the relation I stood in to him in the college.
Such a manner of behavior, I confess, did not become a
Christian; it was taking too much upon me, and did not
savour of that humble respect, which I ought to have
expressed towards Mr Whittelsey. I have long since
been convinced of the falseness of those apprehensions,
by which I then justified such a conduct. I have often
reflected on this act with grief; I hope on account of the
sin of it: and am willing to lie low, and be abased before
God and man for it. I humbly ask the forgiveness of the
governors of the college, and of the whole society; but
of Mr Whittelsey in particular.

After denying that he had ever said that he expected the
rector to drop dead for fining the scholars who followed
Gilbert Tennent to Milford, he continues:

God has made me willing to do anything that I can do,
consistent with truth, for the sake of peace, and that I
might not be a stumbling block to others. For this reason
I can cheerfully forego, and give up what I verily
believe, after the most mature and impartial search is my
right, in some instances. God has given me the disposition, that, if a man has done me an hundred injuries and
I (though ever so much provoked to it) have done him
only one, I feel disposed, and heartily willing humbly to
confess my fault to him, and on my knees to ask
forgiveness of him; though at the same time he should

justify himself in all the injuries he has done me, and
should only make use of my humble confession to
blacken my character the more, and represent me as the
only person guilty; yea, though he should as it were
insult me, and say, 'he knew all this before, and I was
making work for repentance.' Though what I said concerning Mr Whittelsey was only spoken in private, to a
friend or two; and being partly overheard, was related to
the rector, and by him extorted from my friends; yet,
seeing it was divulged and made public, I was willing to
confess my fault therefore in public. But I trust God will
plead my cause.[6]

I believe this lengthy statement is, by any standard, an
adequate apology, not only for Brainerd's uncharitable remark, but for an offence far worse. The college officials should
have responded to Brainerd's early movements towards reconciliation and, taking his youth into consideration, have
welcomed him back to his academic course. But, alas, such
was not to be the case. The psalmist assures us that with God
there is forgiveness, but often in the human heart it is hard to
find.

It was at this point that Edwards met Brainerd for the first
time and became involved in the controversy concerning the
latter's college status. Edwards was in New Haven at the time
of Brainerd's broken-hearted confession and his counsel was
sought. The Northampton pastor was very impressed with
Brainerd's attitude. He found him to be calm, humble and
totally devoid of any resentment against those who, he felt,
were too harsh on him. By then several leaders, such as Rev.
Aaron Burr of Newark, sought to intervene on Brainerd's
behalf to move the college officials to reconsider. Edwards
himself may have sought to help. At this point Clap and
company seemed ready to relent. They appeared willing to

allow him back in school, providing he would return and spend
at least twelve months in residence. But this requirement was
not possible under his contract with the missionary society
with which he had begun negotiations. And so the way to
Brainerd's completion of his college career was blocked once
and for all.

By the autumn of 1743, however, he had become fully
reconciled to his situation. Other doors were opening. His
attention was soon to be diverted from the recalcitrance of
college officials to the spiritual plight of Indians in the wilderness. For this work, to which God had certainly directed him,
he was more than adequately prepared.

There was one positive result which came from Brainerd's
final encounter with the college officials, the one in which he
'ate humble pie' as it were and humbled himself. Jonathan
Edwards' involvement in this consultation revealed to him the
profound spiritual depth of the exiled student. From then on
Edwards took a keen interest in David Brainerd and supported
him fully in his missionary career. Other friends rallied round
him as well, such as Jedediah Mills, Jonathan Dickinson,
Joseph Bellamy and Samuel Hopkins. More importantly, no
one convinced of the reality of divine providence can question
that an unseen hand was leading him through all these troubles
and would bring him out in triumph at last.

9.
Sanctuary

The problems of Brainerd at Yale highlighted the growing gap between the 'New Light', or revivalist, preachers and the standing order as represented by the officials at Yale. The rules of the New Haven Consociation against lay preachers and itinerants forced the New Lights to band together and protect their own interests. If this body would recognize only ministers trained at Yale and Harvard, there was one obvious solution: start their own association and establish their own accreditation procedures. This they did. The Association of the Eastern District of Fairfield County, all of whose members were friends of the Awakening, assumed the right to license and ordain ministers.

One of the leaders in this association was Jedediah Mills who served as pastor at Ripton, ten miles west of New Haven. He was a Yale graduate who was ordained in 1724 and for eighteen years had been involved in training young men for college. He was an excellent teacher but because of his strong evangelical zeal he did not have a good standing at Yale. In the spring of 1742 he invited Brainerd to come and live in his home where they could work together and plan a course of future ministry.

This new position under the tutelage of Mills proved to be an excellent situation for Brainerd. There were several New

Light ministers not far from Ripton and they invited him to preach for them.

One of these pastors was Joseph Bellamy (1719-1790) who served as pastor at Bethlehem. Bellamy, like Mills, was a Yale graduate (at the age of sixteen), following which he had studied for two years with Edwards at Northampton. In 1740, when he was only twenty-one, he was called to the church at Bethlehem. Being about the same age as Brainerd and thoroughly sympathetic with the Awakening preachers, Bellamy was a natural ally.

Bellamy was one of a group of followers of Jonathan Edwards, which included Samuel Hopkins, Jonathan Edwards the Younger and Brainerd himself, who were destined to have a major rôle in shaping the theology of New England. The Bethlehem pastor was a commanding figure, tall and well built, with a powerful and pleasing voice which could fill any building, regardless of its size. He had a gigantic intellect which was unquestionably sharpened and expanded by the two years he had spent at Northampton. He was open-hearted, confident and outspoken, though to some he seemed dogmatic and hot-tempered. Bellamy was totally committed to both the theology and style of the revivalist preachers. Naturally his sympathies were with Brainerd in his college disputes.

At the time Bellamy was unmarried so Brainerd moved in with him and helped him in his pastoral duties to his congregation, which met in a barn. Brainerd was licensed to preach on 29 July by the New Lights, who made him a probationer, which entitled him to preach within the association's district, but not to baptize or administer communion. The day following his licensure he preached at the church of John Graham, another New Light pastor at Southbury, on 1 Peter 4:8: 'And above all things have perfect charity.' The following Sunday he spoke twice in Bellamy's church on Job 14:14: 'If a man die, shall he live again?' He notes in his diary that he began and closed the day with fervent prayer, adding that it was sweet 'to meditate on death'.

Another man who became a friend to Brainerd after he left Yale was Jonathan Dickinson (1688-1747). He was recognized as the leading Presbyterian preacher in New Jersey and, like Bellamy, aligned himself with the friends of the revival. He was keenly aware of the problems Brainerd was having at Yale and went to New Haven in February 1742 to intervene on his behalf. No one apart from Edwards played a greater rôle in Brainerd's career. It was through the influence of Dickinson, who had connections with a missionary society in Scotland, that Brainerd was eventually sponsored as an evangelist to the Indians.

Dickinson not only was a strong supporter of revivals, but also took a keen interest in the education of young men who were preparing for the ministry. The great goal of his life was the founding of a college in New Jersey which would make room for the warm piety advocated by the Awakening preachers, but which would be as academically strong as Yale. He at first supported the 'Log College' of the Tennents, but since the Old Side Presbyterians would not ordain graduates of that school, he 'left the Philadelphia body and organized the Synod of New York'.[1]

Dissatisfied with the formalism of Yale and the lack of acceptance of the Log College graduates, Dickinson embarked on a campaign to organize a college in New Jersey. He convinced many of the New Light pastors of the need for an institution to train men for the ministry, which he was determined would be Presbyterian in affiliation. In October 1746 his dream was realized when the college of New Jersey was chartered with himself as president. When it opened at the end of May 1747 the classes were held in his house.

There is considerable evidence that Brainerd's expulsion from Yale was one important impetus for the founding of the

College of New Jersey, which eventually became Princeton.
David Dudley Field, author of *The Genealogy of the Brainerd
Family in the United States,* states a strong case for this. In
1857 he gave a first-hand report to support his claim: 'I once
heard the Hon. Jon Dickinson ... son of the Rev. Mr
Dickinson, of Norwalk, say, that the establishment of
Princeton College was owing to the sympathy felt for David
Brainerd, because the authorities of Yale College would not
give him his degree, and that the plan of the college was drawn
up in his father's house.'[2]

Archibald Alexander, author of *Biographical Sketches of
the Founder and Principal Alumni of the Log College,* also
bears witness to the connection between Princeton and
Brainerd. After discussing the important rôle Aaron Burr and
Dickinson had he adds, 'Both these distinguished divines were
graduates of Yale College; but just at this time their minds
probably experienced some alienation from their alma mater
on account of the harsh treatment which Mr David Brainerd
had received from the officers of that college.' He concludes
that 'The attachment of all the members of the New York
Synod to Mr Brainerd was warm, and deservedly so,' and that
it was likely that his dismissal from Yale had 'quickened the
zeal of these excellent men to get up a college of their own'.[3]

Norman Pettit adds further confirmation to this position
from the testimony of Alexander: 'Alexander, like Field, also
offered a first-hand account: "Some years ago," he declared,
he had heard "the relict [widow] of the late Dr Scott, of New
Brunswick, say that when she was a little girl she heard the
Rev. Mr Burr declare in her father's house in Newark, 'if it had
not been for the treatment received by Mr Brainerd at Yale,
New Jersey College would never have been erected.'" It was,
however, Thomas Brainerd who in summing up the evidence
made the final claim: "This testimony of the Rev. Dr Alexander so corroborates the statement of the Rev. Dr Field," he

wrote, "that we may regard the question as settled, that the
expulsion of David Brainerd from Yale led to the founding of
Princeton College." The Brainerd tradition — well into the
nineteenth century — remained strong.'[4]

If we accept the evidence of this impressive list of witnesses
(and who today could dispute it?), then we must add another
positive good that came from David Brainerd's treatment at
Yale. For well over a century Princeton College, and also the
seminary which was connected to it, continued as a force for
many of the spiritual ideals which were near and dear to
Brainerd and his friends. It is a pleasing thought that the travail
and sorrow of this son of Connecticut were related, however
minutely, to the mighty efforts of such towering figures as the
Alexanders, the Hodges, Patton and even Warfield.

The months Brainerd spent with Mills, Bellamy and
Dickinson were taken up with preaching, conversations with
the Yale officials and also private study and heart-searching.
Riding his horse through the woods and dales of Connecticut
and New Jersey he pored over the Scriptures, prayed, ministered wherever he could and pondered the meaning of life.

He learned the meaning of forgiveness:

> Oh it is a sweet disposition, heartily to forgive all
> injuries done us; to wish our greatest enemies as well, as
> we do our own souls! Blessed Jesus, may I daily be more
> and more conformed to thee! (25 April 1742).

His life of prayer deepened:

> I retired early this morning into the woods for prayer;
> had the assistance of God's Spirit, and faith in exercise;
> and was enabled to plead with fervency for the advance-
> ment of Christ's kingdom in the world, and to intercede
> for dear, absent friends (18 April).

I set apart this day for fasting and prayer to God for his grace; especially to prepare me for the work of the ministry; to give me divine aid and direction in my preparation for that great work; and in his own time *to send me into his harvest*... In the afternoon, *God was with me of a truth*. O, it was blessed company indeed! God enabled me to so agonize in prayer that I was quite wet with perspiration, though in the shade, and the cool wind. My soul was drawn out very much from the world, for *multitudes* of souls. I think I had more enlargement for sinners, than for the children of God, though I felt as if I could spend my life in cries for both (19 April).

This morning, I spent about two hours in secret duties, and was enabled, more than ordinarily to agonize for immortal souls... (25 April).

I long to enjoy God alone (11 May).

He felt the shame of his sin at college, and his unworthiness, but exulted in the free grace of God:

The disgrace I was laid under at College, seemed to damp me; as it opens the mouth of opposers. I had no refuge but in God. Blessed be his name, that I may go to him at all times, and find him a *present help* (3 July).

Edwards comments, 'He saw clearly that whatever he enjoyed, better than hell, was of free grace' (22 June).

His difficulties and loneliness drove him deeper into intimate fellowship with God and entire devotedness to him:

Had the most ardent longings after God, which I ever felt in my life. At noon, in my secret retirement, I could

do nothing but tell my dear Lord, in a sweet calm, that
he knew I desired nothing but *himself*, nothing but
holiness; that *he* had given me these desires, and he *only*
could give me the thing desired. I never seemed to be so
unhinged from myself, and to be so wholly devoted to
God. My heart was swallowed up in God most of the day
(15 June).

Since his preaching near New Haven made him a fugitive
from justice he sought in his God strength, courage and
protection:

Was informed, that they only waited for an opportunity to apprehend me for preaching at New Haven lately,
that so they might imprison me. This made me more
solemn and serious, and to quit all the hopes of the world's
friendship... Retired into a convenient place in the
woods, and spread the matter before God (6 September).

In the evening, went very privately into town, from
the place of my residence at the farms, and conversed
with some dear friends; felt sweetly in singing hymns
with them; and made my escape to the farms again,
without being discovered by my enemies, as I knew of.
Thus the Lord preserves me continually (9 September).

He longed for heaven:

I hoped that my weary *pilgrimage* in the world would
be *short*; and that it would not be long before I was brought
to my heavenly home and Father's house (4 July).

Through divine goodness, I have scarce seen the day
for two months, in which *death* has not looked so

pleasant to me, at one time or other of the day, that I could have rejoiced that the *present* should be my *last,* notwithstanding my present inward trials and conflicts. I trust, the Lord will finally make me a *conqueror,* and *more than a conqueror*; and that I shall be able to use that triumphant language: 'O death where is thy sting?' And, 'O grave, where is thy victory?' (8 November).

It has often been observed that anyone specially chosen of God for eminent service in his kingdom will be called to suffer. Just as iron when heated becomes soft and malleable, so the believer who has endured the fires of earthly pain becomes, through divine grace, soft, tractable and yielded to God. David Brainerd had gone to college as a high-spirited, ambitious and determined young man. But the spring of 1742 found him humiliated, broken, ashamed and grief-stricken. God was using the rigidity, and even the unkindness, of other people to cast him solely upon divine aid. The keen sense of his own failures, the frequent desertions by God, the bodily weakness — all these trials tested him, refined him, strengthened him, matured him. Like the men of old who were fishing on the Sea of Galilee, the Great Saviour was calling him away now from his own pursuits to a life of fishing for men.

10.
The ingathering of the heathen

Brainerd first recorded an interest in being a missionary to the Indians in August 1742, fourteen days after his licensing as a minister. After a restless night, in which he endured 'sore inward trials', he wrote, 'I had in a great measure lost my hopes of God's sending me among the Heathen afar off, and of seeing them flock home to Christ.' These comments came after he had visited and preached to a group of Indians who lived along the Housatonic River near Kent, about fifteen miles west of Bellamy's home where he had been staying. He spoke from the same text from which he had preached at Bellamy's church, Job 14:14. The Indians were responsive. 'Some Indians cried out in great distress, and all appeared greatly concerned' (12 August). These Indians were remnant Mohegans, Wampanoags and Narragansetts who lived as wards of the provincial government in the common village called Scaticock.

The evangelization of the Indians had been a major concern of the Puritans from the earliest days of their settlement. The Massachusetts charter had charged the governor and company to win them to Christ, but already their work was made more difficult by the successful initiatives of the French Catholics. The Catholics thought that the proper approach would be to introduce them to English civilization and culture, believing this would make their work easier. But the Puritan emphasis on conversion was so strong that gospel preaching normally preceded any concern about the preparatory work of education. Charles Beatty, an early missionary, had argued that conversion should precede civilization. He said, 'They hate civilization and Christianity equally and must be convinced of the misery of their spiritual state before they can realize the misery of their civil state.'[1]

The first Puritan to have substantial success with the Indians was John Eliot (1604-1690), who was dubbed the 'great apostle to the Indians'. Eliot was a native of Hertfordshire in England and migrated to America in 1631 where he was appointed to the pastorate of a Presbyterian church in Roxbury, Massachusetts. His evangelization of the Indians began in 1645. Considering the difficulties of his task, he was eminently successful. He established several Christian Indian towns, translated both the Old and New Testaments into the Mohegan dialect and eventually saw 4,000 make a profession of faith.

John Eliot

King Philip's War wiped out all of Eliot's accomplishments, however, and by 1723 the situation looked hopeless. When Brainerd was five years old Solomon Stoddard expressed deep concern that so little was being done to help the Indians. He published a tract in which he asked, 'Whether God is not angry with this country for doing so little toward the Conversion of the Indians?'

To the Puritans the Indians represented a tremendous challenge because of their demon worship and total ignorance of true religion. Edwards, who ministered for a while to the Mohawks at Stockbridge after being dismissed from his church, considered them to be sunk in 'natural stupidity' and idolatry. He regarded their 'brutish' nature as evidence of the universal depravity of mankind, pointing to their desperate need of the Christian gospel. Of course, their theology put the Puritans, from a human standpoint, at a considerable disadvantage in their Indian evangelism, as compared with the French Catholics, or even the Moravians, who had also begun missionary work among the Indians. For those of Edwards' school much more than mere declaration of allegiances, or attendance at services, was required for acceptance in church membership. Nothing short of evidence of repentance and a thorough reformation of life would make anyone, Indian or otherwise, acceptable in the community of believers.

There was a wide gap between the Indians and the Christian Europeans, particularly the Puritans. Some of them, of course, had from the very first been willing to listen to the Christian message. But certain aspects of the Christian religion were not at all appealing to them. The strangeness of the clothing of the Christians, their habit of kneeling in worship, and the absence of dancing — all these were totally contrary to Indian instincts. But the primary problem was the theology of orthodox Christians, which the Indians found totally baffling. They basically had no concept of sin and thus no felt need for redemption. To them all nature was good, not fallen through some original temptation. Mankind, to be sure, was plagued with many problems, such as disease, witchcraft and death, but these difficulties were thought to come about largely through chance or mishap. The purpose of religion was seen as being to outsmart the demons through incantations or to frighten them off with weird behaviour.

In spite of Brainerd's early interest in the Indians near Bethlehem, it was almost a year before he would preach to them again. As a licensed itinerant of the Fairfield East Association he was able to preach wherever he wanted. He even visited private houses in New Haven and conducted secret meetings, in defiance of the assembly's new law. He had many excellent associations with friends such as Jedediah Mills and Bellamy, and through them many opportunites to share the gospel. He also stayed in contact with some students at Yale, including his brother John, who had just enrolled as a freshman. In the autumn of 1742 he went on a 175-mile preaching tour up the Connecticut Valley, visiting such places as Simsbury, West Suffield, Eastbury (where his brother Nehemiah lived) and Hebron. In November Nehemiah died of tuberculosis, at the age of thirty.

Ten days after the latest tragedy in his life, the death of his brother, Brainerd received a communication from the mission society through which he was destined to minister to the Indians. It was the Society in Scotland for Propagating Christian Knowledge which provided the connection he needed to fulfil his missionary ambitions. This society was organized in 1701 and chartered by Queen Anne in 1709, originally as a means of combating spiritual ignorance and Roman Catholicism in the Scottish Highlands. In 1730 its leaders began to see the need for work in the American colonies, so they turned their attention towards that direction. Money became available from the estate of Dr Daniel Williams for the purpose of sponsoring three missionaries. The society commissioned Governor Jonathan Belcher and 'other gentlemen of character and influence' to form a Boston board of managers, assigning to them £56 as the income from the Williams bequest. The General Court added additional support for five years.

The first volunteers for this missionary enterprise, Joseph Seccombe, Ebenezer Hinsdel and Stephen Parker, went to military posts where Indians came and went. But there were insurmountable difficulties. There was no control at these posts, which made evangelism difficult. Furthermore the Jesuits had already greatly influenced the Indians. The situation was so discouraging that after three years this project was terminated.

The society's next venture was on behalf of the Indians of Mohegan stock in the Housatonic Valley. It was to these Indians that the Boston board sent John Sergeant in 1736 to establish a mission. Unlike the first men to be appointed, Sergeant had an opportunity actually to organize a community of Christian Indians. Sergeant was a Yale graduate; in fact he was the highest-ranked student of the class of 1729. His wife Abigail was the daughter of Ephraim Williams, one of the four English families that lived at the new community named Stockbridge. The house which he built, a three-storied structure with two chimneys, was considered very elegant at the time. The building, which originally stood on Prospect Hill, now graces the main street of Stockbridge.

The Indians in the Housatonic Valley were much more disposed to the Protestant Christianity which Sergeant preached than those who gathered around the military outposts. The English found them mannerly and generally of good moral behaviour. Sergeant, who had lived formerly in the beautiful Berkshire Hills of Massachusetts, laboured faithfully and sacrificially among the Stockbridge Indians. In 1737 he baptized the sachem, or supreme chief, Yokun and fifty of his tribesmen. He diligently studied their 'Moheekanneew' dialect and translated prayers, parts of Scripture and a catechism

of Isaac Watts. In the village of Stockbridge and its environs
there were altogether about four hundred Indians.

The chairman of the New York board of SSPCK was
Ebenezer Pemberton, who pastored the Presbyterian Church
located on the north side of Wall Street between Nassau and
Broadway. He had been one of the few ministers totally in
sympathy with Whitefield, Tennent and the other evangelists
who were active in the Great Awakening. When Whitefield
came to America in 1739 Pemberton was glad to welcome him
into his pulpit. His sermons were very Christocentric and
evangelistic in tone. He once preached at Yale from Paul's
phrase in 1 Corinthians 2:2: 'I am determined to know nothing
among you, save Jesus Christ, and him crucified.' He admonished the students to devote their lives totally to Jesus Christ,
without regard to the consequences. Brainerd heard Pemberton when he preached at Yale and would appear to have been
profoundly impressed. Pemberton's sermon on 'The Knowledge of Christ Recommended' was published and Brainerd
bought six copies.

As a part of the 'New Light' movement, Pemberton certainly looked with sympathy on the situation of the young
student David Brainerd, who had been expelled from Yale.
Their acquaintance was no doubt partially brought about by
Jonathan Dickinson. Dickinson had taken a great interest in
the Indian missions that SSPCK had initiated and he was also
anxious for his friend David Brainerd to find a place of service.
In fact in August 1742 Dickinson was appointed as one of the
commissioners for the society in America, which put him in a
position to be of real use to the expelled student. The SSPCK
had already commissioned Azariah Horton to work among the
remnant Indians on Long Island, and now they were looking
for another man to work in other areas. In all probability Dickinson discussed with Brainerd the new possibilities for Indian
missions when he was in New Haven interceding for Brainerd.

When David Brainerd received an invitation from
Pemberton to come and meet with the missionary society in
New York to discuss missionary work, it was obviously a
turning-point in his life. He says, 'Received a letter from the
Reverend Mr Pemberton, of New York, desiring me speedily
to go down thither, and consult about the Indian affairs in those
parts; and to meet certain gentleman there who were intrusted
with those affairs' (19 November 1742). Knowing that this
was a significant crossroads in his life, Brainerd sought the
counsel and fellowship of his friends. He 'retired with two or
three Christian friends, and prayed'.

There is nothing in his diary about the eighty-five-mile
journey he took to New York City. Since the regular stage to
New York was not inaugurated until forty years later, he of
necessity had to go on horseback. To reach his destination he
simply followed the Housatonic River to Stratford and continued through the old shore towns and across the Saugatuck
River. Then he rode south through White Plains, named after
the white balsam groves which surround it. Leaving White
Plains he continued his course through the Huguenot town of
New Rochelle, arriving in New York on Wednesday, 24
November. The journey had taken him three days.

New York City at that time was a predominantly Dutch-
English town of some 11,000 inhabitants. On the northern
outskirts was Harlem, still a rural district. To reach the
southern tip of Manhattan Island Brainerd rode through
Harlem and on down the pebbled streets to Pemberton's
church where the meeting with the commissioners was to be
held.

As he rode his horse through southern Connecticut and
along the Hudson Valley David Brainerd was weighed down
in spirit with the importance of this trip. When he first
contemplated the meeting his mind was 'seized with concern'
and he was 'oppressed with the weight of that great affair'. Yet

New York in the eighteenth century

he was 'enabled from time to time to "cast [his] burden on the
Lord," and to commit [himself] and all [his] concerns to him'.
As he approached New York he continually prayed for God's
guidance as the time for his appointment drew near. Long
accustomed to quieter communities in Connecticut, he was
'confused with the noise and tumult of the city'. The long ride
took him away from his cherished times of quiet and communion with God. 'My soul longed after him,' he sighed.

But the next day he was able to spend his customary
moments in prayer and supplication for good success on this,
the day of his interview. In the interview he was interrogated
about his Christian experience, his theological convictions
and his aspirations relative to mission work. He was also
required to preach to a group which he described as 'grave and
learned ministers'. During the whole day the melancholy traits
with which he constantly struggled oppressed him heavily:
'Was made sensible of my great ignorance and unfitness for
public service. I had the most abasing thoughts of myself, I
think, that ever I had.' So extreme was his sense of worthless-
ness that it 'pained' him in his heart that anybody should show
him any respect.

In self-confidence and optimism, qualifications so needful
in Christian service, the young missionary aspirant was dread-
fully lacking. But in terms of meekness, humility and dependence on God, graces which divine grace alone can give, David
Brainerd was eminently suitable.

11.
Getting ready to go

Brainerd's interview with the commissioners of SSPCK was successful. He met their approval and he was immediately commissioned to go 'as soon as possible' to minister to the Indians living near the Forks of the Delaware in Pennsylvania and also the tribes who lived along the two branches of the Susquehanna. John Sergeant had already made several long trips to the headwaters of the Susquehanna to take the gospel to these people. Also the Moravians had worked among them, with some success.

With the future course of his ministry finally clear, Brainerd began to make preparations to depart for Indian settlements. There were a few matters to attend to. First he decided to dispose of the money he had inherited from his father's estate. What better way to do so than by using it to pay for the education of a young minister? An acquaintance by the name of Nehemiah Greenman, whom he describes as a 'dear friend', was making preparations for college. Shortly after visiting New York Brainerd went to Southbury and offered to pay the cost of Greenman's education at Yale. Through the largesse of Brainerd Greenman was able to finish his college career and served as a Presbyterian pastor from 1753 till 1779.

Then Brainerd began to make his rounds preaching to the churches who had been so faithful in their encouragement of

him. In December he visited Joseph Bellamy, whose friendship had been so precious. On the 12th he preached at
Bellamy's church in Bethlehem on Matthew 6:33: 'Seek ye
first the kingdom of God...' After prayer together on the 13th
he left Bethlehem with a feeling of 'sweetness and composure'
in his soul. He was confident that he would soon be going into
the wilderness, perhaps never to return, so parting with
Bellamy was an emotional experience. He 'supposed it might
be likely we should not meet again till we came to the eternal
world' (15 December).

As the new year approached melancholy pressed upon him
with a special blackness. Even today our souls reach out in
sympathy with him as we read such pathetic words as those he
wrote on 14 January:

My spiritual conflicts today were unspeakably
dreadful, heavier than the mountains and overflowing
floods. I seemed inclosed, as it were, in hell itself; I was
deprived of all sense of God, even of the being of a God;
and that was my misery. I had no awful apprehensions
of God as *angry*. This was distress, the nearest akin to
the damned's torments, that I ever endured; their torment, I am sure, will consist much in a *privation* of God,
and consequently of *all good*. This taught me the *absolute dependence* of a creature upon God the Creator, for
every crumb of happiness it enjoys. Oh I feel that, if
there is no God, though I might live for ever here, and
enjoy not only this but all other worlds, I should be ten
thousand times more miserable than a reptile. My soul
was in such anguish I could not eat; but felt as I suppose
a poor wretch would that is just going to the place of
execution.

Such times of inner conflict were not unmingled with better
feelings, however. Just prior to this in December he 'enjoyed

a precious season indeed'. He 'had a sweet melting sense of
divine things, of the pure spirituality of the religion of Christ
Jesus… Oh, the sweetness, the tenderness I felt in my soul! If
ever I felt the temper of Christ, I had some sense of it now.
Blessed be my God, I have seldom enjoyed a more comfortable and profitable day than this. Oh, that I could spend all my
time for God' (27 December). Two days after his horrible
sense of God's absence he recovered and had great joy in the
'exercises of religion and christian conversation'. Such ups
and downs are not rare among believers of a decidedly melancholy temperament.

Later in January he was invited to preach at Stonington,
Connecticut, in the parish of Joseph Fish. Here Brainerd
encountered some of the worst manifestations of the radical
elements of the Awakening. Fish had graduated from Harvard
in 1728 and was a well-received minister there. But in 1741
James Davenport came to preach in his church and brought his
extreme brand of revivalism. There were 104 additions to the
church, but the cost was great. Davenport indulged in his usual
intemperate and severely judgemental attitudes. Many of the
people in Fish's congregation became just as fanatical. Fish
tried to calm the troubled waters, but since the people looked
upon Davenport as a kind of apostle many of them left the
church. Even more alarmingly Fish himself began to question
his own relationship to God. He even removed himself from
the pulpit for six weeks.

When Brainerd visited Stonington and witnessed the distress and divisions going on in the church it brought back
painful memories. He recalled how he too had for a while been
caught up in the harsh and vindictive spirit of some of the
radical elements of the awakening, though he never went to the
extremes of Davenport. A great change had come over him
now. He saw clearly the dangers of 'false zeal' and 'bitterness'
and he spoke out forthrightly against such things. He had
conversations with the followers of Davenport and could not

at all agree with them. 'God had not taught them with briars and thorns to be of a kind disposition towards mankind,' he notes in his diary on 28 January.

Brainerd's trip to Stonington seems to have been important in his spiritual development. Witnessing at first hand the terrible fruits of a severe and judgemental spirit convinced him once and for all of the need of patience, tolerance and gentleness in dealing with people. His new-found wisdom and moderate preaching had a soothing effect on the congregation. Soon the tensions were eased and Fish was back in his pulpit.

About this time Brainerd received word that the commissioners had changed their minds about his immediate assignment. They decided that it would not be wise for him to leave for the mission-field in the dead of winter. With their permission he went to East Hampton, Long Island, to serve as a supply preacher for the Congregational Church. Their aged minister, Nathaniel Huntting, was ill and ready to retire. After preaching a farewell sermon to family and friends at East Haddam, Brainerd duly proceeded to Long Island.

The winter of 1743 was fairly mild and the waters of Long Island Sound were open. After a two-day wait he and a messenger from East Hampton crossed by ferry and sailed the ten miles aross the Sound to Oyster Ponds, on the north-east shore of Long Island. Having disembarked he rode about twenty miles to East Hampton on the south side of the island.

Here Brainerd found more evidences of the divisions some of the radical revivals had caused. Pastor Huntting was one of the 'New Lights' himself, but like so many other pastors, he had begun to distance himself from the irregularities of the movement. This created suspicions on the part of some members of the church, in a similar manner to what had happened in Stonington. Davenport, in spite of the obvious imbalances in his ministry, had a nearly hypnotic effect upon many people, especially those untrained in theology.

Brainerd's diary during his stay at East Hampton records some of the experiences which were so typical of his emotional and spiritual state. He often went alone into quiet places to pray and meditate. He studied diligently for preaching responsibilities. Sometimes there was comfort and 'sweetness' (his favourite word again; one often used by Edwards as well) but also alternating descents into gloom and dejection. On 19 February he had a headache and was hardly able to sit up. He 'exceedingly longed to die'. However, these dark moods did not usually last long. Generally, though not always, he enjoyed preaching. On 20 February he preached 'with some life and spirituality'.

On 20 February he recorded in his diary a conviction which not only typified his own outlook on the nature of true religion, but also reflected a particular slant on Puritanism that was beginning to grow in the minds of Edwards and some of his followers. He mentions preaching in the afternoon, at which time he 'was able to speak closely against selfish religion; that loves Christ for his benefits, but not for himself'. At the heart of Edwards' theology was the persuasion that God, or the Supreme Being, as he was wont to be called, should be loved for his inherent loveliness of beauty. Indeed this is the distinguishing mark of true godliness. Everything else can be counterfeited. Even natural or unsaved people can have a sort of fondness for God as long as they think he is benefiting them. But only a genuinely regenerated person can have a deep and profound appreciation of God's inherent glory. Brainerd, Bellamy, Hopkins and many others built on this concept and made it a fundamental part of their evangelistic ministries. 'Selfish religion,' that is, a piety rooted in a persuasion of God's favour towards oneself, is suspect.

Brainerd's visit to Long Island afforded an incidental opportunity for him to gain further experience with Indians. About sixteen miles from East Hampton, at the east end of the island, were two settlements of Indians under the care of the missionary Azariah Horton, who had been sent out by the Scottish missionary society. Horton had graduated from Yale in 1735 and since 1741 he had been employed to work among a struggling group of Long Island Indians who lived along the southern shore. It was a very difficult task. The four hundred or so Indians who were under his care lived along a hundred-mile stretch of sandy coast, a distance that made the ministry there hard to manage. They existed in squalid conditions and were, like so many Indians, victims of the white man's brews: whisky and rum. Horton was faithful in this place, but results were meagre. After leading about thirty-five adult Indians to salvation, he eventually gave up and left.

This visit to Long Island was important for David Brainerd in that during it he was exposed to the kind of difficulties he would soon be facing in his ministry to the Indians further west. After witnessing the destitute conditions of the Indians, physically, socially and morally, he felt his 'flatness and deadness'. Perhaps then more than ever he was impressed with the difficulty of the calling which he had chosen for himself.

But he preached. On 9 March he ministered to some of the 162 Indians who lived here from Isaiah 53:10: 'Yet it pleased the Lord to bruise him.' He enjoyed on this occasion some divine assistance in his delivery and felt God's presence in the meeting. The next day, 'exceedingly infirm' in body, he returned to East Hampton where he remained for the rest of the week.

On Sunday 13 March, although very ill, he preached to the church at East Hampton from Genesis 5:24: 'And Enoch walked with God.' This was his last engagement on Long Island and one gets the impression that it was a poignant occasion for Brainerd. He both 'mourned and rejoiced at the same time' as he made preparations to leave. He mourned because he would soon leave the company of his dear Christian friends to go to the wilderness, but he rejoiced at the great

mission before him, that of sharing the gospel with those who
were lost in sin.

On Monday he rode fifty miles to Brook Haven, an incred-
ible feat considering his physical condition, where he enjoyed
'refreshing conversation with a Christian friend'. On Tuesday
he continued on to New York, where he 'waited on the
Correspondents for the Indian mission'. On Friday he went to
Dickinson's home in Elizabethtown and on Saturday he
stayed with Aaron Burr in Newark. Burr, who was a son of a
Supreme Court judge of Fairfield, Connecticut, had been a
classmate of Brainerd at Yale and like him was a bachelor.
They prayed together and no doubt reminisced over some of
their college experiences.

Brainerd met with his employers at Woodbridge for final
instructions on Monday, 21 March. Once again he heard that
tensions in the frontier Indian settlements over Indian land
claims had postponed his intended commission to Pennsylvania. But the society had been in touch with John Sergeant,
who had recently visited the Indians on the New York-
Pennsylvania border. They now instructed Brainerd to study
the Indian language with Sergeant and to assist him at
Stockbridge. After being 'speedily dismissed' the young
preacher travelled onwards at about fifteen miles a day towards his destination at the Indian outpost, visiting various
places with which he had formerly been associated. He
preached again to the Indians at Scaticock, where he and
Bellamy had preached in August. During the weekend of 26-
28 March he wrote a letter to Joseph Bellamy expressing relief
that the revival excesses had largely passed away, but complaining about the challenges presented by the Moravians who
were ministering in the area.

By the end of March 1743 a year had passed since Brainerd
lived with Jedediah Mills in Ripton. He had accomplished a lot
in that time. He had covered over twelve hundred miles in the
saddle and preached at least sixty sermons in three dozen

towns. He had grown in an understanding of his own heart and the needs of the Indians. His attitude, if not his theology, had moderated as he had seen the devastating effects of religious fanaticism. The missionary recruit was now ready to go with the message of God's grace to the Indians of New York.

12.
Indian mission boot camp

About twenty miles west of Stockbridge, where John Sergeant had laboured faithfully for four years, there resided a group of Indians who were a part of the Mohegan tribe. Nearby was a mountain from which the Indians imagined they heard a sound like Kau-nau-meek, which meant to them that there were deer around, ready for the hunt. To this place on Good Friday, 1 April 1473 came the colonial missionary David Brainerd, not on a mission to find deer, but to hunt the hunters themselves. Kaunaumeek was to be a sort of spiritual boot camp where he could see first-hand Sergeant's methods of Indian instruction and evangelism. This would also be an excellent place for him to get acquainted with the Indian languages.

After a ride through the mountains of Western Connecticut Brainerd first visited John Sergeant and his lovely, but imperious wife Abigail. Their fine home, with its impressive baroque doorway and pine panelling, was a welcome sight for the weary traveller. There was much for the two missionaries to talk about: Brainerd's relationship with the officials at Yale, his commission from SSPCK and the Europeans in the area with whom he needed to make friends. But the primary topic for discussion was the strategy for the evangelism of the Kaunaumeek Indians. He would, of course, need to frequently ride the twenty miles back and forth to Stockbridge. An interpreter would be highly desirable. Together the two men dreamed and prayed about a great work of God among the Indians in these parts.

But Brainerd's stay was brief. After only one night with the Sergeants, he rode to Kaunaumeek and spent his first night on the mission-field sleeping on 'a little heap of straw'. All day long he was distressed with inward trials and distresses. As he reflected upon the awesome task before him he cried out, 'Oh that God would help me!'

During the first week of his work in the new station, he felt lonely and disconsolate. He missed the English people, especially other Christians. Grief over his exile from the college, occasioned as it was by 'pride, selfishness, bitterness, and party spirit', rolled over his spirit. He felt himself frankly inadequate for, and unworthy of, the task which had been assigned to him: 'I thought that I was the meanest, vilest, most helpless, guilty, ignorant, benighted creature living. And yet I knew what God had done for my soul.'

His first encounter with the Indians themselves was on the whole encouraging. The labours of John Sergeant had not only civilized them but made them more susceptible to the influences of the Christian gospel. They were mannerly, polite and well-behaved. On Sunday, 10 April, he preached to the Indians in the morning and evening. Two or three seemed concerned about their spiritual condition. An Indian squaw told him that since she had begun to hear him preach 'her heart cried'.

But in spite of these encouraging signs, as time went on the problems of Indian evangelism seemed awesome. After preaching on 16 April his spirits were low: 'In the afternoon, preached to my people; but was more discouraged with them than before; feared that nothing would ever be done for them to any happy effect.' Afterwards he was temporarily cheered by the appearance of two white men, an Irishman and a Dutchman. They told him that they wanted to hear him preach. But his heart was grieved by their cursing. He went aside and thanked God that he had made him to differ from such people.

The visitors seemed afraid of him, and when he preached to them about sanctifying the Sabbath, they seemed unmoved and returned to their former frivolous conversation. David wrote, 'What a hell it would be, to live with such men to eternity!'

20 April was his twenty-fifth birthday. He set it aside, not for celebration but for fasting and prayer. He reflected on God's goodness to him. He prayed that God would sanctify his spiritual afflictions and soul distress. Wandering alone in the woods he 'poured out his complaint unto God'.

The probable place of these early labours of Brainerd was one which on a modern map is called Brainard, about twenty miles west of Pittsfield, Massachusetts, and approximately the same distance south-east of Albany.[1] It is named after a Jeremiah Brainard, a later member of the family clan who settled in this region. Located at the intersection of Route 20 and Taconic Parkway and nestled in the Berkshire mountain valley, Brainard is picturesque and peaceful to the modern traveller. But if David Brainerd noticed its natural beauties, he never mentioned them in his diary. Cut off as he was from his friends, oppressed by the guilt of his past and overwhelmed by the difficulties he faced as a missionary, this place was to him a desert, a 'wilderness'. The only beauties Brainerd could see, at least during this point in his life, were the attractions of the spiritual world.

In a letter to his brother John, written on 30 April, he gives a fairly detailed description of what life was like here in the Indian frontier: 'I live in the most lonely melancholy desert, about eighteen miles from Albany... I board with a poor Scotchman: his wife can talk scarce any English. My *diet* consists mostly of hasty pudding [oatmeal porridge], boiled corn, and bread baked in the ashes, and sometimes a little meat and butter. My *lodging* is a little heap of straw, laid upon some boards, a little way from the floor; for it is a log room without any floor, that I lodge in. My *work* is exceedingly hard and difficult: I travel on foot a mile and a half, the worst of ways, almost daily, and back again; for I live so far from my Indians. I have not seen an English person this month.'

But the letter was not all complaining. He mentions that the Indians were kind to him, attentive and apparently open to his message. Yet so far there had been 'no apparent success'. He concludes that God was testing him and enabling him to endure hardness for the sake of the gospel. The words of the apostles to the believers of Asia came to mind: 'We must through many tribulations enter the kingdom of God' (Acts 14:22).

His greatest trials, however, were not physical but spiritual. He continued to be oppressed with a consciousness of his own unworthiness. After a particularly painful sense of sinful thoughts he said, 'If I had been banished from the presence of all mankind, never to be seen any more, or so much as thought of, still I should have been distressed with shame; and I should have been ashamed to see the most barbarous people on earth because I was viler, and seemingly more brutishly ignorant than they. "I was made to possess the sins of my youth."' The ghosts of Yale were still tormenting him.

In May, as the weather began to warm up, he made plans to build a cottage for himself. As the work progressed he moved out of the house of the Scottish folk and lived in Indian wigwams. He continued to travel back and forth to Stockbridge where he assisted Sergeant in the observance of the Lord's Supper. He also preached.

Then some help in his ministry came. He secured an Indian interpreter named John Wauwaumpequunnaunt. John was a capable assistant who knew English and Indian very well and was adept at writing. He had been trained by Sergeant and a couple of other Christian leaders. Later he served as Jonathan Edwards' interpreter when the latter went to labour among the Indians. With the help of the Indian Brainerd was able to translate simple prayers and he even learned to pray and sing in their language.

In June he went to New Jersey to discuss with the commissioners of the missionary society the possibility of setting up an Indian school at Kaunaumeek, similar to the one which Sergeant operated at Stockbridge. Wauwaumpequunnaunt was selected to be the schoolmaster. Brainerd reached Aaron Burr's house in Newark on Thursday, 3 June. During this trip the problems at Yale were never absent from his heart. After visiting New York he sought a reconciliation with the rector, Thomas Clap, but received nothing but a stiff rebuff. The door to his coveted college education seemed to be closed more tightly than ever. The proximity of his field of labour to Yale graduates such as Sergeant and Bellamy unquestionably kept the matter fresh in his mind.

After his return to Kaunaumeek he proceeded to establish the Indian school. Progress was encouraging. The Indian youngsters learned the English language quickly, which facilitated instruction in the great truths of the Reformed faith which were so dear to Brainerd.

Thomas Brainerd, the author of the life of David's brother John, claimed that David kept two diaries while at Kaunaumeek. One was the record of his religious experiences which Edwards published, and the other was the history of his conflict with the college authorities. The latter document, which consisted of some 120 pages, was still in existence as late as 1865. Edwards did not divulge very much of the material in this part of the diary. Thomas Brainerd wrote, 'We may yet give it entire, just as Brainerd wrote it. It is justly severe on the college authorities; they broke his heart.' But alas, this intriguing part of Brainerd's memoirs has never seen the light of day. Wynbeek was of the opinion that this diary, had it been published, would have revealed more faithfully the human side of Brainerd than Edwards' doctored diary. It would have disclosed, no doubt, a young man boiling with anger. Edwards' reluctance to print this was unquestionably designed to preserve his young friend's character.

On the last day of July Brainerd moved finally into the humble hut which he had been building. 'Found it much better,' he wrote, 'spending the time alone than in the wigwam where I was before.' On 1 August he continued to make improvements in his house, relishing his new quarters, humble though they were. As Wynbeek says, 'The house, complete with bed-ticking, deer blankets, kettle and teapot, was a boon to his spirit.'[2] Secure now in his snug new quarters, he was conscious of the joy of the Lord beginning to seep into his soul: 'Felt a little of the sweetness of religion, and thought that it was worth while to follow after God through a thousand snares, deserts, and death itself.'

A couple of diary entries in August reveal an interesting aspect of Brainerd's attitude towards evangelism. On the 22nd he demonstrated the compassion that his heart felt for the Indians: 'At night, I spent some time instructing my poor people. Oh that God would pity their souls!' But the next evening, after a day of study and meditation he discloses the real driving force behind his missionary labours. After travailing in prayer for 'for all the world, friends and enemies', he penned the following significant sentiments. 'My soul was concerned, not so much for souls as such, but rather for Christ's kingdom, that it might appear in the world, that God might be known to be God, in the whole earth.' This is without question one of the most significant statements in Brainerd's diary. For him evangelism is seen in military terms. It is an invasion of God's visible sovereignty into the territory of the devil. The conversion of sinners is important, not primarily because people are rescued, although that is involved, but because the kingdom of God is established in human hearts.

There is one final pathetic footnote to the business of his relationship with Yale. In September he made a final trip to

New Haven to attend the graduation of which he himself should have been a part. He went with trepidation, for he anticipated that as he saw his classmates receiving their degrees he would be overwhelmed with grief. Yet when the actual ceremonies took place he was enabled by the Lord to be calm and resigned. His mind was calm, sedate and comfortable, as he said in his heart, 'The will of the Lord be done.'

This time Clap and company were at last willing to reinstate him into the college, but his contractual relations with the correspondents of the missionary society made a further academic career impossible. All indications are that although Brainerd never graduated from Yale, the school has since felt some embarrassment over the way he was treated. There is one physical reminder that the melancholy missionary walked the halls of Yale, pointing no doubt to the fact that many of its leaders have, over the years, recognized his greatness. A house in Yale's Sterling Divinity Quadrangle is named in his honour, bearing the inscription: 'David Brainerd, Class of 1743.'

The pain Brainerd experienced at the Yale Commencement in 1743 was no doubt assuaged by the presence of the man who more than anyone else served as his mentor and guide. Jonathan Edwards had come specifically to intercede with the school officials on the missionary's behalf. Edwards was, after all, the best-known evangelical preacher of New England at the time and was himself a former Yale student.

Although he was not successful in his advocacy Edwards did have an opportunity to observe first-hand Brainerd's conduct during these very difficult days. He was very impressed: 'I was witness to the very Christian spirit which Brainerd showed at that time; being then at New Haven, and one whom he thought fit to consult on that occasion. This was my first opportunity of a personal acquaintance with him. There truly appeared in him a great degree of calmness and humility; without the least appearance of rising of spirit for any ill treatment which he supposed he had suffered, or the

Jonathan Edwards

least backwardness to abase himself before them, who as he thought, had wronged him. What he did was without any objection or appearance of reluctance, even in private to his friends, to whom he freely opened himself.'

It was at this time that Brainerd made the full and frank confession in which he 'abased himself' before the college authorities and asked for their forgiveness.

There is an intriguing human interest development at this point in Brainerd's life which deserves some comment. Practically every historian of the Edwards family and the Brainerd family, as well as modern biographers, has concluded from the relationship David had with Jerusha Edwards during his final days in Edwards' home that they were engaged to be married at that time.[3] From the standpoint of circumstantial evidence, this is certainly not surprising. Jerusha attended him constantly when he was ill and accompanied him on his final trip to Boston. Wynbeek suggests the possibility that an attraction between them may well have begun when the Edwards family were at Yale in 1743. All we can say for certain is that this is a possibility, for there is no mention of Brainerd in his diary of romantic interest in her. If a mutual interest beyond mere Christian friendship developed between Brainerd and Jerusha, the Yale Commencement would have been a natural time for this to have taken place.

It is a known fact that Edwards often took his daughters with him on his speaking engagements. His oldest daughter Sarah went with him to Boston in May when he met Thomas Clap and discussed the uproar caused by Whitefield's preaching. She rode behind him, sitting on a pillow. Did Jerusha accompany her father on this trip to New Haven?

When Brainerd came to New Haven the day before Commencement he wrote, 'Lodged at —' Why did he not identify the place where he stayed? What was his residence on this occasion? Normally Edwards stayed at the home of his brother-in-law James Pierrepoint, a son of New Haven's first minister and one of the founders of the college. He was one of the New Lights and often opened his home for preaching. It is at least possible that Brainerd was a house guest that night at the Pierrepoints.

Edward's second daughter was fourteen at that time, not too young for courting. Her beautiful mother Sarah had been a year younger when she became the object of the attentions of her suitor, Jonathan Edwards. He had spoken of Sarah as 'a young lady in New Haven who has a strange sweetness in her mind'. Jerusha was his favourite and what is more natural than to think that he might have seen in the humble, conscientious student a possible marriage partner for her? The home of her uncle would have been a convenient place for the lovely maiden to have been introduced to Brainerd. He, with his Puritan reticence towards earthly ties and his absorption with spiritual realities, would probably have made no mention of this young woman in his diary. Is it not conceivable also that it was Edwards himself who struck from the diary the place where the missionary stayed on 13 September?

But when all is said and done, we can only guess at what the relationship between the godly Jerusha and the disgraced student was. Whether or not not Jerusha met Brainerd at the Commencement, this was an eventful time for him. Here a friendship and mutual appreciation were cemented between him and the man who would become his model, spiritual father, protector and care-giver when his life was coming to a close.

13.
Developing a theology

On the way home to Kaunaumeek from the graduation at New Haven David stopped to visit Joseph Bellamy. He preached in Bellamy's barn on 19 September and enjoyed considerable liberty and power both in prayer and preaching: 'I felt serious, kind and tender towards all mankind, and longed that holiness might flourish more on earth.' The next day he came down with an illness that appears to have been influenza. His teeth hurt and he shivered with cold all through the night.

These years in which New Lights like Brainerd and Bellamy were beginning their respective ministries were important since a particular theological perspective was being formulated. The tragic events at Yale and their aftermath had mellowed Brainerd somewhat, but at the core he never changed his outlook. These men held high views of the need for a powerful experience with God, as opposed to any liturgical or formal ideas of what a Christian experience is. As students of Edwards they were also keenly interested in the doctrinal issues that revolved around the nature of sin, free will, the decrees of God and the atonement. We can be sure that whenever Brainerd visited Bethlehem, Connecticut, he and Bellamy engaged in detailed discussions of their understanding of these matters.

In October Berkshire forests began to blaze with their brilliant reds, yellows, purples and browns. Brainerd continued to ride back and forth to Stockbridge, amid the falling leaves, calling on Sergeant and preparing for his first winter at Kaunaumeek. On 16 October he received from Col. John Stoddard of Northampton a warning that the strain between Britain and France was rapidly reaching boiling-point and that open warfare might break out at any time. If this should happen Brainerd's welfare might be threatened by the French Indians who could come and take him captive, or even kill him. All citizens friendly to the colonial government were to take means to protect themselves in the event of attack.

Also on the 16th Brainerd entertained a guest. Wynbeek speculates that this might have been Samuel Hopkins who was then considering a call from a church at Sheffield, Massachusetts, which was down the Housatonic River near the Connecticut border. Hopkins was one of the young ministers who, like Brainerd and Bellamy, had been influenced by Gilbert Tennent's preaching.

During the revival at New Haven Hopkins had approved totally of the activities of the New Lights. But he himself had not yet experienced conversion. Then Brainerd began to talk to him about his soul. As David Brainerd pried into his spiritual life Hopkins acknowledged that he 'resolved to keep him in the dark, and if possible prevent his getting any knowledge of my state of religion'.[1] But the probing questions and constant attention of the student succeeded in awakening Hopkins to a deep conviction. He began to experience the agonies that often accompanied awakened sinners. His feelings of wickedness and guilt increased each day. The horrors of hell passed vividly before him. He began to attend the revival services and private prayer meetings and admitted to all that he was not converted. Eventually relief came as Hopkins experienced the witness of divine grace to his heart.

Shortly after his conversion Hopkins went to study at Northampton, Massachusetts, under the tutelage of Edwards.

Here he not only became schooled in the pastor's theology but also he became acquainted with the latter's wife Sarah, who had some remarkable religious experiences. At times she swooned and fainted during emotional ecstasies in which she seemed to be overwhelmed with a sense of God's presence. When under these spells she professed to be elevated above any selfish interests and to be lost in the desire to promote the glory of God.[2] Without a doubt such communications had an impact on Hopkins and moved him towards the concepts of self-abnegation for which he later became famous. We can presume also that the sincere self-effacement demonstrated by David Brainerd, which he observed during such times of fellowship as the visit in October 1743, was a factor in influencing Hopkins.

Hopkins went on to accept the pastorate of the church at Sheffield and in December was ordained to the gospel ministry. It was a difficult field of labour, for the local inhabitants were uncivilized, rowdy and were thought of as 'disreputable ruffians'. In his diary he says concerning these people, 'They are a very wicked people, but I can't tell them of it.'[3] John Sergeant came down to see him on 14 December on a day of fasting in preparation for ordination.

The actual ordination day was 28 December and Brainerd rode down to be present. He wrote afterwards, 'At the solemnity I was somewhat affected with a sense of the greatness and importance of the work of a minister of Christ.' It did not take long, however, for the missionary to realize how hard Hopkins' job would be: 'Afterwards was grieved to see the vanity of the multitude.'

The day after Hopkins' presumed visit to Brainerd at Kaunaumeek David's thoughts turned once again to evangelistic interests, which he described as 'Zion's prosperity'. He longed that 'God would arise and have mercy on Zion speedily'. The ultimate vision, seen from the postmillennial outlook of Edwards, was for the gospel eventually to prevail across the entire globe. 'Oh that I may see the glorious day, when Zion shall become the joy of the whole earth! Truly there is nothing that I greatly value in this lower world.'

Six days later his meditations were still on this theme of the universal triumph of the kingdom of God. He prayed for this glorious day 'with courage and strength of hope'. It was Sunday and he ministered the Word of God to the Indians. He preached 'with freedom and warmth' and the people were attentive. His message in the morning was on 'the glories of heaven'; in the afternoon he preached on 'the miseries of hell and the danger of going there'. Two or three were deeply moved and came to him for further instruction. His heart reached out to them with deep concern. 'Oh that God would be merciful to their poor souls!' he prayed.

He spent 3 November in secret prayer and fasting, while he also pondered the story of Elijah from the book of 1 Kings. His heart was stirred as he read the life of the prophet, and he longed to be like him: 'My soul breathed after God, and pleaded with him, that a "double portion of that spirit" which was given to Elijah' might rest on him. He firmly believed that Elijah's God was still alive and could do the same kind of wonders as he did in the days of old: 'Nothing seemed too hard for God to perform; nothing too great for me to hope for from him.'

The seven months which he had so far spent among the Mohegan Indians had left him somewhat doubtful that much could be done to bring them to salvation. But his studies in the Old Testament during the autumn were reviving hopes. He was swept into ecstasy when he read from the third and twentieth chapters of Exodus on the glory and majesty of God. After reading these chapters he fell on his knees, 'crying to God for the faith of Moses, and for a manifestation of the divine glory'. The accounts of Abraham's pilgrimage and of Israel's deliverance at the Red Sea encouraged him. He longed as never before to live by faith and commune with God like the saints in these stories. As he wrestled in prayer for Christian friends and the unsaved he said that he 'felt more desire to see the power of God in the conversion of souls' than he had done for a long time.

During the next few months he had a lot of riding to do in connection with his personal affairs and missionary labours. In his diary he complains of bodily weakness and pain. The cold and stormy weather of the New York November buffeted his frail body. But he took comfort again in the Scriptures. He was refreshed as he read about David's trials when Saul pursued him, which no doubt reminded him of his own difficulties with the Yale authorities. God took away from him all bitterness and desire for revenge. He even 'mourned for the death of his enemies'.

On 29 November his studies of the Indian language began in earnest with John Sergeant. On 5 December, a day that was bitterly cold, he was back again. But the outward difficulties were not all that troubled him. He struggled with the conflicting emotions within his heart as well. He found the vanity and levity of professed Christians vexatious. An entry on 8 December mentions that not only God but also certain 'objects in the world' invited his heart and affections. What were these things? He was seeking to become 'dead' to some earthly or worldly 'object' which attracted him. In his own mind he was being tempted to idolatry. Perhaps it was Jerusha Edwards who was at the centre of this conflict.

His diary for the next few weeks reveals a man pressing forwards with renewed vigour, not only in the evangelism of the Indians but in the pursuit of holiness. He had a deep concern about 'the improvement of precious time'. Three weeks later he wrote to his brother John at Yale, 'I find nothing more conducive to a life of *Christianity,* than a diligent, industrious, and faithful improvement of *time.*' On Christmas

Day (he makes no mention of the date as a special occasion) he preached and counselled some seekers. On New Year's Day he praised God for his gracious provision, and mentioned with gratitude that he had been able to give one hundred pounds of New England money to charity. 'May I always remember,' he says, 'that all I have comes from God.'

He complained on 3 January that travelling (which took up so much of his time) hindered his devotional life. Such anxiety could come only from one who was contemptuous of the pleasures and attractions of the world. On 4 January he wrote, 'Was in a resigned and mortified temper of mind, much of the day. Time appeared a moment, life a vapour, and all enjoyments as empty bubbles, and fleeting blasts of wind.'

In the entry for 24 January he makes some comments regarding his developing theory on the subject of self-love. In the company of some visitors he 'took pains to describe the difference between a regular and irregular self-love'. When is self-love proper and when is it not? Here are his comments: 'The one [regular self-love] consisting with a *supreme love to God,* but the other [irregular self-love] *not*; the former uniting God's glory, and the soul's happiness, that they become one common interest, but the latter disjoining and separating God's glory and man's happiness, seeking the latter with a neglect of the former. Illustrated this by that genuine love that is founded between the sexes; which is diverse from that which is wrought up towards a person only by a rational argument, or hope of self-interest. Love is a *pleasing* passion, it *affords pleasure* to the mind where it is; but yet, genuine love is not, nor can be placed on any object *with that design of pleasure itself.*'

Brainerd's view was that true love — virtuous love, derives its inherent pleasure from its objective appreciation of the object, not because of the satisfaction the relationship might bring. While love is inherently pleasurable, it must not be sought for pleasure's sake but for the good of the object.

On 3 February he enters one of the few fairly extended theological essays that we encounter in his diary. It was the fruit of his 'meditation' on the 'whispers of the various powers and affections of a pious mind'. Various faculties of the Christian, such as the understanding, the will, the conscience and the emotions, are represented as being in dialogue. An introductory statement pertaining to the poignant problem of sin and man's dependence on God's grace is probably the most significant of all these ruminations.

He begins by affirming the great and pressing problem of 'indwelling corruption'. He attributes all saving grace to the intervention of God. God alone gets the glory of godly thoughts and deeds: 'I am more sensible than ever, that God alone is "the author and finisher of our faith", i.e. that the whole and every part of sanctification, and every good word, work, or thought, found in me is the effect of his power and grace; that, "without him, I can do nothing" in the strictest sense, and that, "he works in us to will and do of his own good pleasure," and from no other motive. O how amazing it is, that people can talk so much about men's powers and goodness; when, if God did not hold us back every moment, we should be devils incarnate! This my bitter experience, for several days last past, has abundantly taught me concerning myself.'

In March a congregation at East Hampton on Long Island issued a unanimous call to him to come and settle as their pastor. The offer was tempting, but he 'knew not what to do'. He sought God's will and committed the matter to him. Three days later a messenger came from another congregation near his home town of Haddam, with a 'feeler' whether he would be interested in coming as their pastor. Once again he was burdened about the proper course he should take.

These invitations to a permanent pastorate in well-established congregations demonstrated that despite the disgrace of his expulsion from Yale there were still many opportunities open to him. But he had in fact become a missionary to the

Indians and this seemed to be God's calling for him. Difficult as this work was, the needs of the ignorant and unfortunate Indians pressed upon his heart. There was no turning back.

Brainerd had now spent about a year at Kaunaumeek. The obstacles in the way of continuing this work were tremendous. The English people continued to steal the lands of the Indians, so he encouraged them to move to Stockbridge where they could come under the care of Sergeant. His work here was done. But it had been a profitable year. He had learned to survive in the wilderness on little food. He had coped with the problem of finding fodder in the forest for his horse. He had successfully built a crude hut for shelter and had become accustomed to sleeping on a bed of straw. More importantly, he had become better acquainted with Indians' language and customs.

On 1 May he received his orders to go to Pennsylvania to the Indians on the Delaware River, his original assignment. A new phase of his life was upon him.

14.
Into the wilderness

On 1 May Brainerd set out on his horse for the place which had originally been his destination for missionary work among the Indians, the Forks of the Delaware. His trip took him through Sharon, Connecticut and Fishkill on the east side of the Hudson River. As he left his homeland behind him and journeyed on through the 'howling wilderness', his heart was heavy. The task he had undertaken seemed tremendous, made more difficult by the fact that he was going alone. On 8 May he said, 'My heart, sometimes, was ready to sink with the thoughts of my work, and going alone in the wilderness, I knew not where; but still it was comfortable to think that others of God's children had "wandered about in the caves and dens of the earth".' He compared himself to Abraham who was called to go forth 'not knowing whither he went'.

On 10 May he reached the ancient Indian town of Minisink where there resided a conglomerate group of tribes known as Munsees. This place, about 140 miles south-west of Kaunau-meek, had been an important trading post for the French for many years.

Immediately Brainerd sought to introduce these people to the gospel of Jesus Christ. He found the sachem and, after a friendly introduction of himself, revealed to him his intention — to introduce him to Christianity. The king simply walked away and turned the interview over to another man who evidently held an important position. Brainerd's conversation with this 'principal' person brought to light one of the prime obstacles to his work, with which he would always have to contend — the bad reputation of English Christians. The Indian wondered why Brainerd had come to convert them to the Christian faith when the Christians he had known were much worse than the Indians.

In a later report to the mission agency Brainerd explained this problem in a frank way: 'The Christians, he [the Indian] said, would lie, steal, and drink, worse than the Indians. It was they who first taught the Indians to be drunk; and *they* who stole from one another, to that degree, that their rulers were obliged to hang them for it, and that was not sufficient to deter others from the like practice. But the Indians, he added, were none of them hanged for stealing, and yet they did not steal half so much; and he supposed that if the Indians should become Christians, they would then be as bad as these.'[1]

Brainerd acknowledged to the Indian that there was far too much truth in this objection and not only joined with him in condemning such conduct, but apologized for such scandalous behaviour. Brainerd assured him that such people were not true Christians at heart. After this explanation seemed to calm the man down somewhat Brainerd asked him if he would be willing for him to come again. 'Yes,' he replied, 'if you will come as a friend and not try to make a Christian out of me.' After that comment, the young horseman bid farewell and resumed his journey for the Forks.

The route Brainerd took was the Esopus Road, a 104-mile wagon path which was 'the first man-made highway of any considerable length in the colonies'.[2] It had been constructed in about 1640 by the West India Company to transport ore to Esopus from the Pahaquarry Copper Mines in New Jersey. As he made his way south Brainerd passed several Dutch settlements and isolated homesteads. In all probability he travelled through the mountains by riding along the river. If so, his route would have taken him through the beautiful Delaware Water Gap where the river cuts through the mountain range. On the north rim of the valley he might have paused a moment to view the waters of the Delaware glistening in the light of the May sun.

Brainerd first camped at Hunter's Settlement, a colony of predominantly Ulster-Scotch or Scotch-Irish folk who had settled fifteen years earlier north of the junction of the Delaware River and the Lehigh or West Branch of the Delaware. Wynbeek says, 'The "Dutch" people who also lived near here were not likely Hollanders such as lived north of the Gap, but Palatinate Germans who after 1725 immigrated in increasing numbers into the region from their original Hudson River settlements.'[3]

Brainerd was wet from rain and fatigued from hard riding, but he could now take comfort from the fact that he was within twelve miles of his final destination. He seems not to have been impressed by the natural beauty of the country through which he had been travelling, but focused instead on the spiritual condition of the settlers around him. He awoke on Sunday, 13 May, still weary but also troubled by sinful talk and behaviour around him. He carefully described the reasons for his gloom: 'There appeared to be no Sabbath; the children were all at play; I am a stranger in the wilderness, and knew not where to go; and all circumstances seemed to conspire to render my affairs dark and discouraging.' He needed an interpreter, but had none. He heard that the Indians were scattered, which would make gathering them for a meeting difficult.

Immediately he plunged into his task of preaching. He shared the gospel with the Irish and the Indians on 13 May. Within a week he had again discovered the deep prejudices of the Indians against Christianity, so on the 20th he preached twice to them, seeking to answer their objections. The following Sabbath he visited the Indians and had an opportunity to witness first-hand their funeral customs. He referred to their behaviour as 'heathenish practices', uttering a prayer, 'Oh that they might be "turned from darkness to light"!'

He greeted the Indian chief and proposed to introduce him to the Christian faith. After consulting with some advisers the sachem agreed to give him an audience. Brainerd was then given an opportunity to preach to a group of Indians who had become curious, and they were 'very attentive and well disposed'. The chief especially seemed very interested and was pleased with the message. Brainerd was invited to come back and preach any time he wished. The house of the chief became Brainerd's church for the rest of the summer.

Attendance at the meetings was at first small, usually twenty or twenty-five. But as autumn approached the numbers had increased to forty or more. More importantly, Brainerd's witness was beginning to show some specific results. Some of them began to renounce their idolatry and refused to take part in the feasts during which sacrifices were offered to mysterious deities. Many became concerned about the state of their souls and began to 'inquire the way to Zion'. Their interest continued to grow. They began to bring their friends to the meetings. They asked questions and showed great respect for the young white missionary. He was encouraged. Now he saw concrete evidence that God had begun a work among them which led him to hope that many of them would eventually be converted.

During the fourteen months or so he had spent ministering to the Indians Brainerd had, of course, worked closely with SSPCK. The next important event they had scheduled for him was ordination to the ministry. On 28 May he left the Forks to go to Newark, New Jersey, where the ordination had been planned. He visited Ebenezer Pemberton at New York and

Jonathan Dickinson at Elizabethtown where he spent eight days preparing for his examination. It was the independent Synod of New York, which had been organized specifically to get around the actions of those opposed to the revival, which was to place its imprimatur on Brainerd.

Brainerd was weak and apparently nervous as he prepared for his examination. He was required to preach and the text chosen for him was Acts 26:17-18. It related Paul's own commission from God to take the gospel to the Gentiles, seeking 'to open their eyes, and to turn them from darkness to light, and from the power of Satan unto God'. He was exhausted after preaching. He wrote, 'Was tired, and my mind burdened with the greatness of that charge I was in the most solemn manner about to take upon me; my mind was so pressed with the weight of the world incumbent upon me, that I could not sleep this night, though very weary and in great need of rest.' He was examined the next day, 12 June, and passed the test.

At the 10 o'clock ordination service Ebenezer preached from Luke 14:23: 'And the Lord said unto the servant, Go out into the highways and hedges, and compel them to come in that my house may be filled.' The sermon, printed in many editions of Brainerd's life, had three points:

I. The *melancholy state* of the Gentile world. They are described as 'in the highways and hedges', in the most perishing and helpless condition.

II. The *compassionate care*, which the blessed Redeemer takes of them in these their deplorable circumstances. He 'sent out his servants' to them, to invite them to partake of the entertainments of his house.

III. The *duty of the ministers* of the gospel, to 'compel them to come in' and accept of his gracious invitation.

'These I shall consider in their order,' Pemberton said as he introduced his subject, 'and then apply them to the present occasion.'

The sermon by Pemberton is worthy of careful study. David Brainerd undoubtedly listened in rapt attention, drinking in every word from this minister whom he admired so much. The last point about the duty of ministers to bring sinners to salvation is particularly significant, because it embodied the rich Puritan theology which Brainerd had preached to the Indians. 'Ministers,' said the New Light minister from the Empire state, 'are to compel sinners in several ways'. First, by setting before them their 'guilty and perishing condition by nature'. Secondly by a 'lively representation of the power and grace of our Almighty redeemer'. Thirdly, by encouraging them to accept of Christ and salvation through his merits and righteousness. And finally, by exhibiting the 'unspeakable advantages that will attend a compliance with the gospel call'.

Here is an example of the solid evangelical and Reformed theology which is typical of the New Light ministers. Brainerd's ordination preacher was holding before him an excellent standard for ministry. He pointed the young minister to the right *goal*: that of leading sinners to salvation through Christ. He stated clearly and positively what the *means* should be: the gospel itself, unadorned and untainted by human philosophy. He instructed him on the proper *method* or *style*: he was to preach with tenderness, zeal and compassion. With such a model before him, it is no wonder that the youthful preacher, with hungry souls waiting for him many miles away, carried out so faithfully the mandate of biblical evangelism.

It took Brainerd about three days to travel the seventy miles from Dickinson's home in New Jersey to the Forks of the Delaware, which was at the site of modern Easton, Pennsylvania. He arrived on 21 June. In July he rode thirty miles west to make contact with a group of Indians who, so he was informed, lived at a place known as Kaukesauchung. This is near the present town of Cherryville, just north of Allentown, Pa. This area was long known to be prime Indian territory. The name survives in the present town of Catasauqua, which is south of the ancient Indian village.

Brainerd found these Indians quite ready to listen to him. While he was preaching they became very sombre and attentive. They appeared to be surprised at the unusual information which Brainerd's message brought. But once again there was an objection to be dealt with. They suspected that Brainerd had some 'ill design' upon them. They let the missionary know that the whites had abused them by taking their lands away from them. They were also afraid that Brainerd would make slaves of them and force them to fight with 'people over the water' (meaning the French and Spaniards).

By the end of June 1745 David Brainerd had seen and heard enough about Indian customs and culture to know that any effectual change in them would have to come by the sovereign grace of God. On the 25th he wrote in his diary, 'To an eye of reason, every thing that respects the conversion of the Heathen is as dark as midnight; and yet I cannot but hope in God for the accomplishment of something glorious among them. My soul longed much for the advancement of the Redeemer's kingdom on earth.' This theme was still upon his mind the next day: 'In prayer, my soul was enlarged, and my faith drawn into sensible exercise; was enabled to cry to God for my poor Indians; and though the work of their conversion appeared impossible with man, yet, with God, I saw, all things were possible.'

He was convinced that God was fully able to bring about the great awakening among the Indians he desired: 'It seemed to me that there would be no impediment sufficient to obstruct that glorious work, seeing the living God, as I strongly hoped, was engaged for it.'

As a student of Pauline theology, as well as that of the Puritan Calvinist Edwards, Brainerd was totally dependent on God's power and grace to give him success in his enterprise of evangelism. On 27 June he recorded, 'While I was riding, had a deep sense of the greatness and difficulty of my work; and my soul seemed to rely wholly upon God for success, in the diligent and faithful use of means. Saw with the greatest certainty, that the *arm of the Lord* must be *revealed*, for the help of these poor Heathen, if ever they are delivered from the bondage of the powers of darkness. Spent most of the time, while riding in lifting up my heart for grace and assistance.'

Puritan evangelism involved more than simply bringing about an external reformation. It also regarded true salvation as being more than compliance with a few rituals. It relied on no techniques of crowd psychology to elicit a momentary decision. The sinner, whether he be Gentile or Jew, European or American pagan, was spiritually ignorant and alienated from God. From such a vantage-point there is no simple or easy relief for the dilemma of the natural man. Only God can bring him salvation.

15.
Passion for the lost

During the summer of 1744 Brainerd continued to labour among the Indians at the Forks. His diary reveals an increasingly intense commitment to the missionary work to which he was called. He knew that in order to be really effective he would need to tear from his heart all attachment to the world and carnal pleasure:

> After I had rode more than two miles it came into my mind to dedicate myself to God again, which I did with great solemnity, and unspeakable satisfaction; especially gave up myself to him renewedly in the work of the ministry. This I did by divine grace, I hope, without any exception or reserve; not in the least shrinking back from any difficulties that might attend this great and blessed work. I seemed to be most free, cheerful, and full in this dedication of myself. My whole soul cried 'Lord, to thee I dedicate myself! O accept of me, and let me be thine forever. Lord, I desire nothing else; I desire nothing more. O come, come, Lord, accept a poor worm...' After this was enabled to praise God with my whole soul, that he had enabled me to devote and consecrate all my power to him in this solemn manner. My heart rejoiced in my particular work as a *missionary*;

rejoiced in my necessity of self-denial in many respects;
and still continued to give up myself to God, and implore
mercy of him, praying incessantly, every moment with
sweet fervency (1 July).

The spiritual darkness in which the Indians dwelt was a
great burden to him. On 21 July he began a day of prayer in the
woods so he could have the courage to confront the Indians
about an 'idolatrous feast and dance' which he knew they were
soon to attempt. He prayed with such earnestness and importunity that when he rose from his knees he was nearly overcome with weakness: 'I could scarce walk straight; my joints
were loosed; the sweat ran down my face and body; and nature
seemed as if it would dissolve.'

Unquestionably David Brainerd was now a man with one
burning passion: to win the Indians to a saving knowledge of
Jesus Christ. 'Indeed, I had no notion of joy from this world;
I cared not where or how I lived, or what hardships I went
through, so that I could but gain souls to Christ.' These words
are reminiscent of the tentmaker from Tarsus who became all
things to all men that he might gain some. On 31 July he wrote
to a 'dear friend', 'I would not change my present *mission* for
any other business in the whole world. I may tell you freely,
without vanity and ostentation, God has of late given me great
freedom and fervency in prayer, when I have been so weak and
feeble that my nature seemed as if it would speedily dissolve.
I feel as if my *all* was lost, and I was undone for this world if
the poor Heathen may not be converted.'

Brainerd had known from the time of his induction into the
missionary calling that the Indians living on the branches of
the Susquehanna in Central Pennsylvania would be a target of
his evangelistic outreach. As the European settlers steadily
encroached on their lands in New Jersey and New York they
migrated in increasing numbers to these relatively unspoilt

Brainerd among the Indians

territories. On 1 October he met with Eliab Byram, pastor of the Presbyterian church at Rockciticus, whom he had asked to accompany him to the Susquehanna region. Byram was a Harvard graduate who served for nine or ten years at Rockciticus, which was about forty miles east of the Forks. He, along with Tattamy, Brainerd's interpreter, and two other Indians, planned a trip in October.

The Susquehanna River, which spreads across the central portion of the state, filling, as someone has said, 'the valleys with beauty and sometimes with menace and turmoil',[1] drains 20,000 square miles. The northern branch begins in New York and breaks through the mountain barriers into the heart of the state. The west branch follows a 200-mile course and runs the divide between two watersheds before joining the northern branch to empty into Chesapeake Bay. The confluence of the rivers is at what is now called Sunbury, and in Brainerd's day was the location of an Indian town known as Shamokin, 'the Indian capital'.

Brainerd's destination for his first trip into this picturesque but rugged and wild region was an Indian village on the north branch of the river which he called 'Opeholhaupung'. This was Brainerd's special spelling for the village that is now called Wapwallopen. The Moravians referred to it as Wamphallobank. It was just across the river from the present Berwick and the former Indian village of Nishebeckon at Nescopeck Creek.

On 2 October he rode twenty-five miles into the wilderness which he describes as 'the most difficult and dangerous travelling, by far, that ever any of us had seen'. He notes that it was a country of 'lofty mountains, deep valleys and hideous rocks'. The horse he was riding broke her leg after getting it hung in one of the rocks and she was in such a miserable condition that he had to kill her. As a result he had to continue the trip on foot. As the sun fell over the western mountains

Brainerd and Byram built a fire with a few bushes and made a shelter from the hard frost. After committing themselves to God they slept on the ground.

A look at the map reveals that Brainerd must have travelled an Indian trail west and then followed the Lehigh River in a north-westward direction through the Blue Mountains and the Lehigh Gap. The awesome beauty of this countryside is ravishing, but Brainerd seemed oblivious to its natural glories. Zinzendorf, the Moravian missionary, travelled this region and stated that it was the wildest he had ever seen. A modern traveller can appreciate this perspective if he can remove himself from the comfort of his car and imagine what it would have been like to climb over these rocky cliffs on foot or on horseback.

When Brainerd arrived at Opeholhaupung three days after beginning his journey he found twelve Indian houses and about seventy people. He saluted the sachem 'in a friendly manner' and announced that he had come to discuss Christianity with them. They seemed receptive so, after some discussion, they gathered to hear him preach. He asked if they would be willing to hear him again and, upon receiving a favourable response, he conducted a second service. They even agreed to allow him to speak on the next day. On 6 October he again preached to these Indians and visited them from house to house.

These Opeholhaupung Indians were polite, evidently, but impassive as Brainerd spoke to them about God's remedy for sin. He was impressed again with how hopeless his task was without the special, sovereign intervention of God: 'I was exceedingly sensible of the impossibility of doing any thing for the poor Heathen without special assistance from above; and my soul seemed to rest on God, and leave it to him to do as he pleased in that which I saw was his own cause' (5 October).

On the banks of the Susquehanna

The next day it was again necessary for him to deal with the objections to Christianity he had so often encountered in New York and New Jersey. Although he does not specify in his diary we can presume that the inconsistent lives of the English Christians were the principal barrier to the Indians' acceptance of the gospel. Yet on 8 October they postponed a hunting trip and came to hear him preach again. On the 9th he and his party, after commending themselves to God in prayer and asking for his special protection, set out for the Forks. Once again they made a fire and rested under a shelter made of bark. 'In the night, the wolves howled around us,' he notes ominously, 'but God preserved us.' On the 12th he was back home where he praised God that he had been supported through this difficult and tiring journey which was made on foot.

With the first of his trips to the Susquehanna region behind him Brainerd continued to minister to the Indians at the Forks of the Delaware. His diary entries for the autumn of 1744 show that the attainment of holiness in thought and life was much on his mind at this time. 'I went to the place of public worship, lifting up my heart to God for assistance and grace, in my great work: and God was gracious to me, helping me to plead with him for holiness, and to use the strongest arguments with him, drawn from the incarnation and sufferings of Christ for this very end, that men might be made holy' (14 October). Two days later he wrote, 'Felt a spirit of solemnity and watchfulness; was afraid I should not live to and upon God: longed for more intenseness and spirituality. Spent the day in writing; frequently lifting up my heart to God for more heavenly mindedness. In the evening, enjoyed sweet assistance in prayer; thirsted and pleaded to be as holy as the blessed *angels...*'

As Brainerd's intense longing for holiness increased he continued to regard himself as one who fell far short of God's absolute standard. On 19 October he speaks of enjoying a 'sweet season of bitter repentance and sorrow, that I had wronged that blessed God, who, I was persuaded, was reconciled to me in his dear Son'. The paradox of a 'sweet season' of bitterness can only be understood by a true believer who knows on the one hand of the preciousness of God's forgiving grace and yet on the other hand is aware of his own shortcomings. To feel grief over one's own moral failures is painful because the new man within strives against all violations of God's law. Yet this very pain has a kind of pleasure to it, because the enlightened Christian knows that the repentance he has experienced has only come by the sovereign grace of God working within. Sensitivity to and bitter regret over sin are themselves important marks of regeneration. Brainerd epitomized the pilgrim who longs for a life of devotion to the Saviour. He strives most for holiness and fears sin most of all. As Brainerd said on 19 October 1744, 'And I was afraid of nothing but sin; and afraid of that in every action and thought.'

Brainerd often expressed a desire to leave the world and take his place among the redeemed who are with Christ in heaven. On 26 October he wrote, 'My soul was exceedingly grieved for sin, and prized, and longed after holiness; it wounded my heart deeply, yet sweetly, to think how I had abused a kind God. I longed to be perfectly holy, that I might not grieve a gracious God; who will continue to love, notwithstanding his love is abused!' His often expressed desire to die was not merely a wish to escape the tribulations and trials of this life, although we cannot eliminate that motive altogether. For him the final state in heaven was the supreme goal for living because it afforded final relief from the weight of sin which hung upon him. Such an attitude was expressed by Paul the apostle when he stated that he had a strong 'desire to depart and to be with Christ' (Phil. 1:23).

On the first Monday of November Brainerd wrote an account of his first year as a missionary and addressed it to

Ebenezer Pemberton. That very day he left his residence at the Forks of Delaware to go to New York to meet with the presbytery. During this two-day trip, on a horse he had borrowed, he was exposed to extreme cold and stormy weather. When he returned from New York to the home of Aaron Burr at Newark, he was ill. One cannot but wonder what the thoughts of the members of the missionary society may have been as they interviewed the weak and sickly man they had employed to take the gospel to the Indians. How true are the remarks of David Wynbeek, 'They had employed the frailest among them for the most arduous task.'[2]

Brainerd stayed ten days with Aaron Burr in order to recuperate for the anticipated trip back to the Forks. At the time Burr was, like the Indian missionary, a bachelor. This was a needed time of rest for the weary traveller and surely must have refreshed him spiritually and physically. Burr later married Esther, the next younger sister of Jerusha Edwards and they became the parents of Aaron Burr Jr, the third vice-president of the United States. In 1804 he had his famous duel with Alexander Hamilton at the Weehawken bluff of the New Jersey shore of the Hudson River. At the end of this contest Hamilton lay dead. As Brainerd and the future vice-president's father shared the precious moments together they little thought that one of them would have a son who would rise so high in the world of politics, or be marked in history as one who brought to an untimely death one of the founders of the American Republic.

David Brainerd loved and appreciated his friends. Having no family and having suffered the disgrace of expulsion from college he naturally found in the fellowship of men like Bellamy, Hopkins and Burr encouragement for the journey of life. He regarded them as fellow soldiers in the battle for truth, fellow pilgrims on the long and difficult path to glory. He especially cherished the fellowship of other ministers of the gospel who shared the joys as well as the reproach of divine service. An illustration of such treasured companionship is found in his trip back to the Forks from New York. He dined at Rockciticus, in the Mendham-Morristown region, with Timothy Johnes, a pastor who many years later was privileged to minister to George Washington when the general had his headquarters in the vicinity. After this visit he said, 'My soul loves the people of God, and especially the ministers of Jesus Christ, who feel the same trials I do.'

Brainerd needed the rest and refreshment with Burr and Johnes for the trip home was arduous and dangerous. Evidently he had not fully recovered from the sickness he had experienced in New York for he complained of pain and cold in his head. He was physically unprepared for the miserable time he experienced in getting back to the Forks. 'About six at night, I lost my way in the wilderness, and wandered over rocks and mountains, down hideous steeps, through swamps, and most dreadful and dangerous places; and the night being dark, so that few stars could be seen, I was greatly exposed. I was much pinced with cold and distressed with an extreme pain in my head, attended with sickness at my stomach; so that every step I took was distressing to me. I had little hope for several hours together, but that I must lie out in the woods all night, in this distressed case' (22 November).

Providentally at about 9:00 he found a home where he lodged for the night. The next day he was back at the Hunters' home, his quarters at the missionary station. As he reflected on the difficulties of the past few days he wrote, 'In this world I expect tribulation; and it does not now, as formerly, appear strange to me.' Also he thought about how much greater the trials of others of God's children had been.

16.
The winter of the soul

Since coming to the Delaware River Brainerd had made his residence with the family of Alexander Hunter, who had settled north of the confluence of the Delaware and Lehigh and owned three hundred acres of land. The colony he established here, consisting primarily of Ulster-Scotch or Scotch-Irish folk was known as Hunter's Settlement. Brainerd was given his own room — the same room which would be occupied five years later by his brother John who also was destined to become a missionary to the Indians. As the winter of 1744 began to approach he decided to build his own house, with the help of others.

By 1 December the house was finished and he moved in. This building was quite substantial and stood intact for more than fifty years. Its location is known: it was at Martin's Creek, about 200 yards from a large bend of the Delaware River, eleven miles south of Mt Bethel. In December 1884 the Brainerd Society of Lafayette College erected a modest granite monument to mark the site. According to tradition Brainerd dug a well at this house which remained in use for a century.

It was a day of joy and delight when he moved into his house on 6 December. He cherished the privacy of his new place where he could have more time to study and pray. He decided to spend this first day in fasting and prayer, reflecting on the 'extreme difficulties' that attended his work and how little success he had thus far. His spirit was almost overwhelmed at the depressing thought that despite all his efforts the Indians to whom he had been preaching were still 'worshipping devils'. He also lamented the fact that he had become too attached to 'earthly objects' and had at times been too desirous of death as an escape from his earthly woes.

But the miserable condition of the Indians did not prevent him from finding solace in reflecting upon God's own essential glory, which is unchangeable and imperishable. 'Towards night I felt my soul rejoice, that God is unchangeably happy and glorious; and that he will be glorified, whatever becomes of his creatures.' This concept that God is himself self-sufficient, happy and devoted to his own glory is a view which permeated the latter-day Puritanism which was coloured so strongly by the theology of Edwards. Preachers such as Bellamy, Hopkins and Brainerd found great delight in dwelling upon this abstract idea. It removed them, at least temporarily, from the inconveniences and discouragements of their own immediate situation.

On Sunday, 9 December, Brainerd travelled about ten miles from his house and preached twice at Greenwich, New Jersey. His first message was delivered without warmth and power. He was concerned about this and went alone into the bushes where he cried out to God for pardon for his deadness. His second attempt came off much better. He felt great fervency and was able to address precious souls with 'affection, concern, tenderness, and importunity'. He sensed that God was present in the service: 'The effects were apparent, tears running down many cheeks.'

He was encouraged by the way some of his hearers were being aroused spiritually through his preaching. Even his interpreter Tattamy apparently began to come under conviction. Commenting on this change he says, 'Found my Interpreter under some concern for his soul; which was some comfort to me; and yet filled me with a new care. I longed greatly for his conversion; lifted up my heart to God for it, while I was talking to him; came home, and poured out my soul to God for him' (12 December). The next day he continued to pray for the interpreter and three or four others who were under conviction.

But then in the very midst of these encouraging developments an unexpected temptation arose which plunged him into one of his most poignant depressions. On 13 December he complained of pride and wandering thoughts. The first of these 'cursed iniquities' was a secret thought that by succeeding as an Indian missionary he might become famous. 'The former of these cursed iniquities excited me to think of writing, preaching, or converting heathens, or performing some other great work, that my name might live when I should be dead. My soul was in anguish, and ready to drop into despair, to find so much of that cursed temper.'

The sense of guilt over these ambitions so tormented him in the next few days that it became an obsession. On Sunday,16 December, he felt himself sinking, as it were, into the very depths of despair: 'Was so overwhelmed with dejection, that I knew not how to live. I longed for death exceedingly: my soul was sunk into deep waters, and the floods were ready to drown me.' He was so discouraged that it was with great difficulty that he was able to preach to the Indians.

But these days of grief were perhaps only preparations for the tremendous blessings which were soon to come upon his ministry. By the middle of December he was now beginning to see the 'first fruits', as it were, of the awakening which would eventually take place among his Indians. His interpreter, though still not formally a Christian, began to become more animated and enthusiastic as he translated Brainerd's messages. Then Brainerd noticed that many of his hearers were becoming deeply moved. An old man who looked to be a hundred years old openly wept as he preached and seemed to be convinced of the truth of his message. He praised God for these developments and exhorted Tattamy to 'strive to enter in at the strait gate'.

In a letter written on Christmas Eve, he laid bare his soul to an unnamed New Jersey pastor, revealing himself to be a man who found little pleasure in life as such, except as it was a means to serve and glorify God: 'I can tell you, that if I gain experience in no other point, yet I am sure that I do in this ... that the present world has nothing in it to satisfy an immortal soul; and hence, that it is not to be desired for itself, but only because God may be seen and served in it... It is no virtue, I know, to desire death, only to be freed from the miseries of life; but I want that divine hope which you observed, when I saw you last, was the very sinews of vital religion. Yet we ought to desire, or at least to be resigned to tarry in it; because it is the will of our all-wise Sovereign.'

The winter of 1744-45 developed into a terrible one for David Brainerd. There were perhaps a number of factors which combined to darken his already sombre moods. Long cold nights, stormy weather and confinement within the walls of a house are notorious for the breeding of negative emotions. What an encouragement a godly wife would have been for him, but he had chosen to walk his pilgrimage alone.

But it was not just his loneliness or the snowdrifts accumulating outside his cabin that made the wilderness witness so miserable. He refers to 'vapour disorders, melancholy, and spiritual desertion' as the causes of his agony as he laboured on in preaching to the Indians. On 27 January he had almost 'the greatest degree of inward anguish' which he had endured thus far. It was Sunday and he was scheduled to preach to the Indians. 'I was perfectly overwhelmed, and so confused, that after I began to discourse to the Indians, before I could finish a sentence, sometimes I forgot entirely what I was aiming at;

or if, with much difficulty, I had recollected what I had designed, still it appeared strange, and like something I had long forgotten, and had now but an imperfect remembrance of.' This mysterious mood of gloom continued until about nine o'clock that night when 'the cloud was scattered' while he was praying for the Indians. On Friday of the same week this melancholy rose 'to an extreme height'. It continued through Saturday, until again he experienced some relief.

On Sunday, 3 February, he reflected on the 'slough of despondency' through which he had been walking. He refers to his Friday agony as 'the wormwood and the gall'. He feared that he would once again be called upon to drink of that 'cup of trembling'. It was, he said, 'inconceivably more bitter than death, and made me long for the grave more, unspeakably more, than for hid treasures, yea inconceivably more than the men of this world long for such treasures'.

These melancholy moods are one of the more significant phenomena which leap from the pages of David Brainerd's diary. This tendency was a human weakness and frailty which he knew well and lamented. There are frailties of the human body and there are frailties of the human spirit. A strong physical frame is a blessing; a sickly body is a burden. A joyful, optimistic spirit is wholesome and useful. Depression is not only a real trial but can be a tool of Satan to inhibit Christian service. Solomon said, 'A cheerful heart is good medicine, but a crushed spirit dries up the bones' (Prov. 17:22). David Brainerd seems for much of his life not to have enjoyed this 'good medicine' which carries a person through the inevitable bumps and bruises of life.

While recognizing that the saintly Indian missionary struggled with negative moods of the foulest and darkest nature, we can see the hand of God even in this. All things, including emotional ills, work together for good to those who love God and are the called according to his purpose. In dark caverns beneath the earth miners find the most precious of jewels. God unquestionably allowed David Brainerd to struggle with terrible inner conflicts, and yet out of his rich soul the most beautiful flowers grew. He tasted the cup of human misery, to be sure, and yet his heavenly Father was using these afflictions to wean him from all earthly comfort, so that he would delight himself totally in God. The world was a barren wilderness to him, and yet this made his longing for the glories of heaven more intense. Edwards, who published his diary, recoiled at some of the desperate statements he made. Yet most of them he left intact so that people could make an honest evaluation of Brainerd's character.

History has enshrined David Brainerd as one of the great believers of history. He loved God intensely. He sacrificed himself for the noblest of causes — evangelism. But he was not a perfect man. His flaws, as well as his virtues, are matter of historical record. He chose to disclose the intermost secrets of his heart in a personal diary which he did not want to be published. But published they were and his frequent fits of gloom are there for all to see. Who could stand if all their inner motivations and attitudes were recorded for all the world? What anger, bitterness, jealousy, and lust torment the greatest of God's people! Paul himself describes the struggle between the flesh and the Spirit in Romans 7. Every Christian fails and struggles with temptation and corruption. Essentially Brainerd was no different from anyone else; he simply chose to write his struggles down. All in all, the world is a much better place because he did so.

Even in the midst of this most miserable of winters Brainerd continued to preach to the Indians at the Forks of the Delaware. For the most part the only witnesses to the public services of this frail but intense man were the Indians themselves who left no record behind. On 17 February, however, he had occasion to speak to a crowd of white people who had gathered on the 'sunny side' of a hill. They had come from as far as thirty miles to hear him. His text was John 7:37, where we read that Jesus stood and cried out saying, 'If anyone thirsts, let him come to me and drink.' It was a blessed time: 'I think I was scarce ever enabled to offer the free grace of God to perishing sinners with more freedom and plainness in my life.' Also he invited those who were already saved to continually come to the fountain of the water of life and drink. Many were moved: 'There were many tears in the assembly; and I doubt not but that the Spirit of God was there, convincing poor sinners of their need of Christ.'

One of the 'white' people who was there lived to report about this memorable service. Jane Wilson, a fifteen-year-old, had come on horseback from Bath, near Craig's Settlement. In the *Reminiscenses* of Dr John C. Clyde she recalls how she stood on that mild winter day under a large apple tree and heard the Indian missionary. In 1810, when she was eighty years old, she still knew the exact spot of Brainerd's pulpit. The green hill, she wrote, was a few yards from the old Presbyterian church at Martin's Creek.

Another hearer may have been Mary Walker, the widow of James King, whose gravestone is the oldest in the Craig's Settlement graveyard. This woman with her four daughters would often 'take a child in her arm and ride to Mt Bethel to hear Brainerd preach in the open air'.[1]

A week later he went back to the Indians to preach, but Tattamy was not present to interpret for him. He secured, however, the help of a 'Dutchman' who substituted for the interpreter, but not very efficiently. He preached on this occasion from John 6:67 on the loving invitation of Jesus Christ to his own people who had drifted away from him or backslidden. He spoke about how gracious God is to welcome his own people back to him after they have for a while succumbed to worldliness. All this came from his own experience for he sensed that he himself had been guilty of a sort of carnality, that of 'laboring for spiritual life, peace of conscience, and progressive holiness, in my own strength'. God seemed to be teaching him that *he* is the fountain of grace, not only for initial forgiveness of sin but for continual supplies of grace for assistance in the pursuit of holiness.

Edwards comments that in the pursuing weeks Brainerd 'had frequent refreshing, invigorating influences of God's Spirit', although he still complained of times of dullness. One can see in these remarks a positive development in the missionary's progress. He was beginning to depend on God more and look to his abundant resources for overcoming power in the Christian warfare rather than relying on his own resolves and strivings.

17.
The harbingers of revival

In the spring of 1745 the war with France was in full progress. The colonies of New England were making frantic preparations for the final assault against the French fort at Louisbourg on Cape Breton. At Northampton, where Jonathan Edwards was leading the Congregational Church, watchtowers were being built for protection against French-Indian attacks. Edwards was so concerned that on 4 April he preached a sermon entitled 'Fast for Success in the Expedition against Cape Breton'. George Whitefield was invited to be chaplain for this expedition, but he refused.

As these turbulent political and military events were taking place, Brainerd, unperturbed by them no doubt, left the Forks of Delaware during March and April and travelled some six hundred miles throughout New England, visiting places in New Jersey, New York and Connecticut. The purpose for this trip was to raise funds to support a colleague to travel with him in his long and arduous evangelistic trips. He notes in his diary that after spending two years 'in a very solitary manner' it seemed necessary to find a helper. Since 'Christ sent out his disciples two and two,' he reasoned, this should be an excellent model for his own ministry. Eight months later he confessed that he had not found anyone 'qualified and disposed' for this good work, although several ministers had encouraged him to believe that money could be raised for his maintenance, should an associate be found.

He was not able to visit Stockbridge on his trip but while at Woodbury, Connecticut, he hurriedly sent a letter to John Sergeant in which he gave an account of some of his experiences since leaving New York. Also he demonstrated not only a continual interest in the Indian work at Stockbridge but a willingness to help in that cause financially:

> I long to hear of your affairs; and especially how things are like to turn out with respect to your plan of a free boarding-school, which is an affair much upon my heart amidst all my heavy concerns, and I can learn nothing whether it is like to succeed or not.
>
> I fully designed to have given something considerable for promoting that good design; but whether I shall be able to give any thing, or whether it will be my duty to do so under present circumstances, I know not. I have met with sundry losses lately, to the value of sixty or seventy pounds, New England money. In particular, I broke my mare's leg last fall in my journey to Susquehannah, and was obliged to kill her on the road, and prosecute my journey on foot, and I can't get her place supplied for fifty pounds. And I lately moved to have a colleague or companion with me, my spirits sink with my solitary circumstances. And I expect to contribute something to his maintenance, seeing his salary must be raised wholly in this country and can't be expected from Scotland.[1]

Brainerd mentioned in this letter to Sergeant several details concerning the sale of certain personal items such as an iron tea kettle and bed-ticking, the proceeds from which he intended to give to Sergeant for his mission work. He instructs that his blankets be turned into 'deer skins' and sent to Samuel Hopkins or Joseph Bellamy. 'Please to remember me to Madam and all friends,' he concludes.

On his way back he stopped at Woodbridge, New Jersey, where he met with several ministers to consult 'about the affairs of Christ's kingdom, in some important articles'. No doubt among these ministers was Jonathan Dickinson who had been installed as the moderator of the newly organized New York Presbyterian Synod.

Brainerd arrived back at the Forks of the Delaware on 13 April and immediately gave thanks to God for preserving him during his five-week excursion into New England. He preached on Sunday, 14 April, from Ezekiel 33:11: 'As I live, saith the Lord Jehovah, I have no pleasure in the death of the wicked; but that the wicked turn from his way and live.' With or without a companion, Brainerd's plans to visit the Susquehanna Indians had to go on. His trip to Opeholhaupung in October of the previous year had convinced him that this was by far the most promising territory in terms of the potential for outreach among the Indian tribes. In fact it seemed to him that before long it would be prudent for him to leave the Forks and settle among the tribes on the Susquehanna.

In order to secure an advantage with the Indians Brainerd decided to go to Philadelphia in the middle of April to see the Deputy Governor, George Thomas. He was a friend of the Chief of the Six Nation Iroquois Confederacy which controlled vast territories in the American frontier, including the Susquehanna region.

The Six Nation Confederacy began in the sixteenth century and consisted originally of five Indian tribes: the Cayuga, Mohawk, Onondaga, Oneida and the Seneca. In 1710 they admitted the Tuscaroras on their southern borders, completing the alliance. Their original land claims were the wedge-shaped territory of their residence, stretching from Lake Erie in the

north-west to the upper Hudson Valley in the north-east and
what is now the north-west corner of North Carolina in the
south. By conquest they dominated a much wider area, taking
in all the Great Lakes region of North America, all of Ohio,
most of Illinois, Kentucky, Tennessee, North Carolina, Vir-
ginia, as well as New Hampshire and Vermont. This alliance
was a force to be contended with throughout the 1700s and no
political decisions were made by the colonial government
without taking into consideration the attitudes of the Six
Nation leadership.

In Brainerd's time various Indian tribes who had been
forced to leave their homes in the white man's colonies lived
all up and down both of the upper branches of the Susquehanna
and the larger river south into which they emptied. The 450-
mile course of the river from New York to Maryland was a part
of the Catawba War Trail that extended from their capital
Onondaga in Central New York to North Carolina. It was one
of their primary highways which the Iroquois used to control
the tribes they had subjugated in the south.

Some of the specific tribes along the Susquehanna were the
Senecas — one of the members of the alliance — the Susque-
hannocks, whom Captain Smith had first discovered in Vir-
ginia, and the Shawnees. Another tribe here were the
Nanticokes, who were greatly feared by the other tribes
because of their reputed skill in witchcraft. One of their
unusual customs was that of removing the bones of their dead
from place to place during their migrations.

Another important tribe was the Lenni Lenape, more com-
monly known as the Delawares. They had originally resided in
the region of the Mississippi, but they migrated to the
Allegheny region and settled along the Susquehanna river
because this valley abounded in wild life, water-fowl and fish.
However, the Delaware Indians were conquered by the Iroquois confederation and were reduced to a sort of vassalage.

In the language of the Indians the Delaware tribe had to become 'women', that is, they were forced to completely give up any territorial claims and cease any war-making endeavours. This was the greatest humiliation an Indian nation could endure.

On 8 May, though somewhat tired from the recent journey to New England, Brainerd set out with Tattamy for the Susquehanna region. Edwards does not quote any of Brainerd's diary notes during this twenty-four-day trip but summarizes what happened:

> The *next day*, he set out on his journey to the Susquehanna, with his interpreter. He endured great hardships and fatigues in his way thither through a hideous wilderness; where, after having lodged one night in the open woods, he was overtaken with a north-easterly storm, in which he was almost ready to perish. Having no manner of shelter, and not being able to make a fire in so great a rain, he could have no comfort if he stopped; therefore he determined to go forward in hopes of meeting with some shelter, without which he thought it impossible to live the night through; but their horses — happening to eat poison, for the want of other food, at a place where they lodged the night before — were so sick, that they could neither ride nor lead them, but were obliged to drive them, and travel on foot; until, through the mercy of God, just at dusk, they came to a bark hut, where they lodged that night.
>
> After he came to the Susquehanna, he travelled about a hundred miles on the river, and visited many towns and settlements of the Indians; saw some of seven or eight tribes, and preached to different nations, by different interpreters. He was sometimes much discouraged, and sunk in his spirits, through the opposition which appeared

in the Indians to Christianity. At other times, he was
encouraged by the disposition which some of these
people manifested to hear, and willingness to be instructed. He here met with some who had formerly been
his hearers at Kaunaumeek, and had removed hither;
who saw and heard him again with great joy. He spent
a fortnight among the Indians on this river, and passed
through considerable labours and hardships, frequently
lodging on the ground, and sometimes in the open air. At
length he felt extremely ill, as he was riding in the
wilderness, being seized with an ague, followed with a
burning fever, and extreme pains in his head and bowels,
attended with a great evacuation of blood; so that he
thought he must have perished in the wilderness. But at
last coming to an Indian trader's hut, he got leave to stay
there; and though without physic or food proper for him,
it pleased God, after about a week's distress to relieve
him so far that he was able to ride. He returned home-
wards from Juncauta, an island far down the river; where
was a considerable number of Indians, who appeared
more free from prejudices against Christianity, than
most of the other Indians. He arrived at the Forks of
Delaware on Thursday, May 30, after having rode in this
journey about three hundred and forty miles.

On the first Sabbath after his return he preached from Isaiah
53:10 on the expression: 'It pleased the Lord to bruise him.'
Some were aroused by this message.

Early in June Brainerd was back in his familiar and much-
beloved residence where he could again spend a lot of time in
prayer and meditation. On 5 June he remarked that he 'felt
thirsting desires after God'. Fellowship with God was precious
during these days. He described how he felt:

In the evening, enjoyed a precious season of retirement: was favored with some clear and sweet meditations upon a sacred text; divine things opened with clearness and certainty, and had a divine stamp upon them. My soul was enlarged and refreshed in prayer; I delighted to continue in the duty; and was sweetly assisted in praying for my fellow-christians, and my dear brethren in the ministry. Blessed be the dear Lord for such enjoyments. O how sweet and precious it is, to have a clear apprehension and tender sense of the *mystery of godliness*, of true holiness and of likeness to the best of beings. Oh what a blessedness it is, to be as much like God, as it is possible for a creature to be like his great Creator! Lord give me more of *thy likeness*; 'I shall be satisfied, when I awake with it' (5 June).

On 7 June he rode nearly fifty miles to Neshaminy to assist Charles Beatty in his communion service. He was tired from the journey but the next day he preached from Isaiah 40:1 on the text: 'Comfort ye, comfort ye my people, saith your God.' The Lord was with him and he preached with great freedom. Reflecting on this service later he commented in his diary, now swelling with information about his fascinating experiences, 'Blessed be the Lord, it was a sweet melting season in that assembly.'

Brainerd had now spent about a year at the Forks of the Delaware and the results had not been significantly different from those of his earlier labours in New York. The Indians had for the most part been attentive and respectful, but their hearts seemed strongly prejudiced against the gospel he loved. One can sense, however, in the missionary a growing confidence in his preaching and increased power in the meetings. That power was demonstrated in a fresh and unusual way when he visited Beatty at Neshimany. The 'melting season' the day before the Sabbath was a precursor of things to come.

The first two years of Brainerd's Indian ministry were not unlike those of Elijah the Tishbite in the time of the wicked King of Israel, Ahab. Just as there was no rain for three and a half years in those ancient times, producing a terrible drought, so from a spiritual standpoint Brainerd's ministry among the Indians had so far been without the refreshing ministry of the Holy Spirit in the abundant fashion he had hoped for. He had seen nothing of the traumatic convictions and marvellous conversions that had taken place under the ministry of Gilbert Tennent when he was a student at Yale. Certainly there had been no massive movement towards God such as Whitefield had experienced. But there were some signs that this was about to change, although we cannot be sure Brainerd was aware of what was happening.

The first indication that the rains were about to come in Elijah's day was the passing of a cloud from the sea over the top of Mount Carmel following the prophet's victory over the prophets of Baal. On 9 June 1745 a cloud of mercy appeared over the head of the prophet of the American wilderness, David Brainerd. It was at the long anticipated communion service at Neshaminy. The previous day was a 'melting season' but this was more. Brainerd preached on that day from Isaiah 53:10, one of his favourite texts, on the substitutionary work of Christ. He had a huge audience of over three thousand people, the most he had ever ministered to so far. He laid his notes aside and spoke extempore. As he addressed the great throng he lost himself in the theme. It was an unusual service. 'The word was attended', he later wrote, 'with amazing power.' Hundreds were 'much affected' by the message and there was much weeping. As he saw the deep concern of his hearers Brainerd thought about the promise of Zechariah 12:10-11 in which God promised to pour out the spirit of grace and supplication upon the house of Israel. When that happens they will mourn for him 'as a man mourns for his only son'. 'In that day,' said Zechariah, 'there shall be a great mourning in Jerusalem, like the mourning at Hadad Rimmon in the plain of Megiddo.'

This was indeed a small cloud coming over the land. Here were the first signs of the revival power that David Brainerd had for so long prayed and longed for. This was the firstfruits of a great awakening.

18.
Springs in the desert

First there was Kaunaumeek, which Brainerd had described as a 'lonely melancholy desert'. Then he went to the Forks of the Delaware, where he built a house and gained the respect of the Indians, but saw little in the way of real results from his preaching. He had also been to the Susquehanna, the river of many Indian tribes where hearts were desperately hard. By June 1745 he felt very discouraged. On the 19th he made a frank confession of a sense of failure relative to his preaching at the Forks and to the Indians to the west: 'Not having had any considerable appearance of special success in either of those places, my spirits were depressed, and I was not a little discouraged.'

Then he heard about some Indians living at a place called Crossweeksung, in New Jersey, about eighty miles south-east of the Forks. After reflecting on the matter a while, he decided to go there and 'see what might be done towards christianizing them'. Crossweeksung is now known as Crosswicks and is seven to eight miles south-east of Trenton. It was settled originally in 1681 by Quakers, the same year as Philadelphia. There had been an extensively used iron ore bog at Crossweeksung and when Brainerd arrived four mills and a tannery were in operation.

The situation in which the Indians of New Jersey found themselves at this time is described by Wynbeek: 'After a

Sign of the town of Crosswicks (formerly called Crossweeksung)

The post office at Crosswicks

century of white occupation, few Indians lingered in New Jersey, especially after the veritable flood of immigrants arrived between 1700 and 1745. Only a few remnant Delawares lived as beggars on the fringes of the white man's villages. Decimated by epidemics of smallpox and the flow of firewater, they eked out their livelihood from the fields and woods by making baskets, brooms, and wooden utensils to sell to their white neighbors. In varying degrees they understood or spoke English, and intermarriages with runaway Negro slaves was not uncommon. However they maintained some contact with the Forks of Delaware and interior Indians.'[1]

On the basis of what he knew about them Brainerd had no reason to expect any different reception from these Indians than from those to whom he had formerly preached. In fact some of them, a few months previously, had expressed strong opposition to Brainerd's interpreter who had sought to teach them about the Christian gospel. They had demonstrated as much hostility to Christianity as any he had seen.

When Brainerd came to Crossweeksung to preach he found few Indians. There were not more than two or three families in any specific location, and these few were in small settlements several miles from each other. But from the first time he began to speak to them, they had a different attitude from others he had met. They were 'well disposed, serious and attentive, and not inclined to cavil and object, as the Indians had done elsewhere'. His first audience consisted of a few women and children. When he told them that he would be back to speak again the next day they eagerly went to invite their friends, ten or fifteen miles away, to come and hear him. These first hearers seemed to Brainerd like the woman of Samaria in wanting others to come and see the man who had told them about the folly of a life of wickedness and ignorance of God. He went to bed that night very tired but encouraged. The next day he preached again to those who had been invited by the women. These also were 'attentive, orderly and well disposed'. An even larger crowd was present that evening to hear his message.

Perhaps to refresh himself, or to fulfil a previous commitment, he went on 21 June to visit William Tennent Jr, who was pastor of the Presbyterian Church at Freehold. William was the brother of Gilbert, the famous evangelist who had stirred New England when Brainerd was at college. The people of Freehold had sided with the New Light revivals and seven thousand gathered on 1 May 1740 to hear Whitefield.

On 22 June Brainerd came back to Crossweeksung and found that the Indians had increased in numbers from six or seven to nearly thirty. They listened with 'solemn attention' when he preached to them — an indication that they had been impressed with the power of his message. Several demonstrated conviction for sin and an earnest desire for salvation, even to the point of weeping because of their longing to become true Christians. The next day was the Sabbath and Brainerd preached to a crowd that had swelled to even greater numbers. He could not but be impressed with the fact that none of them cavilled against the message he preached to them.

The interest among the Indians in his ministry increased to the point where they asked him to preach to them twice a day. He was delighted at this growing hunger and of course cheerfully responded to their request. After preaching to them twice on Monday, 1 July, he spoke to many of them privately to see how much they had absorbed. It was with immense satisfaction that he recorded: 'It was amazing to see how they had received and retained the instructions given them, and what a measure of knowledge some of them had acquired in a few days.'

This awakening at Crossweeksung was encouraging, but Brainerd still had a heart for the Indians at the Forks, so he decided early in July that he would visit them again. When they heard this, the New Jersey Indians said in effect, 'Hurry back,' and promised to travel throughout the territory and bring many others to attend on his ministry when he returned. They even agreed to live in the same village as long as he remained among them and were willing to recognize him as their spiritual leader. As he prepared to depart for the Forks of Delaware a woman said to him, tears streaming down her face, 'I wish God would change my heart.' Another woman expressed a desire to 'find Christ' and an old man, formerly one of their chiefs, 'wept bitterly with concern for his soul'.

All of this was encouraging. Brainerd was very hopeful that the blessing for which he had long prayed and laboured was beginning to come about. Yet he had seen good signs before which had come to nothing. More than ever he was suspended between hope and fear — hope that many of the Indians would come to Christ for salvation, but also fear that the good impressions and convictions would pass away and that they would return to their pagan ways. Of one thing he was absolutely convinced: only God could effectually do a work of grace among the Indians. 'I have learned,' he remarked, 'that he only can open the ear, engage the attention, and incline the hearts of poor benighted, prejudiced pagans to receive instruction.'

His daily labours among the Indians at Crossweeksung had left the missionary exhausted, so he determined to take a break. He spent about a week in New Jersey, visiting several other ministers, including no doubt Burr and Dickinson, who were directors of the missionary society. On 12 July he arrived back at his house at the Forks. The melancholy which had dogged him in days past seemed in a great measure to have left him now. Without a doubt the good results of his preaching in New Jersey were part of the reason. His diary for 18 and 19 July reveals that his times of quiet and meditation were now delightful seasons of praise and thanksgiving. He spent some time reflecting on Revelation 3:12: 'Him that overcometh will

I make a pillar in the temple of my God.' Afterwards he wrote, 'This was then a delightful theme to me, and it refreshed my soul to dwell on it. O when shall I go no more out from the service and enjoyment of the dear Redeemer! Lord hasten the blessed day!' (19 July).

Although there was obviously a work of God going on among the Indians in New Jersey, the Forks of the Delaware had the distinction of yielding the first open profession of faith for Brainerd's missionary labours. In the summer of the previous year Moses Tattamy, Brainerd's interpreter, had shown significant signs of interest in the Christian gospel. Brainerd noticed that he became very enthusiastic as he translated the missionary's words to the Indians. This initial response had matured by the summer of 1745 into a positive commitment. Brainerd had the privilege of baptizing Tattamy and his wife on 21 July and his children on 26 July. As a pædo-Baptist Brainerd followed the form laid down in the *Westminster Confession* which states that 'Not only those that do actually profess faith in, and obedience unto Christ, but also the infants of one or both believing parents are to be baptized.' When Tattamy's children were baptized, they were, in the usual Presbyterian-Congregationalist fashion, brought into the visible church through baptism, the 'sign and seal of the covenant'.

Tattamy, who had gone to work for Brainerd in the summer of 1744 when he was about fifty years old, was well equipped for this work. He was fluent in the various Indian dialects and in English. He was also thoroughly familiar with Indian manners and customs and recognized their need for better education and culture. But he had no interest in religion as such either from a theoretical or practical standpoint. Although during the first months of his employment by Brainerd he had given up the 'hard drinking' in which he had formerly indulged, he 'seemed to have no concern about his own soul'.

Brainerd and his interpreter

As his association with Brainerd continued, however, Tattamy became increasingly concerned about his spiritual state. Soon conviction of his lost condition became acute and he even lost sleep from anxiety. Brainerd described his feelings at this time as follows: 'After he had been some time under this exercise, while he was striving to obtain mercy, he says there seemed to be an *impassable mountain* before him. He was pressing towards heaven, as he thought; but "his way was hedged up with thorns, so that he could not stir an inch further." He looked this way and that way, but could find no way at all. He thought if he could but make his way through these thorns and briers, and climb up the first steep pitch of the mountain, that then there might be hope for him; but no way or means could he find to accomplish this... He saw it was *impossible*, he says, for him ever to help himself through this insupportable difficulty. "It signified just nothing at all for him to struggle and strive any more."'

Later on Tattamy came to be strongly convinced, not only that he was without any real power in this spiritual struggle, but that he was utterly guilty in his sins and unworthy of God's grace. He came to see that he had never done a single good thing, as far as recommending him to God was concerned. Brainerd says, 'He knew he was not guilty of some wicked actions of which he knew some others guilty. He had not been accustomed to steal, quarrel, and murder; the latter of which vices is common among the Indians. He likewise knew that he had done many things that were right; he had been kind to his neighbors, etc. "But still his cry was, that he had *never done one good thing*." "I knew," said he, "that I had not been so bad as some others in some things; and that I had done many things which folks call good; but all this did me no good now." ... "And now, I thought," said he, "that I must sink down to hell; that there was no hope for me, because I never could do anything that was good: and if God let me alone ever so long, and I should try ever so much, still I should do nothing but what is bad.'''

Like produces like. One can see in the feelings and attitudes of Tattamy some of the struggles, and particularly the sense of hopelessness, that Brainerd himself felt in his pursuit of peace with God. Eventually Tattamy seemed to hear a voice, almost as if it had spoken audibly to him, which said, 'There is hope, there is hope.' He came then to rest on this hope, which was in God's mercy, and peace filled his heart.

Brainerd described with great delight the remarkable change that came upon his interpreter after his initial moment of conversion:

> But these exercises of soul were attended and fol-lowed with a very great *change* in the man; so that it might justly be said he was become *another man*, if not a *new man*.
>
> His change is abiding, and his life, so far as I know, unblemished to this day... He seems to have a very considerable experience of *spiritual exercise*, and dis-courses feelingly of the conflicts and consolations of a real Christian. His heart echoes to the soul-humbling doctrines of grace, and he never appears better pleased than when he hears of the *absolute sovereignty of God*, and the salvation of sinners in a way of *mere free grace*. He has lately had also more satisfaction respecting *his own state*; and has been much enlightened and assisted in his work; so that he has been a great comfort to me.

Brainerd, like all those who were directly affected by the Great Awakening, required a high standard for those whom they were willing to acknowledge as real converts. They must know and feel their own unworthiness and ill-deserving and depend solely on the grace of God. They were expected to manifest a positive change of character and conduct and abandon any sinful practices of their past life. Brainerd was satisfied that Moses Tattamy had passed the test. In a somewhat official way, he recorded the following analysis on 21 July, the day of Tattamy's baptism: 'After a strict observation of his serious and savoury conversation, his christian temper, and unblemished behaviour for such a length of time, as well as his experience, of which I have given an account; I think that I have reason to hope that he is "created anew in Christ Jesus to good works".'

Jonathan Edwards, who had himself seen many such conversions in his own ministry at Northampton, introduced the section of Brainerd's diary dealing with this fruitful period of his life with considerable pathos. Commenting on Brainerd's success among the Indians he writes, 'Long had he agonized in prayer and travailed in birth for their conversion. Often had he cherished the hope of witnessing that desirable event; only to find that hope yield to fear and in the end disappointment. But after a patient continuance in prayer, in labour, and in suffering, as it were through a long night, at length he is permitted to behold the dawning of the day... He went forth weeping, bearing precious seed; and now he comes rejoicing, bringing his sheaves with him.'

The missionary's spirit soared after the conversion of Tattamy and his wife. His own preaching had begun to bear fruit. His prayers were more intense and joyful. He writes, 'My soul was drawn out for the encouragement of Christ's kingdom, and for the conversion of my poor people, and my soul relied on God for the accomplishment of that great work.' He still had longings for death, but not so much because of misery in this world but because of the glorious anticipation of the ecstasy of heaven: 'How I longed to be with Christ, to be employed in the glorious work of the angels, and with an angel's vigor and delight! Yet how willing was I to stay a while on earth, that I might do something, if the Lord pleased for his interest in the world. My soul, my very soul, longed for the ingathering of the poor Heathen; and I cried to God most willingly and heartily' (26 July).

Such confessions need no commentary. For pathos, for intensity, for purity of intent and motive, where can they be equalled in all of Christian literature? Philosophers have spoken of the 'God-intoxicated' man. If anyone deserves this distinction, the wilderness preacher David Brainerd does.

19.
The windows of heaven open

The passion to save souls from eternal misery through the preaching of the gospel is a feeling so intense that it can really be understood only by those who have felt it. The prophets and apostles of Holy Scripture, touched as they were with the compassion of the God who sent them, were not hesitant in expressing this emotion. Jeremiah, who was called upon to stand in the gate of the temple and watch the ill-fated people of Jerusalem, cried out, 'Oh, that my head were waters, and mine eyes a fountain of tears, that I might weep day and night for the slain of the daughter of my people!' (Jer. 9:1). The soul of Paul was so moved by the needs of the same wayward nation that he affirmed in a solemn manner — his conscience witnessing that he was not lying — that he could even wish himself accursed from Christ for them (Rom. 9:3).

For the psalmist the ecstasy of leading men to God was like the joy of the farmer, who after long hours of hard work in the fields returns during the harvest with sheaves of wheat cradled in his arms (Ps. 126:6). Jesus compared the evangelist to a fisherman who 'catches men' (Luke 5:10) by throwing out the gospel net. What greater work is there, what yields greater reward, than knowing that one has been a means of saving a soul from death and hiding a multitude of sins? (James 5:19-20).

In August 1745 David Brainerd, who was called by God to share the life-giving message with people who were as far removed from the light of truth as can be imagined, experienced in an abundant way the soul-winner's reward. Shortly after his return from the Forks of the Delaware, in the last days of July, Brainerd went alone, as he had so often done before, and poured out his soul on behalf of the Indians of Crossweeksung. There was a difference this time, however. Up till now his prayers had gone up to God without much visible hope of success. In the early months of his ministry he had faithfully shared the word with the Mohegans of New York and the Delawares of Pennsylvania, but with meagre results. But now there were signs everywhere that the sovereign Spirit of God was stirring the hearts of the savages as he did the dead, dry bones of Ezekiel's vision.

Brainerd had left the Delawares in New Jersey under strong convictions and earnest pleas that he return to them. His expectations were high, and yet what was taking place seemed almost too good to be true: 'If the blessed work might be accomplished to the honor of God, and the enlargement of the dear Redeemer's kingdom; this was all my desire and care; and for this mercy I hoped, but with trembling; for I felt what Job expresses (9:16): "If I had called, and he had answered me: yet would I not believe that he had hearkened unto my voice." My rising hopes respecting the conversion of the Indians have been so often dashed that my spirit is, as it were, broken and my courage wasted, and I hardly dare hope' (2 August).

William Tennent had looked after the Indians in his absence and under his leadership there had been no diminution of the intensity of interest. They were still 'under deep concern for an interest in Christ'. His first message after returning was taken from the final invitation of the Bible: 'And whosoever will, let him take of the water of life freely' (Rev. 22:17). He felt strong compassion and tenderness as he spoke. The immediate result was a significant increase in the level of distress on the part of those who listened. 'A surprising concern soon became apparent among them.' All but a couple had eyes filled with tears.

A visible change now began to come over the Indians. They refused to eat until the missionary came to give thanks for the food. This gave him an occasion to remind them about how just recently they had eaten their feast in honour of devils and failed to give thanks to the true source of blessing, God. This gentle rebuke only increased their agony. They began to discuss now nothing but 'religious matters' and Tattamy, who had followed Brainerd back from the Forks, was there with them day and night to give counsel. One woman who had been awakened from the time he first came gained assurance of salvation and was 'filled with love to Christ'.

The numbers of the Indians who listened regularly to him was steadily growing. The half dozen or so that first encountered him in June had become twenty, then thirty, and now were about fifty-five. They all seemed in 'agony of soul' to know the joy of forgiveness. Interestingly, this distress they felt was not because his preaching was on the harsher aspects of the Bible such as the wrath of God or hell. On the contrary, his constant emphasis was on the abundant mercy and love of God in giving Christ as the Saviour and inviting guilty sinners to find peace in him: 'They all as one seemed in an agony of soul to obtain an interest in Christ; and the more I discoursed of the love of God in sending his Son to suffer for the sins of men; and the more I invited them to come and partake of His love, the more their distress was aggravated, because they felt themselves unable to come. It was surprising to see how their hearts seemed to be pierced with the tender and melting invitations of the gospel, when there was not a word of terror spoken to them' (6 August).

On the day when Brainerd gratefully recorded these words in his diary two came to Christ for salvation. Brainerd asked them what they wished God to do further for them. They replied that they wanted Christ to 'wipe their hearts quite clean'. David was satisfied now that indeed the 'arm of the Lord' was being revealed in the lives of his hearers.

The next day, after a message on the cross of Christ from Isaiah 53 a 'remarkable influence' attended the preaching of the Word. A few were so 'affected' that they seemed nearly paralysed. 'Some few could neither go nor stand, but lay flat on the ground as if pierced to their heart, crying incessantly for mercy. Several were newly awakened; and it was remarkable that, as fast as they came from remote places round about, the Spirit of God seemed to seize them with concern for their souls' (7 August).

The archives of the State of New Jersey record that the summer of 1745 was hot and dry. In such times the grass turns to straw and crunches underfoot, the streams shrink to a trickle and even the leaves on the trees begin to shrivel. No doubt the weather was following the usual pattern in the Indian settlement at Crossweeksung on 8 August. But it was a day in which there was definitely to be no lack of refreshment spiritually.

It was Thursday. Charles McKnight, who pastored the Presbyterian Church at Cranberry, a small settlement about fifteen miles north-east of Crossweeksung, was with him. An afternoon service of preaching had been scheduled and the Indians hurried about to gather as many of their number as possible to attend. The ministers prepared themselves for the occasion with earnest and expectant prayer.

There were about sixty-five Indians who sat quietly as Brainerd read his text from Luke 14:23: 'Go out into the highways and hedges, and compel them to come in, that my house may be filled.' It was the same text that Ebenezer Pemberton had used in the Newark church on the day of David Brainerd's ordination. What followed was a time of special divine visitation. It was never to be forgotten.

Only the words of an eyewitness, the preacher himself, are adequate to express what happened:

Brainerd preaching to the Indians

There was much visible concern among them, while I was discoursing publicly; but afterwards, when I spoke to one and another more particularly, whom I perceived under much concern, the power of God seemed to descend upon the assembly *'like a mighty rushing wind,'* and with an astonishing energy bore down all before it. I stood amazed at the influence, which seized the audience almost universally; and could compare it to nothing more aptly, than the irresistible force of a mighty torrent or swelling deluge, that with its insupportable weight and pressure bears down and sweeps before it whatever comes in its way. Almost all persons of all ages were bowed down with concern together, and scarcely one was able to withstand the shock of this surprising operation. Old men and women, who had been drunken wretches for many years and some little children, not more than six or seven years of age, appeared in distress for their souls, as well as persons of middle age. It was apparent that these children, some of them at least, were not merely frightened with seeing the general concern; but were made sensible of their danger, the badness of their hearts, and their misery without Christ, as some of them expressed it. The most stubborn hearts were now obliged to bow.

Normally a Christian evangelist or missionary must be contented with seeing individual cases of conversion. But what Brainerd described seemed to be one of those rare cases in history when God saves a whole group of people together. There were, however, some remarkable individual cases of conversion among these Indians. One of those who was saved on this memorable day was a 'secure and self-righteous' Indian who had formerly thought he was a Christian. On this day he was shaken out of his false security. He was 'brought under solemn concern for his soul and wept bitterly'. Another subject was one who had lived long in the worse kind of spiritual darkness. An old man, who had formerly been a drunk and had practised conjuration, cried out for God to have mercy on him.

A young woman's experience was, perhaps, the most unusual of all. She had come to see Brainerd simply because she had heard that something strange was going on at Crossweeksung. Prior to this she had never thought at all about her relationship to God, or even heard that she so much as had a soul. She visited the missionary at his lodging and when he stated that he had come to preach to the Indians, she began to mock. Yet, out of curiosity, she went to hear him. He had hardly begun to preach when she began to scream out as one who had been pierced through with an arrow. She could neither sit nor stand without being supported by someone else. After the service she lay on the ground praying, all the while oblivious to those who were standing around watching her. From her lips came the words, *'Guttummaukalummeh wechaumeh kmeleh notah,'* which mean, 'Have mercy on me, and help me to give you my heart.' She continued to pray like this for many hours.

After witnessing this pentecostal scene Brainerd wrote, 'This was indeed a surprising day of God's power, and seemed enough to convince an Atheist of the truth, importance, and power of God's word.'

On the next day, 9 August, he spoke to about seventy of the Indians. Once again, as in the former days, his theme was not the terrific and terrible truths about God's holiness of the dangers of hell. He addressed them from Matthew 12:28, 'Come unto me all you that labour...', emphasizing the fulness and all-sufficiency of Christ's redeeming work for the worst of sinners. He pressed upon them their responsibility to come to him without delay. And, just as the day before, 'a Divine influence' seemed to attend what was spoken. All but two or three were melted into tears and cries. Even some who had not been touched by the power of the previous day were now 'deeply affected and wounded at heart'. Each one of these precious Indian people was praying and crying out to God for himself, saying, *'Guttummauhalummeh; guttummauhalummeh'*, 'Have mercy upon me! Have mercy upon me!' 'What a sight this was,' wrote Brainerd, to see poor Indians, 'who the other day were hallooing and yelling in their *idolatrous* feasts and *drunken* frolics, now crying to God with such importunity for an interest in his dear Son!'

Although there were physical manifestations of distress among these Indians, corresponding to the depth of their concerns, such as falling down on the ground and crying out for salvation, their feelings were 'rational and just'. They were not just afraid of the anger of God but were convicted of the wickedness of their lives. They did not remain, however, in this condition. One by one they began to announce that peace had come to their hearts and they were trusting in God's mercy alone to save them. 'They appeared calm and composed,' Brainerd said, 'and seemed to rejoice in Jesus Christ.'

One young girl, converted while living at Crossweeksung, was a special case and became a significant part of evangelical Indian lore. On 5 August, three days before the 'rushing mighty wind' event, she had obtained comfort for her soul, affirming a solid, well-grounded hope in Christ. She appeared, according to Brainerd, to be 'afraid of nothing so much as of offending and grieving him whom her soul loved'. This woman was in reality the first one who made a public profession of faith at Crossweeksung. 120 years later the true story of her life came to light.

It seemed that she was the daughter of Weequehela, who had been the last great Indian sachem among the Delawares in New Jersey. Here is how the story unfolds: Thomas Brainerd was a descendant of an uncle of David Brainerd and his brother John. In 1864 Thomas was preparing a biography of John

Brainerd, who eventually took over Brainerd's ministry among the New Jersey Indians. He decided to write to an Indian missionary in Wisconsin named Cutting Marsh, and ask him if any of the Delaware Indians who were living in that region could remember David or John Brainerd. Marsh did some private investigation and discovered, providentially it seems, some fascinating information. A Delaware woman of his acquaintance lived with some people who were descendants of the Indians of the settlement at Stockbridge, Massachusetts. Marsh asked her if she had heard of David Brainerd? She had.

It seems that her father, Bartholemew S. Calvin, had told his children much about both David and John Brainerd. Indeed it was her grandmother, who had married Stephen Calvin, that was Brainerd's first convert at Crossweeksung, the one who had been so afraid that she would offend her Redeemer. Her father, Weequehela, was a wealthy and powerful Indian chief who lived in New Jersey in the early 1700s. He owned a lot of land, horses, cattle and silverware and even had negro slaves. But a neighbouring white man, Captain John Leonard, had trespassed on his land and claimed it as own. According to the Delaware woman, Leonard extorted large tracts of land from her great-grandfather after getting him drunk. The Delaware code of honour demanded that such a vicious deed could only be dealt with in one way: the offender had to be shot. So Weequehela killed Leonard.

The great sachem knew that he would be tried and executed by the white man's government and he made no attempt to escape. He simply submitted himself to the authorities and advised his Indian subjects to go west. According to the *American Weekly Mercury* for 6-13 July 1727, Weequehela, the Indian king, was executed for living a base, inhuman life and murdering some of his own Indian kin and the Englishman John Leonard. The report also stated that two militia of soldiers were present to protect the sheriff and execution officers from any insults from the mob that saw the hanging of the Indians.

According to Cutting Marsh's informant, Weequehela left behind a widow and four or five children, one of them being only a few days old. After the sachem's execution his family was mistreated and their property taken. In fact in a short time all of this family had died except one three-year-old girl. This little girl had lived a very rough life. She saw her aunt killed by a white man and grew up hating and fearing all white men.

But there was one white man she came to love and respect, according to the account of the Delaware squaw living in Wisconsin. A missionary had come to preach the Christian gospel to the Indians at New Jersey and she loved him very much. 'He loved his heavenly Father so much that he was willing to endure hardships, travelling over mountains, suffering hunger, and lying on the ground that he might do her people good; and she did every thing she could for his comfort.' In fact, she became a Christian through his gentle and patient persuasions. The missionary's name was David Brainerd. It was she who had been converted on 5 August 1745. It was she who was the 'firstfruits' of Brainerd's missionary labours at Crossweeksung, New Jersey.[1]

Thus was converted the grandmother of the Delaware Indian whom time and distance had removed far away from the scene of the New Jersey revival. Thomas Brainerd recounted this story as told to him by the missionary Cutting Marsh. So we today, living two and a half centuries after the memorable events at Crossweeksung itself, know about the long-standing and wonderful fruit of the evangelistic labours of David Brainerd, the true friend of Indians.

20.
The fruits of conversion

As in the case of the New Testament church at Jerusalem, Brainerd's Indians experienced on 8 August a pentecostal power which was not repeated. The phenomenon of the moving of God which seemed to Brainerd like a 'rushing mighty wind' was unique, but its effects continued and in a more subdued way they were perpetuated in the days that followed. Just as Pentecost was followed by wonderful times of divine blessing in Samaria, Caesarea and beyond, so God continued to work day after day at Crossweeksung.

On 10 August Brainerd gathered some of the young converts together in a house in order to teach, caution and encourage them. He explained to them that when a believer dies his soul goes directly to be with Jesus Christ, at which time the believer will be perfectly purified from all sin and will enter into perfect enjoyment of the Saviour. Anticipating that some of them might cherish their present life too much, he suggested that some might have difficulty with the thought of parting with the body. *'Muttoh, Muttoh,'* they cried out meaning, 'No, No!' 'They did not regard their bodies, if their souls might be with Christ.'

Following his instruction of the believers he spoke to other Indians who had pressed in upon the assembly because of their eager desire to hear. His text was Luke 19:10: 'For the son of man is come to seek and to save that which was lost.' Before long the house was filled with cries and groans. These Indians felt themselves totally undone and without hope. He assured them that Jesus Christ had great compassion on the lost and was willing to save them, but this only heightened their distress because 'They could not find and come to so kind a Saviour.' One man, who especially seemed to be pierced to the heart, stated that all the wickedness of his past life came before him and he saw all his vile actions as if they had been only yesterday.

11 August was a Sunday, and Brainerd preached not only to the Indians, but also to some white people, including Quakers, who had come to see what was going on. These ceased to be 'idle spectators' and were greatly moved as they heard that they too had souls to save or lose, just like the Indians. 'This also appeared to be a day of God's power,' Brainerd observed.

The number of Indians regularly listening to him was now about seventy. Quite a few were confident of their salvation and were rejoicing in the hope of the gospel. The missionary was especially pleased to see that their way of living and acting was changing drastically. They 'appeared humble and devout, and behaved in an agreeable and Christian-like manner'. One of the things that encouraged David the most was how sensitive the new believers were becoming on moral issues. One woman seemed very sad. He asked her what was troubling her. It seemed that she had become angry with her child and was tormented that this anger was excessive. She sobbed uncontrollably for several hours.

Brainerd also took great satisfaction in the change taking place among the Indians in the matter of the marriage relationship. Of course, he shared with them from the Scriptures God's standards pertaining to monogamy, fidelity and divorce. The Indians, rooted as they were in animistic traditions, were ignorant of such ideals. Yet when they came to Christ they began immediately to comply. One man who had put away his wife and taken another woman (without any just cause), as was a common practice, was convicted that his conduct was wicked. He wanted to know what his responsibility was. After some instruction from Brainerd he readily and cheerfully accepted God's will. He publicly renounced the sinful liaison and promised to live with, and be kind to, his wife. 'I suppose a few weeks before, the whole world could not have persuaded this man to a compliance with Christian rules in this affair.'

As the days of summer wore on Brainerd continued to preach every day to the Crossweeksung Indians, with growing success. On 16 August his subject was from John 6, where Jesus Christ is set forth as the Bread of Life. Just as in previous days there was deep concern in the audience and two people particularly came under strong conviction. He was amazed at how powerfully God was working: 'Sundry *old* men were also in distress for their souls; so that they could not refrain from weeping and crying aloud; and their bitter groans were the most convincing as well as affecting evidence of the reality and depth of their inward anguish. God is powerfully at work among them. True and genuine convictions of sin are daily promoted in many instances; and some are newly awakened from time to time; although some few, who felt a commotion in their *passions* in days past, seem now to discover their hearts were never truly affected.'

Trained as he was in Puritan theology and methods of evangelism, Brainerd sought to do everything possible to effect a change in the lives of the Indians. He believed that it is the truth of God, plainly explained, illustrated and applied, that is the instrument used to convert the lost. No fatalist, he knew that there is no substitute for faithful, diligent, sacrificial work if a minister is to succeed. He prayed, preached and counselled the Indians with all the strength of his body and soul. But the marvellous work of God in New Jersey which he was now enjoying seemed to him, in a remarkable manner, above or apart from methods and techniques: 'I never saw the work of God appear so independent of means, as at this time,' he remarked.

Brainerd could see very little connection between what he was doing and what God was doing:

> God's manner of working upon them seemed so entirely supernatural, and above means, that I could scarcely believe he used me as an instrument, or what I spake as means of carrying on his work. For it appeared, as I thought, to have no connection with, or dependence on means, in any respect. Though I could not but continue to use the means, which I thought proper for the promotion of the work, yet God seemed, as it apprehended, to work entirely without them. I seemed to do nothing, and indeed to have nothing to do, but to 'stand still, and see the salvation of God'; and found myself obliged and delighted to say, 'Not unto us,' not unto instruments and means, 'but to thy name be glory.' God appeared to work entirely alone, and I saw no room to attribute any part of this work to any created arm.

How should we regard these words? Was David Brainerd unnecessarily self-deprecating? Some might conclude that he refrained from taking the credit for the awakening because of a theological bias, or perhaps even because of an affected humility. Brainerd stated that God worked directly and sovereignly on his Indians, seemingly without any effort on his part. Is this the calm and rational witness of someone simply reporting the facts, or is modesty at work? Such questions will inevitably be asked by many evangelicals living in a day when strategies for success in converting people have reached a high level of expertise. Are we not all familiar with the 'laws of church growth' and the 'keys to effective evangelism'? The 'felt needs' of the pagan world must be met, so many say, in order to reach the lost. And then the preacher must be trained in crowd psychology and sales tactics in order to sweep people into the gospel net. But can personal charisma, communication skills, technology and marketing concepts effect a genuine revival of the church?

The absence of serious Bible study and personal godliness in many products of modern religion is leading many in our own day to conclude that something is desperately wrong with our evangelistic strategies. Perhaps a remedy for the awful moral and spiritual decline in contemporary Christianity can be discovered by pondering the ministry of this frail preacher to the Indians. Here was a man who carried on his evangelistic labours with none of the advantages of our modern culture. The setting for his efforts was one which featured every inconvenience. Those he sought to win were, for the most part, totally ignorant of even the simplest biblical principles. Their customs, concepts and ways of living militated in every way against the way of the cross. But they came in contact with a power that was permanently and powerfully effective. It was the power of the Holy Spirit.

Jesus and the apostles used every convenience and tool at their disposal to convey the life-giving message of salvation. So did David Brainerd. But they did not depend upon them. Experience shows that while techniques may generate a temporary interest, increased crowds and produce superficial converts, only God can save. The marvellous ministry of David Brainerd to the Crossweeksung Indians and the sudden and astounding changes that took place among them bear witness to the truth affirmed by the psalmist that unless the Lord builds the house they labour in vain who build it, and unless the Lord guards the city the watchman stays awake in

vain (Ps. 127:1). The Crossweeksung revival stands as a
perpetual memorial to the wonderful agency of God in saving
sinners. It leaves behind a powerful witness, as far as credible
history can do so, to the fact that in the day when the arm of the
Lord is bared there is nothing that can effectually stand in the
way. Brainerd could, and indeed did, take his place with Paul
in affirming that while an 'earthen vessel' may convey the
treasure of the gospel, the excellence of the power and the
glory of redemption belong to God alone (2 Cor. 4:7).

For almost three weeks Brainerd had been constantly
engaged in preaching to the Indians and counselling the new
converts. This undoubtedly was beginning to take its toll on
his energy, so he decided to take a break. On 19 August he went
to William Tennent's church at Freehold where he preached to
a large crowd about 'Poverty of Spirit' from Matthew 5:3. His
analysis of this sermon is interesting. The people at Freehold
had, of course, heard about the tremendous happenings at
Crossweeksung and no doubt were expecting to share in these
blessings from the presence among them of the man who had
been God's instrument. So they came expecting a powerful,
moving sermon. But they were disappointed; at least it appeared to the preacher that way: 'It pleased God to leave me to
be very dry and barren; so that I do not remember to have been
so straitened for a whole twelvemonth past. God is just; and he
has made me to acquiesce in his will in this respect. It is
contrary to flesh and blood to be cut off from all freedom in a
large auditory, where their expectations are much raised; but
so it was with me: and God helped me to say amen to it. Good
is the will of the Lord. In the evening I felt quiet and composed,
and had freedom and comfort in secret prayer.'

Only three days previously Brainerd had commented on the
fact that when God began to work among the Indians he was
more or less just a bystander. In his own eyes this marvellous
work of God was carried on using such a weak instrument so

that none would be tempted to give any human being the glory. His efforts at Freehold reminded him that the heart of the preacher is cold and his lips dead without the dynamic power of God taking control. Had he been tempted in the least to think that his own natural talent or oratory was responsible for the tremendous awakening he had seen, the failure at Freehold would have disabused him quickly. One is reminded of Paul's testimony concerning his 'thorn in the flesh'. God gave him this humiliating burden, whatever it was, to keep him from being 'exalted above measure' (2 Cor. 12:7). Three times he pleaded that it be removed. But God never took it away. Instead he gave him strength to bear it, so that God's strength might be made perfect in Paul's weakness. What preacher, indeed what Christian, has not at times experienced the same sense of weakness and failure through some human infirmity? Yet God's glory is promoted and his strength is manifested in such circumstances.

On 20 August David Brainerd went from Freehold to Elizabethtown to spend some time with Jonathan Dickinson. The concern much upon his mind now was how he might improve the lot of the converted Indians by settling them into a more stable community. He knew that if they were to be properly instructed and developed, some changes in their political, economic and social customs would be necessary. Such matters were discussed during the visit to Dickinson. Also while at Elizabethtown he wrote to his brother John at Yale.

He returned to Crossweeksung on 23 August. After gathering the Indians together he spoke from John 6:44 about the absolute necessity of God's drawing for souls to be saved. Brainerd, with his roots deep in the Calvinism of his Puritan forebears, would have waxed bold in ascribing all the glory for conversion to God's sovereign grace. The Indians listened attentively and showed great love for the preacher. But the amazing power that had been so much in evidence earlier had now abated considerably, though they still retained their 'deep impressions'.

The next day Brainerd initiated discussions with the new believers about the need for a formal profession of faith and baptism. The nature of the ordinance (according to the Presbyterian method of sprinkling) and the obligations of those who experienced it were among the subjects he addressed. He also spoke to them about the wonderful privilege of having a covenant relationship with the Lord. A church of Jesus Christ was now in the process of being formed.

On the same day a group of newcomers were present who had come under the influence of European civilization and the 'light of the gospel'. They had experienced some of the advantages of education and were civil in their manners. But Brainerd sensed immediately that they knew nothing of the real power of religion and the doctrines of grace. He discerned that they were ignorant of their own sinful condition and were seeking to be saved according to the 'law covenant', that is through their own works. He spoke directly to their needs in this area. One Indian did seem convinced that 'By the deeds of the law no flesh can be justified.' This person wept bitterly and wanted to know how to be truly saved.

Two days in August 1745 must be recorded as 'red-letter days' in the life of David Brainerd. 8 August was the day on which the Holy Spirit came in great power upon the Indians at Crossweeksung. The effects of that event, when many were brought into the kingdom of God, were to last for ever. The second day was 25 August, when twenty-five Indians, fifteen adults and ten children, were baptized. Prior to this ordinance he spoke on the parable of the lost sheep from Luke 15:3-7. The scene was marred by the bad behaviour of some of the white people who were present. They walked around gawking at the preacher and his flock and 'behaved more indecently

than any Indians I have ever addressed'. It was in fact a kind
of harassment which made him very discouraged, so much so
that he could hardly go on.

But the whites eventually left and he joyfully gathered his
congregation of converted Indians together and pressed upon
them their obligations to God. He warned them about the
dangers of careless living and encouraged them to press
forward in obedience to God, the only way of happiness for a
Christian. The results of this message were enough to cheer the
heart of any pastor: 'This was a desirable and sweet season
indeed! Their hearts were engaged and cheerful in duty; and
they rejoiced that they had, in a public and solemn manner,
dedicated themselves to God. Love seemed to reign among
them! They took each other by the hand with tenderness and
affection, as if their hearts were knit together, while I was
discoursing to them; and all their deportment towards each
other was such, that a serious spectator might just be excited
to cry out with admiration, "Behold how they love one
another."'

David Brainerd had known the toils and trials of sowing
the seed of the gospel. He had watered the soil, as it were, with
the tears of his own compassion. Finally, the time for reaping
had come. He had faithfully, patiently laboured and suffered
for the good of the Indians he loved. The bountiful harvest was
now spread out before him.

21.
Region of the shadow of death

As Brainerd continued to instruct the Indians who now made up his spiritual flock — some ninety-five by the end of August — his mind ever and anon turned to the Susquehanna region which he had already visited twice. He had seen the large number of Indian tribes living along both branches of the river, as well as further south, and had also observed their desperate spiritual needs. He considered it to be his duty to go to them again. The time of the year was approaching when they would be gathered together after their summer activities.

In April he had gone to Philadelphia to obtain official permission from the governor for his efforts among the Susquehanna Indians. Once again he needed such a commission. In late August authorization for the trip was obtained, so he departed for the western fields, by way of the Forks of the Delaware. Five days after leaving Crossweeksung he was back at the Forks.

He preached for several days at this place where he had formerly resided and found many signs of spiritual interest. On 5 September he sensed a special power as he spoke, similar to what he had experienced in New Jersey. One man, who gave solid evidence of conversion, sat and wept as he listened to the message. Brainerd asked him directly why he was crying. He quoted the man's exact answer: 'When he thought how Christ was slain like a lamb, and spilt his blood for sinners, he could not help crying, when he was alone.' After saying this he began to sob again. A woman expressed grief that the Indians here would not come to Christ as well as those at Crossweeksung.

The fact is that to some degree the revival in New Jersey had spread to the Forks, for as Brainerd continued to preach in September on numerous occasions the same deep concern and weeping were manifested. But others, unfortunately, who had in the past refused to hear Brainerd preach and demonstrated anger at the growing Christian movement in their midst, became even more hostile. They scoffed at the Christian message and taunted the Indian believers, asking them 'whether they have not now cried enough to do their turn'. So the new believers had to endure the 'cruel mockings' of their fellows.

On 9 September Brainerd began the 130-mile ride west to the Susquehanna region, arriving on the 13th at Shamokin, a major Indian town at the junction of the branches of the Susquehanna, the site of modern Sunbury. Shamokin was known at the time as 'the Indian capital'. At this place was the largest community of Indians in the east. More than half the area of Pennsylvania can be reached by waterways from this spot and no less than ten Indian paths converged here from all directions.

Two of the most famous Indian chiefs of this era lived at Shamokin. One was Sassoonan, also referred to in colonial times as Allumpapees and Swantane. He originally had himself lived at the Forks of the Delaware but moved the council fires to Shamokin, on the western side of the river. He was reputed to be the son of the great chief Tamanend, who had met with William Penn and entered with him into a treaty of eternal friendship at Shackamaxon. Sassoonan was old and not well at the time of Brainerd's visit to Shamokin, as the Moravian bishop Jacob Spangenberg, who visited him the same month as Brainerd, had reported: 'He is very old, almost blind, and very poor, but withal has still power over and is beloved by his people; and he is a friend of the English.' Two weeks later the famous Indian agent Conrad Weiser wrote, '[He] has been drunk for these two or three years almost constantly.'[1]

Nothwithstanding his age and addiction to drink Sassoonan was still held in respect by the Indians and was regarded by the white government as an intelligent and trustworthy leader. In reality he had in the past sought to curtail the liquor traffic among his people. At a meeting of the Provincial Council in August 1731, he made the following request to the white people: 'He desires that no Christian should carry any rum to Shamokin where he lives, to sell; when they want any, they will send for it themselves; they would not be wholly deprived of it, but they would not have it brought by the Christians.'[2]

The principal Indian chief living at Shamokin was Shikellamy, sometimes called Swatany, which means 'the Enlightener'. Shikellamy is thought to have originally been a Cayuga, or even a Frenchman, but was captured and adopted by the Oneida tribe (one of the Six Nations Confederacy) and was baptized by a Jesuit priest in Canada. In the very year of Brainerd's visit he had been promoted to executive deputy of the Grand Council of the Six Nations. His responsibility was to exercise control over all the subjugated nations who lived along the Susquehanna, including the Delawares.

Unlike Sassoonan, Shikellamy was a man of strict sobriety and abstinence, and thus avoided the degraded state into which many of the Indians had fallen. A wise and dignified leader, he had served as a valuable liaison officer during the critical negotiations that had gone on between the Indians and the colonial government during the second quarter of the eighteenth century. Count Zinzendorf, the Moravian, said of him, 'He was truly an excellent and good man, possessed of many noble qualities of mind, that could do honor to many white men, laying claims to refinement and intelligence. He was possessed of great dignity, sobriety and prudence, [and] extreme kindness.'[3]

Brainerd gave one of the best descriptions of the Indian village Shamokin that is found in all colonial literature, one that is highly prized by all historians:

> I was kindly received, and entertained by the Indians; but had little satisfaction by reason of the heathenish dance and revel they then held in the house where I was obliged to lodge; which I could not suppress, though I often entreated them to desist, for the sake of one of their own friends who was sick in the house, and whose disorder was much aggravated by the noise. Alas! how destitute of natural affection are these poor uncultivated Pagans! although they seem somewhat kind in their own way. Of a truth the dark corners of the earth are full of the habitations of cruelty. This town, as I observed in my diary of May last, lies partly on the east side of the river, partly on the west, and partly on a large island in it; and contains upwards of fifty houses, and nearly three hundred persons, though I never saw more than half that number in it. They are of three different tribes of Indians, speaking three languages wholly unintelligible to each other. About one half of its inhabitants are Delawares; the others called Senekas and Tutelas. The Indians of this place, are accounted the most drunken, mischievous, and ruffianlike fellows, of any in these parts; and Satan seems to have his seat in this town in an eminent manner.

Brainerd had the opportunity to meet and spend some time with Sassoonan on 14 September. The chief was not only sober on this occasion but was very cordial and seemed open to Brainerd's ministry. The Indian chief's friendliness was the first real encouragement the missionary had received since his first visit here in May. It gave him hope that this might be the first crack of an opening door for a great work of God at Shamokin.

That night his soul was 'enlarged' in prayer, as he pleaded with God to 'set up his kingdom in this place, where the devil now reigns in the most eminent manner'. He even recorded the words of his prayer. They are powerful: 'Lord, set up thy kingdom for thine own glory; glorify thyself, and I shall rejoice. Get honour to thy blessed name, and this is all I desire. Do with me just what thou wilt: Blessed be thy name for ever that thou art God, and that thou wilt glorify thyself. O that the whole world would glorify thee! O let these poor people be brought to know thee, and love thee, for the glory of thy ever blessed name.'

Here in this prayer is a fine mixture of the two elements that should be at the heart of the evangelistic vision: a burning desire to see the true God glorified on the earth, and a longing for men to know and enjoy the blessings of God's grace. Surveying the Indian capital, where Satan had long held an unchallenged sway, and where every vice of depraved human nature was exhibited so glaringly, had aroused in Brainerd's heart as never before the desire for the Spirit of God to work mightily. One writer characterized the Indian rum towns as 'outlets of hell', and with this assessment Brainerd would have totally agreed. What a contrast he had experienced in the last few months between the world of light which had flooded the Crossweeksung Indian camp and the dense darkness of Shamokin! If ever a community needed the gospel, this one did.

15 September was a Sunday. After visiting Sassoonan, who gave him a very gracious reception, Brainerd gathered some Indians together in the afternoon and preached to them. It was

a difficult task. Although he had great hopes that God would open their hearts to receive the gospel, so many were drunk that it was impossible to communicate with them. In the evening he conversed with one who understood the languages of the Six Nations. This individual seemed willing to hear the gospel message, and Brainerd thought about the possibilities of evangelism among these 'far remote' people.

On 17 September the Indians of Shamokin left on a hunting expedition, so Brainerd also departed to visit some tribes who lived further south along the Susquehanna. He travelled alone, for his interpreter Tattamy had left for 'official business'. Since both Brainerd and Tattamy had come to this region through a commission from the governor it is possible that the Indian was running an errand for the governor. This of course meant that Brainerd's ministry for the rest of the trip would have to be without the aid of a translator.

On Thursday the 19th he arrived at an Indian village called Juniata which is at the mouth of a river by that name. Just below this site the Susquehanna flows between high cliffs on either side, since here it cuts through Peters Mountain. At the mouth of the Juniata is also an island called Duncan's Island, near the present town of Duncannon. The place is important both in Indian and colonial history. John Harris, for whom the city of Harrisburg was named, came here as a trader, cleared land and built a house in 1742. The island was the home of several Indian tribes, including the Shawanese. Their alliances with the French were a constant source of difficulty to Shikellamy, whose responsibility it was to keep them under control.

Another tribe much in evidence here were the Nanticokes, who were much feared by the other Indian tribes. Brainerd refers to their strange approach to handling their dead: 'Their customs, in various respects, differ from those of the other Indians upon the river. They do not bury their dead in a common form, but let their flesh consume above ground, in closed cribs made for that purpose. At the end of the year, or sometimes a longer space of time, they take the bones when the flesh is all consumed, and wash and scrape them, and afterwards bury them with some ceremony. Their method of charming or conjuring over the sick, seems somewhat different from that of other Indians, though in substance the same.'

The unusual customs and manners of the Nanticoke Indians were much in evidence when Brainerd arrived at Juniata and he was very distressed. He had visited this place in the spring and their pagan ways had left a strong impression upon him then.

Brainerd spent the night somewhere around Duncan's Island and the next day was one he would not soon forget. The Indians were busy preparing for a dance and a sacrifice. In the evening about a hundred gathered around a large fire where they had prepared ten deer for this purpose. As the fire grew they threw in the fat of the deer, causing flames to rise to a tremendous height. What a sight this fire must have been, as it shone across the waters and illuminated the distant mountains! While the fire raged they danced about the fire screaming and yelling so as to be heard 'two miles or more' away.

The next day had been dedicated by the Indians to the witchdoctors and medicine men who were seeking a cure for a disease which was raging through the tribes. Many had been stricken with high fever and were bleeding. The medicine men put on a demonstration. For several hours they lay flat on the earth, sat up, bowed with their faces to the ground and gesticulated in wild motions. They howled, they sang and made other hideous sounds. They extended their arms into the air, spreading all their fingers, and then did a pushing motion, as if designed to drive something away, or keep it away. They stroked their faces with their hands and squirted a fine mist of water into the air. At times they writhed and jerked as if in the greatest of agony, twisting and distorting their faces, and turning up their eyes while grunting and puffing.

Some of the Indians seemed to have a special function as leaders or motivators of the others. They were, as Brainerd put it, more 'fervent and devout' than the others. They chanted, peeped and muttered with such 'vigor and warmth' as to, if possible, awaken and engage the very powers of hell. In fact, it seemed to Brainerd that this was the very purpose of these strange antics. All the missionary could do was sit in the shadows and watch with extreme shock, dismay and grief. He held his Bible in his hand and prayed, hoping if possible to spoil their sport and prevent any direct contact with Satan. After the dance Brainerd sought to talk to them about the gospel of Jesus Christ, though his interpreter was himself one of the natives who had no appreciation of the message he delivered. But the Indians left, thus removing his only opportunity to get inside their minds. He retired that night deeply distraught at what had taken place.

He pondered the events of the day and wrote, 'A view of these things, while I was entirely alone in the wilderness, destitute of the society of any one who so much as "named the name of Christ", greatly sunk my spirits, and gave me the most gloomy turn of mind imaginable, almost stripped me of all resolution and hope respecting futher attempts for propagating the gospel, and converting the pagans, and renders this the most burdensome and disagreeable Sabbath which I ever saw.'

It was here on Duncan's Island that Brainerd met a remarkable man whom he had first seen on his previous trip in May and who claimed to be a 'devout and zealous reformer', or a restorer of 'what he supposed was the ancient religion of the Indians'. His garb was boarskins which hung down to his feet. He wore bearskin stockings and had a wooden face-mask painted half black and half light brown, with a mouth cut at an angle so as to give it a grotesque appearance. The mask was fastened to a bearskin cap which was drawn over his head. As he approached Brainerd he shook a rattle made from a dry tortoiseshell filled with dry corn and attached to a piece of wood which served as a handle. As he danced and shook his rattle his gestures gave him a 'prodigiously frightful' appearance.

He informed Brainerd that his aim was to revive the ancient religion of the Indians which had recently been corrupted. He lamented their addiction to strong liquor and had sought with all his might to turn them from its addictive powers. The reformer claimed to have had an intimate acquaintance with the true God, whom he loved and served. After an experience with God he had come, he said, to love humanity in a way he had never done before. He denied the existence of the devil and believed that when people died they all went south where they lived in the same general vicinity. Good people were admitted into a beautiful town with spiritual walls, whereas the wicked hovered about these walls, unable to get in.

He treated the young missionary with what seemed to be sincere courtesy, and enjoyed talking to him about religion. Brainerd shared the basic tenets of the Christian faith with this man, some of which he liked and some of which he disliked very much. He assured Brainerd that he was very confident of his religion which he had received from God and would never abandon it. The Indians at Juniata generally looked upon this man as somewhat of a fanatic, though Brainerd saw some aspects of his 'temper and disposition' which 'looked more like true religion' than anything he had seen among the other tribes. The Christian missionary and the Indian reformer spent a considerable amount of time together, but they parted each believing the same as he did before their encounter.

Brainerd's trip to the Susquehanna, one he had begun with such bright hopes and optimism, was, at least in his own estimation, failing. His heart was breaking with compassion for these poor ignorant Indians. He trembled as he thought about how they were dishonouring the true God through their ignorant and foolish rituals. But there was seemingly nothing he could do except weep in private and pray.

After the Nanticokes had exhausted themselves with their feverish ceremonies on 20 September they went to bed. The shadows of the night that drew around the river scene were nothing, however, in Brainerd's view, to the horrible spiritual darkness which enveloped these tribes who still practised their mysterious rituals from the past. Their superstitions, their extravagant orgies and sacrifices made him think of 2 Timothy 2:26. With all his might he pleaded with God 'that they may come to their senses and escape the snare of the devil, having been taken captive by him to do his will'. As far as Brainerd was concerned, these Indians sat 'in the region of the shadow of death'.

22.
A time for reflection

Brainerd left the Susquehanna region on 23 September with a sad heart as he contemplated the desperate spiritual conditions of the Indians he left behind him and how little he had accomplished in changing them. He was also in a 'weak state of body', for incessant riding, preaching and sleeping in uncomfortable quarters had taken their toll.

After spending a few days with the Indians at the Forks of Delaware he returned to Crossweeksung, arriving on 5 October. What a joy it was to be home again among his Christian Indians! Their enthusiastic response to his preaching and their fervent love for the Lord were a reminder of just how remarkable the awakening had been: 'How great is the change lately made upon numbers of those Indians, who, not many months ago, were as thoughtless and averse to Christianity as those upon the Susquehanna; and how astonishing is that grace, which has made this change' (5 October).

Two years previously Brainerd had received a call from a church at East Hampton on Long Island to consider coming to be their pastor. Because of his commitment to Indian missions he had refused. Now the church was having some severe problems, so great in fact that a number of respected ministers were called to come and seek to deal with the situation. The church had apparently been unable to agree on securing a

minister and was seriously divided. Aaron Burr led the del-
egation to East Hampton, which included David Brainerd and
William Tennent.

The situation was very unsettling to Brainerd, so much so
that he was unable to sleep on several nights. But during this
trip he had several seasons of 'sweet refreshments' and 'his
soul was enlarged and comforted with divine consolations in
secret retirement'.

Brainerd was back at Crossweeksung on 24 October and he
continued to be carried along, as it were, by the strong revival
winds that were blowing across the Indian villages. He
preached on 24 October from John 4:13-14 about the living
water which will spring up for ever in the hearts of believers.
There was an 'unaffected melting' in the assembly. The new
converts exulted as he spoke the next day from Luke 20:27-36
about the resurrection and the glories of heaven.

On the Lord's Day, 27 October, an Indian woman who had
till then been totally ignorant about religion came to hear him,
having been persuaded to attend the service almost against her
will. She was 'seized with a distressing concern about her soul'
and immediately left for her home, some forty miles away, to
bring her husband to hear this preacher. Some English believers were present at this service and were delighted to see this
amazing sight — Indians worshipping the God of Israel with
sincere devotion and solemnity. They thought of the phrase in
Acts 11:18: 'Then hath God also to the Gentiles granted
repentance unto life.'

On 28 October Brainerd preached about the parable of the
marriage feast in Matthew 22:1-14. On this occasion God
seemed to give him a special ability to adapt the profound
truths of Holy Scripture to the capacities of the Indians,
without the least difficulty. 'The word of God, at this time,
seemed to fall upon the assembly with a divine power and
influence, especially toward the close of my discourse. There

was both a sweet melting and bitter mourning in the audience. The dear Christians were refreshed and comforted, convictions revived in others, and several persons newly awakened, who had never been with us before.'

The presence of God was so abundantly manifested that Brainerd thought about Jacob's testimony at Bethel: 'This was no other than the house of God and the gate of heaven.' Every person present who had a relish for the gospel of God's grace was blessed and they all confessed, 'Lord, it is good for us to be here.' The converted Indians appeared to David Brainerd like the New Jerusalem, which came down from heaven 'as a bride adorned for her husband'. The service was so powerful and moving that he reluctantly brought it to a close and went to his lodging.

On Sunday, 3 November, he baptized fourteen Indians, a number that included eight children. Among this group were a woman who was nearly eighty years old and a couple of men aged about fifty who had been notoriously wicked. One was a murderer and both were quarrelsome and boisterous drunks. But now they gave real evidence of conversion, though Brainerd had delayed their baptism to give a kind of trial period to see if this amazing change was truly valid.

The next day he spoke about the resurrection of Lazarus from John 11, comparing this remarkable event with God's sovereign grace in delivering dead souls from their spiritual bondage. Some in the audience on this occasion had come from a great distance to the meeting. One had experienced such a remarkable change as to awaken astonishment in everyone. The first time she attended the meeting she was half drunk and railed at Brainerd, trying if possible to disturb the worship service. But she quickly came under such conviction as to be unable to have any peace until she rested in Jesus Christ.

The total number who had been baptized now was forty-seven, including twelve from the region of the Forks of the

Delaware. With deep gratitude he recorded, 'Through rich grace, none of them, as yet, have been left to disgrace their profession of Christianity, by any scandalous or unbecoming behavior.'

Brainerd had a strong penchant for recording in writing the experiences he had while working among the Indians. He kept a daily diary in which he described in some detail his manner of living and travelling and the people with whom he came in contact. He recorded the texts he preached and the results of each message, as far as he was able to determine it. He wrote down with remarkable frankness the feelings he had during the various phases of his work, including the depths of his discouragements and periods of depression.

On 4 November 1745, in the midst of the most encouraging time in his life, he sat down to review the course of his missionary travels among the Indians. It had been a little over two and a half years since his arrival at Kaunaumeek in New York. He had travelled some three thousand miles, most of them in going to and fro between the Forks of the Delaware and Crossweeksung (some seventy miles distance) and visiting the Susquehanna region which was 120 miles away. This had required him to spend a disproportionate amount of his time in travel, time which could have been spent in studying the Indian languages. The year he had spent in trying to learn the language of the Indians of New York had proved to be of no help to him since there was no similarity between this language and that of the Delaware Indians to whom he had ministered in the last eighteen months.

In addition to his brief review of the statistical data regarding his missionary experience Brainerd felt a need to give a careful evaluation of the remarkable work of God which had taken place among the Crossweeksung tribes. He did so under six major heads, each of which highlighted one aspect of the astounding, marvellous and divine nature of this awakening.

In two and a half years he had travelled some three thousand miles

1. The timing of the revival

First, the awakening came at a time when his own hopes for such a work were at their lowest ebb, and he was physically at his weakest. The time he had spent labouring among the Indians up till the summer of 1745 had been largely without visible result. He had made friends of some of the Indians, to be sure, and many seemed to respect him, but there had been no clear-cut cases of conversion. He had been seriously considering abandoning his enterprise, thinking that the SSPCK was wasting its money in supporting him. Here is how he put it: 'Hence I was ready to look upon myself as a burden to the honorable society which employed and supported me in this business, and began to entertain serious thoughts of giving up my *mission*; and almost resolved, I would do so at the conclusion of the present year, if I had then no better prospect of special success in my work than I had hitherto had.'

The remarkable character of this work of God was also seen in the fact that he was personally worn out and exhausted from long and tedious trips to the Susquehanna. The hardships of travels to these distant regions, on horseback and sometimes on foot, had left him very weary. Also the lack of success he had experienced in his labours had left him in a very low mental state. Optimism, emotional energy and confidence are always assets in any enterprise and are conducive to success. David Brainerd admitted he did not possess these qualities when God took hold of the situation. And yet at this very season when the prospects seemed as bad as could be and he was the least disposed to be successful God intervened in a powerful way.

Brainerd, as always, was ready to make a practical application of all this: 'Thus he "ordained strength out of weakness," by making bare his almighty arm at a time when all hopes and human probabilities most evidently appeared to fail. Whence I learn, that it is good to follow the path of duty, though in the midst of darkness and discouragement.'

2. *The awakening was sudden*

The second fact taken note of by the missionary, as demonstrating the truly miraculous nature of the revival,was the remarkable and providential way the Indians had been called together, and how quickly and unaccountably they were seized with concern about their souls' interests. When he first visited Crossweeksung there was not a single man present, but only four women and a few children. But in just a few days they were coming from as far as forty miles away to listen to the gospel message. Many of these people came purely out of curiosity with no design whatever of becoming Christians. And yet, all of a sudden, in a way surprising to themselves, the Indians came under conviction and began to enquire the way to Zion. Brainerd likened the coming of these people to Saul and his messengers who, when they came among the prophets, began immediately to prophesy. Even total strangers, people who were totally ignorant of the meaning of true religion, were immediately awakened and enquired 'with great solicitude', 'What must we do to be saved?'

3. *The way the prejudices of the Indians were overcome*

A third remarkable aspect of the awakening was the way God preserved the Indians from their accustomed prejudices against the gospel. From the beginning Brainerd's attempts at evangelizing the Indians had been hampered by the attempts of white people to put them on guard against Christianity, and even to frighten them away from religious services. These people had told the Indians that they were good enough already and should not be disturbed by the 'noise' about Jesus

Christ. They accused Brainerd of being a knave and a deceiver who taught lies to the Indians. When this did not work they insinuated that he was disguising his real purpose in coming among the Indians, and that was to sell them to the English as slaves.

Brainerd was certainly at a disadvantage in seeking to answer his accusers because he was a total stranger to them, while his opponents were well known among the Indians. But the Indians had observed that these enemies of the gospel were not only unconcerned about their spiritual interests, but were also obviously interested in profiting from them by selling them strong drink. It soon became evident that it was David Brainerd who was really telling the truth and was genuinely interested in helping them. As a result the tactics of the enemies failed and the Indians continued to listen with open hearts to the preaching of the good news. When Brainerd saw God intervening on behalf of his own cause he often said, 'If God will work who can hinder?'

4. God's provision of an interpreter

In the fourth place, Brainerd was amazed at how God overcame his own limitations through a lack of a knowledge of the Indian languages. Had he been forced to communicate the truths of the gospel through someone who was totally disinterested in the content of the messages, a natural and artificial barrier would have been raised at the outset. But God had touched the heart of Moses Tattamy and had given him a genuine love for the Saviour, and he had come to understand and appreciate the great doctrines taught by the missionary. He was not only able to transmit accurately the content of Brainerd's messages, but he also felt the same pathos and fervency as the speaker: 'It is remarkable that when I was favored with any special assistance in any work, and enabled to speak with more than common freedom, fervency, and power, under a lively and affecting sense of divine things, he was usually affected in the same manner almost instantly, and seemed at once quickened and enabled to speak in the same pathetic language, and under the same influence that I did.' Tattamy aided him not only in translation, but also by repeating and reinforcing in private the truths which Brainerd had taught in the public meetings.

5. *The content of the preaching*

Fifthly, the awakening among the Indians was accomplished without an appeal to the truths of Scripture which are particularly harsh and alarming. Although the Indians were often overwhelmed with conviction and demonstrated visibly their distress over their spiritual condition, it was not such truths as hell or judgement which caused such emotion, but the preaching of the wonderful mercy of God in Jesus Christ. No one could say that the preacher was disturbing them with threats of eternal fire. The 'continued strain of gospel invitation to perishing sinners' was the cause of their seeking the Lord.

Brainerd was also grateful that there was no cause for objection to the revival based on excessive emotional disturbances or disorders. Various physical manifestations, such as screaming, convulsions and swoonings, often accompany strong religious feelings. In the Great Awakening Edwards, Whitefield, the Tennents and other leaders interrupted such tendencies whenever they began to appear, since in their judgement these manifestations tended to discredit what they were trying to do. They wanted the spiritual feelings of awakened sinners and believers to be based on a clear apprehension of truth. They knew that the truth can make a powerful impression on the mind and induce people to intense zeal and great joy, but always within the bounds of propriety. The behaviour of Brainerd's converts was well within these guidelines. Their convictions came from a knowledge of gospel truth, not visions, trances or supposed prophetic inspirations which promote theological error and pride.

6. *The practical results in the lives of the Indians*

Finally, Brainerd was grateful that the practical results of the awakening at Crossweeksung were very positive. The Indians who were converted in the summer of 1745 received with great enthusiasm all the great truths which were unapologetically proclaimed by the Puritan missionary. 'I doubt not,' said Brainerd, 'that many of these people have gained more doctrinal knowledge of divine truths since I visited them June last, than could have been instilled into their minds by the most diligent use of proper and instructive means for whole years together, without such a divine influence.'

The changes in the Indians were not just theological however, but also moral and practical. They abandoned their pagan notions and idolatry upon conversion. They began immediately to seek to carry out biblical standards for marriage, which had formerly been totally foreign to their patterns of behaviour. Drunkenness, which was the 'darling sin' of practically all the Indians, became rare in Brainerd's converted community. This is the more remarkable when we consider that it was not unusual for some of them to indulge excessively in alcohol every day. There were other manifestations of a true and powerful spiritual change in them. They took up cheerfully with the Christian standards of honesty and justice and tried to discharge their old debts which they had contracted. But Brainerd was especially delighted with the spirit of love and fellowship among the new converts. 'Love seemed to reign among them, especially those who have given evidences of having passed a saving change; and I never saw any appearance of bitterness or censoriousness in these, nor any disposition to "esteem themselves better than others".'

And so now Brainerd was able to record with deep satisfaction and with profound thanks to God, to whom alone he attributed such blessings, that a great work of God had taken place among the Indian tribes of Crossweeksung and surrounding communities. By any standards the professions of faith made by these Indians were credible. He concludes his reflections on what had happened with a prayer, so characteristic of his own desires: 'May the *great Author* of this work maintain and promote the same *here*, and propagate it *everywhere*, till "the whole earth be filled with his glory"!'

23.
The wicket gate

In his immortal allegory of the Pilgrim, John Bunyan pictures Christian as setting out towards the Celestial City with a heavy load on his back. The first part of the story tells about some of the struggles the seeking soul has as he determines to leave the world behind and pursue the goal of eternal life. First he has to escape from a terrible swamp called the 'Slough of Despond'. Then other people become a hindrance to him. Some mock him, others threaten him and still others give him false information as to how he should succeed.

A character known as Evangelist points him towards a 'Wicket Gate' where he is to receive further instructions about his eternal interests. After a brief detour as a result of listening to the corrupt advice of a man called Worldly Wiseman, he comes at last to the Wicket Gate. Not far from this gate stands a strong castle where a captain called Beelzebub shoots arrows at those seeking to enter. The gatekeeper counsels Christian as he continues on his journey.

The Wicket Gate has become proverbial in Christian parlance to describe the first stage in the journey for a convicted sinner in his quest for relief from the awful load of his sin. If this Wicket Gate concept is idealized it can become a subtle form of error, for no such intermediate stage is demanded in Scripture for one coming to God. But it certainly does picture what actually happens in the experience of most people. Not infrequently the lost sinner, usually coming from a background of total ignorance as to the nature of his own soul and the gospel, struggles through various misconceptions and obstacles before he looks to a crucified Saviour, the only true remedy. And, of course, the great enemy of mankind Satan, ever jealous of his territory and eager to secure those who are in his control, makes the struggle from the darkness to the light as difficult, painful and as long as possible.

We can see from the recorded experiences of some of the Crossweeksung Indians what a violent experience it is when a pagan, long deluded by idolatry and superstition, passes from the kingdom of Satan to that of God. The devil had for centuries held unrivalled sway over the Native Americans. But now one stronger than he, Jesus Christ himself, had come to overcome him, take his armour from him and divide the spoil he had taken. But when a redeemed sinner is in the process of experiencing this marvellous exorcism, the struggle can often be intense.

In the late autumn of 1745 and the early winter of 1746 Brainerd saw the Spirit of God continue to work powerfully upon the hearts and lives of the Indians who came to hear him, often from great distances. He chose during this period to record in some detail the feelings and attitudes of some the Indians during their spiritual birth-pains. These testimonies are highly interesting and merit specific examination. Much of what follows is from the pen of Brainerd himself, including his own record of dialogue with the Indians.

Nov. 26. I was favored with some special freedom and fervency in my discourse, and a powerful energy accompanied divine truths. Many wept and sobbed affectionately, and scarcely any appeared unconcerned in the whole assembly... The persons lately awakened were some of them deeply distressed for their souls, and appeared earnestly solicitous to obtain an interest in Christ: and some of them, after public worship was over, in anguish of spirit, said, 'they knew not what to do, nor how to get their wicked hearts changed.'

On 28 November, after preaching from Luke 9:28-36 on the transfiguration he remarked,

> Observed some, that I have reason to think are truly such [real Christians] exceedingly affected with an account of the glory of Christ in his transfiguration, and filled with longing desires of being with him, that they might with open face behold his glory. After public service was over, I asked one of them, who wept and sobbed most affectionately, What she now wanted? She replied, 'O, to be with Christ. She did not know how to stay,' etc. This was a blessed refreshing season to the religious people in general. The Lord Jesus seemed to manifest his divine glory to them, as when transfigured before his disciples; and they were ready with the disciples universally to say 'Lord it is good for us to be here.'

On 22 December he preached from Matthew 19:16-22 about the rich young ruler. It was a season of 'comfort' to many, and one woman in particular came forth to give a remarkable testimony which Brainerd cited in her own poor imitation of the English tongue:

> When I came to discourse particularly with her, and to inquire of her, how she obtained relief and deliverance from the spiritual distresses which she had lately suffered; she answered in broken English, 'Me try, me

try save myself; last, my strength be all gone (meaning her ability to save herself); could not me stir bit further. Den last me forced let Jesus Christ alone send me hell; if he please.' I said, 'But you was not willing to go to hell; was you?' She replied, 'Could not me help it. My heart, he would wicked for all. Could not me make him good' (Meaning, she saw it was right she should go to hell, because her heart was wicked, and would be so after all she could do to mend it). I asked her, how she got out of this case. She answered still in the same broken language, 'By by, my heart be glad desperately.' I asked her, why her heart was glad? She replied, 'Glad my heart, Jesus Christ do what he please with me. Den me tink, glad my heart Jesus Christ send me to hell. Did not me care where he put me; love him for all.' She could not readily be convinced, but that she was willing to go to hell if Christ was pleased to send her there; although the truth evidently was, that her will was so swallowed up in the divine will, that she could not frame any hell in her imagination which would be so dreadful or undesirable, provided it was the will of God to send her to it.

Here is perhaps the clearest example of the kind of selfless conversion which later matured into the system known as Hopkinsianism. Jonathan Edwards and his followers believed that the essence of faith is a divine light in the soul enabling the believer to see the essential glory of the Redeemer. True worship is not so much an attempt to secure some blessing from God, even such a noble one as salvation, but love to God for his own inherent worth. Brainerd at this point does not seem to be demanding this kind of faith as a standard; he simply reports what he observed in the Indian woman. Hopkins, however, eventually made willingness to be damned for the glory of God a condition of salvation. Did this view-point germinate, or at least receive confirmation, in the con-versions which took place in the Indian settlements under the preaching of his friend David Brainerd? Undoubtedly Hopkins was one of the early readers of the writings of Brainerd.

> *Dec. 25.* The Indians having been used on Christmas-days to drink and revel among some of the white people in this parts; I thought it proper to call them together and discourse to them upon divine things; which I accord-ingly did from the parable of the fig tree, Luke 13:6-9. A divine influence, I am persuaded, accompanied the word at this season... The power attending divine truths seemed to have the influence of the earthquake rather than of the whirlwind upon them... The impressions made upon the assembly in general, seemed not super-ficial, but deep and heart-affecting. O how ready did they now appear universally to embrace and comply with everything which they heard, and were convinced was their duty. God was in the midst of us of a truth, bowing and melting stubborn hearts!

The following day, 26 December, an eighty-year old lady came to Brainerd and related to him an experience which he considered the most remarkable he had ever come across. She had had a dream-like encounter which, according to her own witness, resulted in a a profound struggle to receive spiritual peace. Brainerd was naturally suspicious of religious emo-tions which were based on 'mental disorders and delusions' or 'visionary scenes', but since this case took place under his own preaching he was forced to at least give her a fair hearing. She had listened to his messages many times without feeling any particular conviction or interest, until the previous Sabbath.

Then something happened. All at once it was as though a needle had been thrust into her heart, after which she could have no rest day or night:

> On the evening before Christmas, a number of Indians being together at the house where she was, and discoursing about Christ, their talk pierced her heart so that she could not set up, but fell down in her bed, at which time she went away, as she expressed it, and felt as if she dreamed, and yet is confident that she did not dream. When she was thus gone, she saw two paths; one appeared very broad and crooked, and that turned to the left hand. The other appeared straight, and very narrow; and that went up the hill to the right hand. She travelled, she said, for some time up the narrow right hand path, till at length something seemed to obstruct her journey. She sometimes called it darkness; and then described it otherwise, and seemed to compare it to a block or bar. She then remembered what she had heard me say about striving to enter in at the strait gate, although she took little notice of it at the time when she heard me discourse upon that subject; and thought she would climb over this bar. But just as she was thinking of this, she came back again, as she termed it, meaning that she came to herself; whereupon her soul was extremely distressed, apprehending that she had now turned back, and forsaken Christ, and that there was therefore no hope of mercy for her.

Brainerd was somewhat perplexed by this experience of the aged Indian woman. He was not sure what was the source of this vision, trance, or whatever it was, though he could not rule out the possibility that God was doing a work in her. He presented to her as clearly as possible the gospel invitation. He shared with her the fact that Christ was able and willing to

Old Indian woman and child

'save to the uttermost all, old as well as young, that come to him'. But this did not seem to comfort her, for she steadfastly affirmed that her heart was so wicked that she could not come to Christ. 'I know not how to come,' she moaned.

> This she spoke in anguish of spirits, striking on her breast, with tears in her eyes, and with such earnestness in her looks, as was indeed piteous and affecting. She seems to be really convinced of her sin and misery, and her need of a change of heart. Her concern is abiding and constant, so that nothing appears why this exercise may not have a saving issue. Indeed there seems reason to hope such an issue, seeing she is so solicitous to obtain an interest in Christ, that her heart, as she expresses it, *prays day and night.*

Cases such as this, through varying in some details, have been common in seasons of revival. There always seem to be some who come under intense convictions and become suspended in a state of uncertainty and despair. Sometimes the lost, under true preaching, do feel themselves unable to fulfil the conditions of salvation. Yet the 'inability' of the sinner is not some physical handicap (as Brainerd would have been the first to confess) but an inability of will, or purpose, rooted in the sinner's pride and unbelief. How about people who 'want' to come to Christ but 'cannot'? No doubt each case is different and there is often something peculiar which causes the seeker to be unable to find relief. Ultimately the evangelist must leave some cases to the great Discerner of hearts. The gospel itself demands no specified period of mental torture for the soul before it embraces Christ but encourages the immediate acceptance of the gospel invitation.

On 29 December Brainerd preached to the Indians from John 3:1-5. It was to be another day when God's presence was manifested in a definite way:

A number of white people were present, as is usual upon the Sabbath. The discourse was accompanied with power, and seemed to have a silent, but deep and piercing influence upon the audience. Many wept and sobbed affectionately. There were some tears among the white people, as well as the Indians. Some could not refrain from crying out; though there were not so many exercised.

It is impossible to give a just and lively description of the appearance of things at this season; at least such as to convey a bright and adequate idea of the effects of this influence... At the same time both of men and women, old and young, might be seen in tears, and some in anguish of spirit appearing in their very countenances, like condemned malefactors, bound towards the place of execution, with a heavenly solicitude sitting in their faces; so that there seemed here, as I thought, a lively emblem of the solemn day of account: a mixture of heaven and hell; of joy and anguish inexpressible.

On 19 January Brainerd preached to the Indians that in order to appreciate and receive the gospel of God's grace it is necessary for a person to feel totally undone and unworthy. An Indian man became convinced that it was necessary for him to work up within himself this proper 'frame of mind', as it were, to get himself ready for salvation. But after some 'strivings' and attempts to get this attitude for himself, he at last despaired of ever mending or changing his heart in any manner at all:

He was amazed that he had never before seen that it was utterly impossible for him, by all his contrivances and endeavors to do anything in that way, since the matter now appeared to him in so clear a light. Instead of imagining now that God would be pleased with him for the sake of this frame of mind, and this view of his undone estate, he saw clearly, and felt that it would be just with God, to send him to eternal misery; and that there was no goodness in what he then felt; for he could not help seeing, that he was naked, sinful, and miserable, and that there was nothing in such a sight to deserve God's love or pity.

Following this the Indian was given an inward and spiritual impression of the greatness of God and the glory of Christ. When this happened, without any strivings or struggles on his part, automatically his heart, 'went out,' as it were, to Christ.

He did not, he said, know what it was that he saw. He did not say, 'This is Jesus Christ'; but it was such glory and beauty as he never saw before. He did now give away his heart, as he had formerly intended and attempted to do; but it *went away of itself* after that glory which he then discovered. He used to make a bargain with Christ, to give up his heart to him, that he might have eternal life for it. But now he thought nothing about himself, or what would become of him hereafter; but was pleased, and his mind wholly taken up with the unspeakable excellency of what he then beheld.

The point has already been belaboured, but it recurs so often in Brainerd's ministry that we shall miss a significant aspect of his emphasis if it is overlooked. The type of preaching and teaching practised by Brainerd produced a uniquely God-centered experience. All the teachers influenced by Edwards proclaimed that Jesus Christ is inherently glorious and great. True conversion, in their view, is the ability to rest in that essential goodness, without regard particularly to one's own benefit or happiness. The less one even thinks of oneself the better.

By any account the depth of the understanding of Brainerd's converts is amazing. Their transportation from demonic animism to a solid relish for spiritual verities, their appreciation for the inherent glory and beauty of the Redeemer and their hearty approval of the way of salvation through him can only be attributed to the enlightenment of the Spirit of God. The specific business of the Third Person of the God-head, according to Jesus' own teachings, is to glorify the Son of God.

24.
Bethel, the house of God

There is no force in the universe which can elevate and ennoble human nature like the gospel of Jesus Christ. When the sovereign Spirit of God awakens the soul of man to the need of redemption and recreates it in the image of God's Son, every dimension of life is changed. The ferocious and selfish nature of man is softened and quickened to every good work. A true Christian is a better neighbour, family member, or employee. Although the deliverance of sinners from guilt and hell was the primary mission of Jesus to earth, the incidental influences of the Christian mind are numerous. The message of Jesus Christ not only delivers individual people from eternal destruction, but also brings domestic tranquillity, educational stimulus, social improvement, political stability and commercial incentive.

David Brainerd without a doubt had the solution for the colossal problems of the Native Americans. The positive changes that took place immediately upon their acceptance of the gospel under his wise and gracious administrations show how effective true Christianity can really be. Had his policies and programmes been followed the tragic history of the American Indians would have been different. Many of the American settlers had adopted only too readily the motto: 'There is no good Indian but a dead Indian.' This prejudice was ill-conceived and unjust on many accounts. When changed by the gospel of Christ the Indians were as capable of making a positive contribution to the world as any other ethnic group. Brainerd's ministry among the New Jersey Indians alone demonstrates the truthfulness of this fact.

Like every true revival, the awakening at Crossweeksung, brief as it was and limited as it was to one Indian encampment, continued to bear fruit for several generations to come, even after its subjects were forced to leave New Jersey for the open spaces to the west. These people not only manifested the normal and essential characteristics of good citizenship, but they became loyal and patriotic citizens of the colonial community. They had no sympathies with the dangerous and deceitful French and their savage Indian allies who waged war against the English in the horrendous wars which stained the American frontier with blood in the 1750s.

John Brainerd, who succeeded David as pastor of the Crossweeksung Indians, reported that at least twenty of Brainerd's converts died fighting for the English in the battle at Lake George, New York, at the height of Pontiac's War in 1763. A notice, signed by John, appeared in *The Pennsylvania Journal* for 5 September of that year: 'Whereas a report has been spreading that the Christian Indians in New Jersey, under my care, were many of them gone back to join the murdering Indians on the frontiers; this is to inform and assure the public that such report is wholly without foundation; that these Indians evidently discover a great abhorrence of the perfidious and inhuman proceedings of their remote Savage brethren, and that there is not one of them missing, or that discover a contrary temper.'[1]

After the Brainerd brothers passed from the scenes many of the Christian Indians moved west, sharing in the fate of their kind. The Calvinistic faith in which they were trained was not always available to them, so frequently they merged with the Moravians. Two members of the Crossweeksung community,

Samuel Moore and Tobias, were Moravian elders who were
murdered in the tragic slaughter at Gnadenhutten, Ohio, in
March 1782. Some white men fell upon these helpless believers and wantonly killed the entire congregation of ninety-six,
including many women and children.

The ministry of the Yankee missionary was talked about for
many generations, even among the Indians who settled far
west of the Mississippi. In 1834 the *Missionary Herald* reported a conversation a mission worker had with two Christian
Delaware sisters who lived among the Shawnees near the
Kansas River, six hundred miles west of the Mississippi.
'Their grandmother, their mother, and their father Jacob Stakit
had all been members of David Brainerd's congregation in
New Jersey. Their grandmother, they said, had often told them
about their beloved Yankee.'[2]

'He was a young man — he was a lovely man; he was a staff
to walk with... He slept on a deer-skin or a bear-skin. He ate
bear meat and samp: then we knew he was not proud. He would
come to my grandmother and say, "I am hungry — make
haste!" Then she would take down the kettle and he would eat.
But some of the people did not like him, and said, "What has
this white man come here for? we don't want him here!" and
they told him to go off... After a while they found he was an
honest man and they would do anything he said.'[3] These aged
Indians, their memories kindled by a tender tradition spanning
many decades, had known David Brainerd to be an evangelist,
a reformer and finally a pastor.

His duties were not only spiritual, but because of the
uncivilized state of the converts, he also had to assume a much
broader rôle and to manage many of their temporal interests as
well. It was necessary for him to 'take care of all their secular
affairs, as if they were a company of children'. He often acted
as a judge to settle their petty disputes. He taught them the
necessity of industry and faithfulness in ordinary business and
secured money to discharge their debts. He intervened when

outsiders sought to encroach on their property or frighten them away from their lands.

Four days before Christmas 1745 he began a serious and concerted attempt to instruct them in a deeper knowledge of the basic truths of the Christian faith: 'My people having now attained to a considerable degree of knowledge in the principles of Christianity; I thought it proper to set up a catechismal lecture among them; and this evening attempted something in that form; proposing questions to them agreeably to the Assembly's Shorter Catechism, receiving their answers, and then explaining and insisting as appeared necessary and proper upon each question.'

The teacher was surprised and delighted at how far they had come in understanding the great truths of the gospel. Their answers were clear and came readily: 'I found their doctrinal knowledge to exceed my own expectations.' The Crossweeksung converts had come a long way from their days of demon-worship and superstition. The gospel of Christ had overcome all the barriers to the cross that heathenism had erected.

But on the day after the catechetical instruction, 22 December, Brainerd was aware of another kind of problem he had to face, more subtle to be sure, but perhaps even more difficult. Recently several Indians who had lived among the Quakers had moved into the area. This exposure to Quaker influences had corrected many of their barbarian social customs and made them polite and civilized. They had, however, imbibed some of the theological opinions of the Quakers, one of which was exceedingly troublesome to David Brainerd. They taught that no one need fear suffering the judgements of God if he lived soberly and honestly according to the sincere understandings of his own heart. This is the famous 'inner light' doctrine which had caused such grave concern among all the Puritans, not only the leaders in the new land of America but also in England.

The idea that a person can recommend himself to God by

his own righteous deeds is a delusion that is often more difficult to counteract than out-and-out paganism. David Brainerd found this to be so in confronting these reformed and self-confident disciples of the Quakers. 'These persons,' he said, 'I found much worse to deal with than those who are wholly under pagan darkness; who make no pretences to knowledge in Christianity at all, nor have any self-righteous foundation to stand upon' (22 December). But Brainerd's faithful teaching soon began to change the direction of their thinking. Under his persistent instruction these people soon saw, in the light of the Word of God, that a sober and honest life was not itself sufficient for the salvation of the soul. Before long they became convinced, just like those who had never been exposed to the theory of works salvation, that a true change of heart was necessary for entrance into the kingdom of God.

Brainerd's rôle among the Indian community went, at times, far beyond instructing them in correct theology. In January 1746 he had occasion to befriend them in very practical ways. Some of the white settlers had previously run them into debt through their excessive drinking. A few of the Indians had been arrested and claims were made against their lands. The loss of their land would have been a great calamity, for not only would this have taken away their means of livelihood, but it would also have jeopardized Brainerd's hope of settling them into a stable community where they could enjoy the advantages of a church fellowship. As soon as the danger became real he sought to intervene. After a consultation with the leaders of the missionary society it was decided to use some of the funds which had been intended for purely evangelistic purposes for discharging the debts of the Indians and thus securing their lands. The society responded with 'eighty-two pounds, five shillings, "New Jersey currency", at eight shillings per ounce.' With the proper payment the problem was solved.

During the early months of the new year Brainerd began to implement his plan of bringing his new converts into the full benefits of a civilized Christian community. The first thing absolutely essential was a schoolmaster to instruct them in the English language and other basics of education. On 31 January the teacher arrived and was heartily welcomed by the Indians. Immediately he distributed several dozen primers. His classes consisted at first of thirty children and young people in the daytime and about half that many in the evening school. It is interesting to note the procedure followed by the Puritan missionary in his efforts to promote change among the Indians. The more ordinary method would have been to civilize and educate them in preparation for proper evangelism. But under Brainerd's leadership this order was reversed. First they became Christians, and then they were introduced to the amenities of learning and culture.

He was pleased and grateful that Indians were coming from great distances to Crossweeksung to hear the gospel and be educated. But their scattered situation was incompatible with a stable community life. They needed to move into one particular area where public meetings would be more convenient. The first reference in his diary to a suitable place for a permanent community was on 29 October, when he 'viewed the Indian lands at Cranberry'. He decided to move the entire Indian community to this place.

Cranberry (now known as Cranbury) is fifteen miles south of New Brunswick, halfway between that city and the original site of Crossweeksung (modern Crosswicks), which is about eight miles south-east of Trenton. Cranberry had been settled in 1689 by Scotch Calvinists who named their settlement after the emblem of the Grant clan. Charles McKnight ministered among these Presbyterians and Brainerd often stayed with him while travelling back and forth to Crossweeksung. McKnight eventually became a patriot in Washington's army. He later served as pastor of a church near Shrewsbury, New Jersey,

The Presbyterian manse at Cranberry, where Brainerd slept when in the vicinity.

which was burned during the revolutionary war. McKnight himself was imprisoned and died in 1778 as a result of the hardships he endured.

The specific location for the future Indian community 'was a pleasant, level country of light sandy soil, between one and two miles north-east of Cranberry, at the head of Wigwam Brook. The stream was fed by two or three good springs, and a few miles toward Freehold was a medicinal spring which the Indians frequented. Close by Cranberry was a small lake.'[4] John Brainerd later gave this Indian settlement the name of Bethel, 'the House of God'. The name was appropriate, for here at Cranberry the Indians were in close proximity to a community of supporting white Christians who would assist David Brainerd in his pastoral care of them.

By March the procedure of clearing the land for the new village was well under way. Brainerd recorded on 24 March his satisfaction in leading the 130 or so Christian Indians in this enterprise: 'My people were out this day with the design of clearing some of their land, above fifteen miles distant from this settlement, in order to their settling there in a compact form, where they might be under the advantages of attending the public worship of God, of having their children taught in a school, and at the same time have a conveniency for planting: their land in the place of our present residence being of little or no value for that purpose.'

With 'his people' (as he often affectionally referred to them) thus busily occupied in building a new community, Brainerd saw an obvious opportunity to instruct them in some basic biblical principles on the need for hard work and industry: 'The design of their settling thus in a body, and cultivating their lands, of which they have done very little in their Pagan state, being of such necessity and importance to their religious interest, as well as worldly comfort, I thought it proper to call them together, and show the duty of labouring with faithfulness and industry, and that they must not now "be slothful in business" as they had ever been in their Pagan state. I endeavoured to press the importance of their being laborious, diligent, and vigorous in the prosecution of their business; especially at the present juncture, the season of planting being now near, in order to their being in a capacity of living together, and enjoying the means of grace and instruction.'

The expression, 'the means of grace', fundamental to a Puritan concept of Christian maturity, refers to the regular disciplines of the church, such as preaching, private instruction (usually by catechism) and observing the formal ordinances such as the Lord's Supper. David Brainerd believed with all his heart that the redemption of souls is a divine work from beginnning to end, rooted in God's sovereign purpose in election and manifested in the redeeming work of Christ and the regenerating power of the Holy Spirit. But he also knew that the ordinary way for God to bring his grace home to the human heart and apply it in the day-by-day walk of the believer is through the means of biblical instruction and training in the church. There was no fanatical dependence upon special revelations of God through ecstatic experiences. Nor was there any fatalistic repudiation of the need for diligence in personal striving for holiness through the study and practice of the Word of God.

By May 1746 the move to Cranberry had been completed. The converted Indians were living together in one vicinity where they were under the regular instruction of a competent educator. Here too David Brainerd was able to spend time with them on a continual basis, helping them to grow in the knowledge of the Saviour they had found and to learn that true faith always results in proper living. The picture before us is powerful yet tender, spiritual yet intensely practical. The evangelist had now become the pastor, or at least had an opportunity to do so. His location would no longer be Crossweeksung, but Cranberry.

25.
False accusations

To trouble, in a variety of types and shapes, David Brainerd was no stranger. As a youth he faced the trauma of the loss of both his parents. His college career was terminated through the excessive and misguided harshness of authoritarian leaders. The inherited melancholy strains in his personality never ceased to vex and torment him as he struggled in the path upward to fellowship with his Lord. He left behind the comforts of a settled life as a colonial pastor to live in the wilderness as a missionary to the Indians, often travelling long miles in bitter cold and driving storms. He often wept tears of grief over the awful blindness of the Indians who refused to open their hearts to the Saviour he loved.

In the autumn of 1745 a new type of difficulty fell across his path from an unexpected source. Just on the heels of the great awakening among the Indians, a phenomenon which should have merited the highest praise from all good men, the missionary and his converts became the target of desperately unfair and malicious accusations. Complicity in turbulent events involving politics and land claims was imputed to him — charges of which he was totally innocent. An interesting comparison can be seen, in this phase of his life, between the charges against Brainerd and the treatment received by his Lord, who was charged with insurrection against the Roman government of his day.

Near Newark, New Jersey, there lived a settler named Samuel Baldwin. One September day he was cutting trees on a tract of land which he claimed as his own when local authorities came and arrested him for trespassing. Refusing to give bail, he was jailed. Baldwin was one of many who were involved in disputes over the legitimate ownership of land. The problem was caused by the unsettled state of things at the time.

When the province of New Jersey was separated from the governorship of New York in 1738 there was much confusion over land rights. Many of the settlers had purchased land directly from the Indians but had not obtained proper titles to it. Later on more prosperous and influential people moved into the territory and secured legal rights to large sections of land, often ignoring any prior claims. Who owned what became a hotly contested issue. Many farmers and poorer settlers, like Samuel Baldwin, were losing their land to the wealthy. A kind of class warfare began to develop as the homesteaders quarrelled with their richer rivals.

When Baldwin was jailed the anger of the original claimants was aroused to a fever pitch. His arrest and incarceration symbolized the threat they all felt. Feeling that justice had been denied their friend, 150 of them, armed with clubs, axes and crowbars, forced their way into the Newark jail and released Baldwin. Several of the rioters promised that this would not be the end, but that they would come again with twice their number and a hundred Indians.

The threat to involve Indians in this uproar was ridiculous on the surface of it. There were not more than fifty Indian males who lived within thirty miles of Newark. Beyond that, by about twenty miles, was Brainerd's Christian Indian community. It was reported that an Indian named Andrew who lived 'near Cranberry on the Navesink Side of the Raritan' had told the rioters that he expected that a large number of Indians, perhaps 300, would come ere long and live on land from which he had been wrongfully dispossessed. Thus the citizens of Newark, because of these idle rumours, faced the spectre of an invasion by an Indian tribe. Alarm was aroused throughout the Newark area, including the members of Aaron Burr's congregation. The fact is that the only Indian settlement of any size was the church of David Brainerd.

Frightened by the prospect of an Indian war, many of the citizens drew up petitions to the legislature for protection. When the governor Lewis Morris received the petitions he too was agitated and proceeded to take action. He wrote to the House of Representatives saying, 'I send you also an Account of a Notorious Riot, Lately Committed at Newark, if it be not Something worse, If the Indians can be prevailed on to joyn in Attempts of the Kind, we may soon have a war with them in our own bowells, encouraged by the King's Subjects; The threat is of Dangerous Consequence.'

Eventually someone, no doubt a person unsympathetic to the evangelistic success of Brainerd, circulated the report that the missionary had been sent into the region for the specific purpose of leading the Indians into insurrection. A more daring lie could not have been invented. Not one Indian had taken part in any of the land-claim scuffles. When a group of whites invaded Newark in January, twice as many in fact as had liberated Baldwin, there was not a single Indian among them. Brainerd's converts had been peaceable and well-behaved and had not given legitimate grounds for the least suspicion. These charges were unquestionably a satanic device to undermine the advance of the spiritual awakening at Crossweeksung.

As if these agitations were not sufficient, another circumstance compounded the problem and fanned the flames of unrest. On 8 January a ship from Great Britain brought the news that a rebellion had broken out in Scotland against the king's government. It seemed that the supporters of James Edward Stuart (known as the Old Pretender), the son of James II, were on the move. James II had been deposed and his son passed over in favour of the Protestant William III and James' daughter Mary during the 'Glorious Revolution' of 1688. In September 1745 the Old Pretender's son, Charles Edward, known in ballad as 'Bonnie Prince Charlie', had gathered a Highland force to restore his father to the sovereignty. His army had invaded England and proceeded as far as Derby, causing panic in the city of London.

Brainerd's enemies, ever ready to find any reason to preju-dice anyone, especially the civil authorities, against him, claimed that he was an agent of the Scotish 'Pretender'. This charge implied that Brainerd was a covert Roman Catholic who had come to organize the Indians for the purpose of making war on the Protestant English.

He first heard of the charge following a sermon he preached on 2 February. The news fell with crushing weight upon him: 'After public worship, my bodily strength being much spent, my spirits sunk amazingly, and especially on hearing that I was generally taken to be a Roman Catholic, sent by the Papists to draw the Indians into an insurrection against the English, that some were in fear of me, and others were for having me taken up by authority and punished. Alas, what will not the devil do to bring a slur and disgrace on the work of God!'

The next day (3 February) the same problem was much upon his mind: 'My spirits were still much sunk with what I heard the day before of my being suspected to be engaged in the Pretender's interest. It grieved me, that after there had been so much evidence of a glorious work of grace among these poor Indians, as that the most carnal men could not but take notice of the great change made among them, so many poor souls should still suspect the whole to be only a Popish plot, and so cast an awful reproach on this blessed work of the divine spirit, and at the same time wholly exclude themselves from receiving benefit from this divine Influence.'

Now the conscientious missionary began to search his past conduct to determine if he had done anything, even something trivial, to give rise to the cruel calumny being hurled against him. How could anyone accuse him of stirring up the Indians against the English? He recalled that he had at times intervened on behalf of his flock when some unscrupulous white people had tried to steal their lands. Could he be blamed for this? He had complained loudly of the vicious practice of giving them liquors and making them drunk. Was this a crime? Had he been too animated and zealous in his advocacy of them? These were the only things he could think of that might by any pretence be used as an excuse for the charges. He remembered the counsel of his Lord that his messengers must be wise as serpents and harmless as doves. This humiliating experience made him aware again of how careful he needed to be.

But David Brainerd had much work to do; therefore he could not let the political agitations deter him. He decided to select six of the converted Indians at Crossweeksung and take them with him on an evangelistic mission back to the Forks of the Delaware. The advantages of taking part of his Indian congregation with him were obvious. In the first place, their testimonies to their own race about how the gospel had changed their lives would in themselves be a powerful attraction. Furthermore, these Indians were, of course, skilled in the Delaware dialect, an achievement that Brainerd had not been able to manage due to his busy schedule.

On 16 February he conducted a service accompanied by the six Indians. Some who had formerly been extremely averse to Christianity now seemed to listen very intently. Others, however, laughed and mocked. Soon the Word of God came with great power on the assembly and many appeared stunned. Some of the white people began to weep. Others who appeared to be disposed to listen sympathetically had been so ridiculed by the pagans that they were obviously ashamed to appear friendly.

Four days later Brainerd had an opportunity to preach to some of the High Dutch people who had come eight or ten miles to hear him. They were among the early Lutheran and Reformed peasant folk who had come from the upper provinces of Germany. He also spoke later to the Low Dutch who had come from the Palatinate and the Lower Rhine Valley provinces. The High Dutch especially were receptive: 'They gave wonderful attention; and some of them were much affected under the word, and afterwards said, as I was informed, that they never had been so much enlightened about the way of salvation in their whole lives before' (20 February).

On 22 February he wrote, 'God has been very gracious to me this week. He has enabled me to preach every day; and has given me some assistance and encouraging prospect of success in almost every sermon — Blessed be His name.'

By 1 March he was back again in New Jersey and was reminded once more what a marvellous thing God had done among the Indians in this place. He could think of no place he had ever been where there were so many manifestations of a true work of God in the hearts of people: 'I know of no assembly of Christians, where there seems to be so much of the presence of God, where brotherly love so much prevails, and where I should take so much delight in the public worship of God in general, as in *my own congregation*; although not more than nine months ago they were worshipping *devils* and *dumb idols* under the power of Pagan darkness and superstition.'

Brainerd's diary reveals very clearly that God had developed in him a special kind of devotion, which has through the years made his testimonies so appealing to many. There were a number of factors which combined to make him the spiritual giant he was. He was constitutionally inclined to being sensitive, sad and introspective. Add to this a highly imaginative mind, trained in the rigours of Puritan logical analysis, and we have a fertile soil for the development of divine grace. His deep trials and sufferings softened him, broke his will and gave him a servant heart. His spirit, enlightened by constant contemplation of the glory of God and deepened by prayer, was aroused to selfless consecration. Frequent association with the unfortunate and helpless awakened in him profound sympathy and compassion for the unconverted Native Americans.

It should be no surprise that those who were awakened and converted under his ministry caught the spirit of their teacher and shared some of his own unique tenderness and devotion. In his personal writings he took special note of some of the more remarkable experiences of those who came to know his God. They too confessed to extreme feelings of unworthiness, expressed their willingness to be dealt with by God in any manner suitable to him and not infrequently recounted rapturous flights of divine love such as Brainerd himself had known.

The beautiful spirit of an Indian woman who attended on his ministry was given in some detail in his diary for March 1746. He had mentioned on 9 February that a woman had been brought to a 'comfortable calm' and bowed to divine sovereignty. She told Brainerd that she now felt and saw that it was right for God to do with her as he pleased. On 9 March while the congregation were singing she was so visibly moved as to lead him to say of her that she was 'filled with joy unspeakable and full of glory'. She cried out, sometimes in English and sometimes in Indian: 'O blessed Lord! do come, do come! O do take me away; do let me die and go to Jesus Christ! I am afraid if I live I shall sin again. O do let me die now! O dear Jesus, do come! I cannot stay, I cannot stay! O how can I live in this world? Do take my soul away from this sinful place! O let me never sin any more! O what shall I do, what shall I do, dear Jesus? O dear Jesus!'

This woman seemed to the missionary to epitomize the believer who is so enamoured with the preciousness of the love of Christ as to find it hard to remain in the world where she was physically absent from the Redeemer and where sin tormented her. He talked with her at length, quizzing her about her feelings. She constantly complained of the hardness and rebellion of her heart. For quite a while she groaned constantly because she could not love Jesus as he ought to be loved. When relief and comfort came her spiritual ecstasy was as dramatic as her conviction for sin had been poignant.

What especially pleased Brainerd was the fact that her joy came as a result of a spiritual perception of the loveliness of the Saviour. He described the source of her inner peace in terms especially pleasing to him, for they exhibited the utter absorption in God which in his estimation represented the highest level of Christian devotion: 'This sweet and surprising ecstasy appeared to spring from a true spiritual discovery of the glory, ravishing beauty, and excellency of Christ; and not from any gross imaginary notions of his human nature, such as that of seeing him in such a place or posture, as hanging on the cross, as bleeding and dying, as gently smiling, and the like; which delusions some have been carried away with. Nor did it rise from sordid, selfish apprehensions of her having any benefit whatsoever conferred on her; but from a view of his personal excellency and transcendent loveliness; which drew forth those vehement desires of enjoying him which she now manifested, and made her long, "to be absent from the body, that she might be present with the Lord".'

It is highly probable that Brainerd's reference to those who were taken up with imaginations about the physical sufferings of Christ concerned the teachings of the Moravians. In the early days of their settlement in America they were especially impressed with the torments Jesus experienced while dying on Calvary. They dwelt and preached much upon the crown of thorns, the nails, the long hours of agony and the shedding of his blood. Often such meditations, profitable in themselves, were taken to excess. Imaginary and perhaps even exaggerated pictures were added to the simple biblical narratives, and personal experiences of seeing the crucified Jesus in visions and trances were encouraged.

The Congregationalist and New Side Presbyterians such as the Tennents, as well as George Whitefield, discouraged such sentimentalism and stressed the spiritual nature of Jesus' sufferings. Their emphasis was upon the penal, substitutionary and vicarious nature of the cross, not so much just the physical misery endured by the Son of God. As we can see from his commendation of the rapturous devotion of this Indian woman, Brainerd approved of a faith that appropriates Christ's whole divine person, rather than just the human dimension. His brother John later expressed a fear shared by many of the Calvinistic pastors that the Moravians 'worshipped the human nature of Christ'.

Notwithstanding the terrible opposition and accusations which had been levelled against him, Brainerd was a happy pastor as the spring of 1746 approached. The storm from without was terrible, but within the fellowship of his Christian flock there was relative peace and contentment.

26.
Community of faith

From the time that the Spirit of God came so powerfully upon the Indians at Crossweeksung in the summer of 1745 David Brainerd's labours had been crowned with uninterrupted blessing and success. A steady influx of both white people and Indians came to hear him preach and many hearts gladly opened to hear the saving message of Christ. The Indians were especially hungry to hear the Word and kept him busy preaching publicly and privately applying and illustrating what he had taught them. The demands upon him were so great that at times it was difficult for him to find adequate energy for the task. On 16 March he wrote, 'My house being thronged with my people in the evening, I spent the time in religious exercises with them, until my nature was almost spent. They are so unwearied in religious exercises, and insatiable in their thirsting after Christian knowledge, that I can sometimes scarcely avoid labouring so as greatly to exhaust my strength and my spirits.'

Unlike the early days of his evangelistic efforts, when long weeks and months of preaching went by without visible result, the time came when public meetings resulted in immediate professions of faith. Diligent effort and carefully designed strategies to arouse the attention of the Indians had in the past failed, but now the interest was so great that no special effort was needed. After a particularly moving meeting on 23 March he took note of the astounding change which took place in the behaviour of some 'Pagans' who were formerly rough and disorderly. In the past they would walk away when he or one of the converts began to discuss the gospel. 'But now there was no need of using policy in order to get an opportunity of conversing with some of them about their spiritual concerns; for they were so far touched with a sense of their perishing state, as made them voluntarily yield to the closest addresses which were made them respecting their sin and misery, their need of and acquaintance with, and interest in the great Redeemer.'

By the end of March the hundred or more Indians under his charge were a sheer delight to teach and lead. Especially encouraging was their delight in the preaching of the Word and their hunger to learn more. After a catechism session on 29 March he could not fail to notice how eager they were to learn more about God's plan for them: 'There appeared such a liveliness and vigor in their attendance upon the word of God, and such eagerness to be partakers of the benefits mentioned, that they seemed not only to be "looking for", but "hasting to the coming of the day of God". Divine truths seemed to distill upon the audience with a gentle, but melting efficacy, as the refreshing "showers upon the new mown grass".'

As the new converts grew in the faith they increasingly become a source of fellowship and encouragement for the missionary himself. The pastoral bonding of love and affection grew deeper and stronger. On 5 April he said, 'After public worship a number of my dear Christian Indians came to my house; with whom I felt a sweet union of soul. My heart was knit to them; and I cannot say I have felt such a sweet and fervent love to the brethren, for some time past. I saw in them appearances of the same love. This gave me somewhat of a view of the heavenly state; and particularly of that part of the happiness of heaven which consists in the communion of saints; and this was affecting to me.'

Notwithstanding such precious seasons, there were times when he felt useless and fruitless, as he had in earlier days. He never felt satisfied with either his own level of accomplishment as a soulwinner, or with his personal attainment in spirituality. On 2 April he wrote, 'I was somewhat exercised with a spiritual frame of mind; but was a little relieved and refreshed in the evening with meditation alone in the woods. But alas! my days pass away as the chaff; it is but little I do, or can do, that turns to any account; and it is my constant misery and burden, that I am so fruitless in the vineyard of the Lord. Oh that I were a pure spirit; that I might be active for God... God deliver me from the clogs, fetters, and a body of death, which impede my service from him.'

Occasionally the cloud of depression which often plagued him would return, though such periods seemed not to be so frequent or intense. While attending a presbytery meeting at Elizabethtown he complained that he was 'very vapory and melancholy, and under an awful gloom which oppressed his mind'. About a week later he wrote, 'O, my barrenness in my daily affliction and heavy load! O how precious is time, and how it pains me to see it slide away, while I do so little to any good purpose. O that God would make me more fruitful and spiritual!'

David Brainerd complains here of 'barrenness'. The dictionary defines 'barren' as 'unproductive, fruitless, desolate, and lacking'. If this man was lacking in love for the souls of men and zeal for God, where can these things be found?

Two days after this pitiful lament we find him expressing emotions which contradict his self-abasing estimate of himself. After preaching from Psalm 73:28 on the expression, 'But it is good for me to draw near to God,' he wrote, 'My heart was melted for the dear assembly; and I loved every body in it; and scarcely ever felt more love to immortal souls in my life. My soul cried, "Oh that the dear creatures might be saved! Oh that God would have mercy on them."'

Brainerd's self-deprecating statements are, of course, manifestations of that poverty of spirit and humility which are commended in the Scriptures. The truth is that these qualities exist only in those who breathe the atmosphere of heaven and walk with God. His passionate love of the Saviour, his self-denying spirit and his intense commitment to service for God are a model for those who are in pursuit of holiness.

His burning love for his fellow men and his great longing to see them converted are just such traits as have qualified the true heralds of the cross for their missions of mercy through the centuries. We find such tender compassion in the hearts of preachers such as Jeremiah, Paul, Henry Martyn, M'Cheyne and Spurgeon. These men imbibed the spirit of Jesus of Nazareth, who was moved with compassion when he saw the multitudes 'weary and scattered, like sheep having no shepherd'. Those who have a similar spirit and a willingness to 'spend and be spent for perishing souls' are God's chosen instruments to bring the lost sheep home to the fold.

What work in this world is so noble as that of turning perishing sinners from the error of their ways? And what joy so great as that of being the instrument of this marvellous, miraculous work? Clearly Brainerd's success at Crossweeksung had intensified his zeal for the lost and made him even more hungry for conversions. Leading people to God was a passion: 'Oh that the kingdom of the dear Lord might come. Oh that the poor Indians might quickly be gathered in great numbers!' (21 April). The next day after an evening of secret prayer for God's blessings he wrote of his great desire 'that Zion might prosper, and precious souls be brought home to God'.

True evangelism is concerned not merely with the *conversion* of the lost, but also their *instruction* and *training* in the Christian faith. Wherever Christianity has made a lasting impact churches have been established, for it is in the church that the teachings of Christ and the apostles are incorporated into community life. Individuals come and go, but institutions tend to have a more abiding quality. Brainerd wanted to establish an Indian church, which observed the ordinances of worship and was organized in accordance with his understanding of biblical order. A congregation of believers, and a remarkably lively one at that, had been raised up by God through his faithful labours.

At the end of April, just before removing the Indians to Cranberry, he made preparations for the observance of the Lord's Supper. Careful instruction, much prayer and even a time of 'solemn fasting' were, in Brainerd's view, necessary before this sacred time was to be experienced. He was convinced that the Indians were now ready.

The Indians listened with rapt attention on 25 April as their leader told them that they were about to renew their covenant with God. They were counselled to walk together in the fear of God, in love and Christian fellowship, and to pray earnestly that God's presence would be with them as they approached the table of the Lord. They were to humble themselves before God because of 'the apparent withdrawment' of the blessed influence which had been so manifest only a few days before. They were to confess any carelessness in their behaviour and repent of any known sin in their lives.

Then he led them in a solemn reaffirmation of their baptismal covenant, in which they had explicitly and publicly given themselves up to the service of God. Once again they renounced the pagan superstitions and idolatrous festivals which were a part of their dark past. They promised anew to make the Word of God the rule of their lives and to love and watch over one another with seriousness and devotion. There was much 'gravity and seriousness' during this time of preliminary instruction, but also freedom, cheerfulness and joyful anticipation of the coming blessing of sitting at the feet of Christ in communion.

The actual day of the observance of the 'sacred ordinance' began with a message from Titus 2:14 on Christ's substitutionary work for sinners. Several of the Indian community had gone away on that day to the Forks of the Delaware, but there were still twenty-three who were judged qualified to receive the elements. The presence of the Saviour whose blood was being symbolized was felt powerfully: 'The ordinance was attended with great solemnity, and with a most desirable tenderness and affection. It was remarkable that in the season of the performance of the sacramental actions, especially in the distribution of the bread, they seemed to be affected in a most lively manner, as if Christ had been really crucified before them ... there was a sweet, gentle, and affectionate melting without any indecent or boisterous commotion of the passions' (27 April).

Following the meeting Brainerd rested for a while and then visited from house to house discussing with the Indians their feelings about the communion service. They had been 'almost universally refreshed at the Lord's table, "as with new wine".' He was especially pleased with the love that the Indians demonstrated towards each other: 'Never did I see such an appearance of Christian love among any people in all my life. It was so remarkable that one might well have cried with an agreeable surprise, "Behold how they love one another."'

It seemed to Brainerd that the tenderness, love and warm fellowship among these new believers equalled that of the early converts to Christ as recorded in the book of Acts. As far as he was concerned this had to be the 'doing of the Lord'. There was no human ingenuity, skill or strategy which could have accomplished what his eyes had seen.

The establishment of the Indian church under the leadership of Brainerd is an amazing testimony to the power of the Christian gospel and a witness to the credibility of the Christian faith. The message and methods of this faithful servant of

God are worthy of careful study and emulation in our own day when many are casting about to bring life into their Laodicean congregations. The transformation of dozens of lives which were formerly steeped in the most hopeless type of pagan religion is indeed miraculous, but not a miracle in the physical or visible sense.

In every age 'sign seekers' have sought to impress the world with demonstrations of physical healings or other impressive external marvels. Visible appearances of Jesus or angels, weeping statues, even cloud formations are appealed to as evidences of the reality of God's presence. But no sign or miracle can compare with the powerful evidence of a changed life and hearts aflame with the love of Jesus Christ. Almost any kind of physical marvel can be passed off by the power of sleight of hand or the adroitness of the magician. The Indian witch-doctors were masters of the cunning arts, including claims for physical healing. But when greedy, violent, super-stitious, idolatrous souls are transformed suddenly into loving and obedient followers of God, a true and authentic manifes-tation of grace is in operation. When people are willing to cast away traditions and practices which have been handed down over many generations and, ignoring the curses of neighbours and former friends, press forwards in a path of service to an unseen God, there is without question a credible verification of the new faith.

Brainerd believed that there is nothing which can bring about such changes except the proclamation of the gospel of Jesus Christ, applied by the inward and effectual working of the Holy Spirit. He did not seek to *educate* the Indians into the kingdom, or *reform* them into the kingdom. They were *born* into the kingdom, frequently after violent emotional struggles. He sought no new schemes for delivering the Delawares from their satanic bondage but relied upon the time-tested methods of the apostles and evangelists such as Whitefield and Tennent.

Not the least source of his satisfaction as a spiritual leader was the readiness of the Indian converts to receive willingly and quickly the doctrinal truths of Scripture. They gave evidence of a clear grasp of the necessity and meaning of Christ's vicarious work on Calvary, as symbolized in the Lord's Supper. 'They were also acquainted with the end of the ordinance, that they were therein called to commemorate the dying love of Christ.' He speaks of the 'competency of doctrinal knowledge' of his people, who had come to the Christ only a few months earlier. Clearly the souls of these Indians, ploughed as they were by the initiative of the sovereign Spirit of God, were fertile soil for the truth.

Brainerd took the time in his journal to report some of the more remarkable of the conversions among his Indian community. Often something unusual about their faith was a reason for them to receive special mention. Sometimes a unique lifestyle, or position in the pagan community before conversion, made the case worthy of notice. On 9 May Brainerd had the pleasure of baptizing a man who was perhaps one of the most astounding examples of divine grace he was to come across in all his missionary labours.

On the day when the Spirit of God was first poured out in great power, 8 August of the previous summer, Brainerd mentioned that an Indian *powwow*, or conjuror, who was also a drunkard and had even been guilty of murder, was brought under conviction. As a *powwow* this man had great standing in the Indian community and was greatly respected as one who had supernatural power. Although he frequently attended Brainerd's preaching services, he continued to engage in his trade, which involved the use of various charms and tricks. Shortly after witnessing the baptism of Brainerd's interpreter he felt 'the word of God in his heart', as he expressed it, and his spirit of conjuration left him. He later acknowledged that he had no idea how he possessed this former power.

As the months progressed this man came under a greater and greater burden because of his spiritual condition. At last he came to the conclusion that his struggle for salvation was useless and he became calm and sedate while professing that all his strivings were useless. Brainerd recorded the following conversation with him:

> I observed him to appear remarkably composed; and thereupon asked him how he did it? He replied, 'It is done, it is done, it is all done now.'
>
> I asked him what he meant? He answered, 'I can never do any more to save myself; it is all done for ever. I can do no more.'
>
> I queried with him whether he could not do a little more, rather than go to hell? He replied, 'My heart is dead. I can never help myself.'
>
> I asked him what he thought would become of him then? He answered, 'I must go to hell.'
>
> I asked him if he thought it was right that God send him to hell? He replied, 'Oh it is right. The devil has been in me ever since I was born.'
>
> I asked him if he felt this when he was in such great distress the evening before? He answered, 'No; I did not then think it was right. I thought God would send me to hell, and that I was then dropping into it, but my heart quarrelled with God, and would not say it was right he should send me there; but now I know it is right, for I have always served the devil; and my heart has no goodness in it now; but it is as bad as ever it was.'

This remarkable brokenness and submission to the sovereign good pleasure of God proved to be the prelude to a marvellous conversion experience in which the old magician received full assurance of salvation. He was given a 'lively soul-refreshing view of the excellency of Christ and the way of salvation by him, which melted him into tears and filled him with admiration, comfort, satisfaction and praise to God'. He became a strong and confident member of Brainerd's congregation and was often very useful in bearing witness to others who had come under the spell of the *powwow*'s sorceries.

27.
A fateful choice

In all the history of the church of Jesus Christ few saints have opened the door into the inner sanctum of the spirit as David Brainerd did. Not intentionally, of course, for his diary was designed as a journal for self-reflection, not as a narrative to inspire others. Yet these meditations, written from a heart often broken, often burdened, yet often carried away into ecstasy of joy at the sight of the great Redeemer, are before us. They have nurtured many a pilgrim on the way to heaven, and they have been a particular source of encouragement to those who, like their author, are prone to the especially poignant affliction known as melancholy.

Some of Brainerd's reflections are especially interesting and helpful to preachers. Only those who have the responsibility week after week of preparing for, and then actually occupying, the pulpit can understand the peculiar trauma that is usually involved. In the mind of the preacher success is often measured not only by the visible response on the part of the people but by his own sense of power in delivery. At times the preacher, although he might have prepared and prayed mightily before delivering his message, will plod along heavily without any sense of freedom. At other times a certain indefinable inspiration will come upon him and he will soar with his subject, fired by such feelings that he is scarcely conscious of his audience.

Brainerd was fully aware of the importance of his theme each time he preached to his Indians, and he wanted his feelings to reflect this. He felt ashamed if he was not fervent, bold and overflowing in his delivery, thinking that somehow he had failed his Lord. When the sermon, in his own perception, was dry and empty, void of the anointing of the Lord, he would sink afterwards into deep sadness.

On 10 May he went to 'Allen's-town' to assist in the administration of the Lord's Supper. In the afternoon he spoke from Titus 2:14, a text which speaks of the substitutionary work of Jesus for his people. Although he had some 'freedom' he did not have the 'enlargement and power' for which he longed. Afterwards he said, 'In the evening my soul mourned, and could not but mourn, that I had treated so excellent a subject in so defective a manner; that I had borne so broken a testimony for so worthy and glorious a redeemer. If my discourse had met with the utmost applause from all the world, it would not have given me any satisfaction. Oh it grieved me to think, that I had no more holy warmth and fervency, that I had been no more melted in discoursing of Christ's death and the end and design of it!' Brainerd's reaction to his rather dull performance shows how sensitive he was to his obligation to handle his magnificent subject with proper enthusiasm.

The very next day, after serving communion to the gathered congregation, he was called upon to preach again. He feared that he would fail miserably for he was 'weak and sick in soul, as well as feeble in body'. Yet he longed that the people might be edified with divine truths. He wrestled in prayer for God's blessing, claiming the promise that God would be present where two or three had gathered in his name. His subject was the transfiguration, based on Luke 9:30-31. Everything was totally different from the previous day. He 'enjoyed special freedom from the beginning to the end without interruption'. As he dealt with the points of his message each of them seemed so full and powerful that he scarcely knew how to leave one behind and go on to the next. Clearly he enjoyed the anointing of the Lord, as seen by the fact that 'The word of God seemed to awaken the attention of a stupid audience to a considerable degree.'

From the time of his expulsion from college Brainerd had felt an unwavering call to spend his life in pioneer missionary work among the Indians. Like Paul his commission was to take the gospel to the 'regions beyond', not entering into other men's labours. But now it seemed that perhaps the situation had changed. God had crowned his efforts with abundant success, as seen in the growing community of believers who were now building a settlement at Cranberry. He had led them to God by his faithful witness and had become their spiritual father. The ties with them were strong and tender. Should he settle among them and abandon his long and wearisome travels to the west? The thought had some appeal.

He recorded on 16 May that he was in the process of looking to God for guidance relative to his 'worldly circumstances'. Did God's 'providential dealings' point to a new rôle for him, that of a settled pastor? There were some compelling reasons to look in this direction. In the first place, his health would have to be a factor. The hardships of incessant travel in all types of weather, with little sleep and poor food, had taken their toll. Furthermore the fellowship with the converted Indians would have been a great comfort and encouragement to him. Although they made heavy demands upon him, not only spiritually but as a manager of their temporal affairs, still he was never happier than when sharing with them in their mutual worship of the great Creator and Redeemer.

Yet somehow he could not be completely comfortable with the thought of a change. The tribes on the Susquehanna desperately needed the gospel and had thus far not responded to his preaching. No doubt as he lay on his bed at night the scenes of Shamokin and Duncan's Island were replayed in his mind. The savage darkness of these places haunted him. To be sure, the

Jesuits would soon travel to these tribes, but he regarded their ritualistic emphasis as little better than the incantations of the Indian witch-doctors. The Moravians would continue to share their faith with the Indians, but this too fell short of the confessional Reformed theology so dear to him.

His journal for the third week of May 1746 reflects the dilemma he was in. The needs of his mind and body, as well as his natural sympathies with the Cranberry Indians, dictated that he establish a permanent residence at Cranberry. But the call to missions still tugged at him. What should he do? On 16 May he prayed, 'Lord, if it [to stay at Cranberry] be most for thy glory, let me proceed in it; but if thou seest it will in any wise hinder my usefulness in thy cause, Oh prevent me from proceeding; for all I want respecting this world is such circumstances as may best capacitate me to do service for God in the world.' 'What possible harm could there have been for him to settle down?' we may well ask. Realistically a stable home life would have strengthened him for the service of God, whereas the brutal schedule of the missionary would most certainly put a great strain on his body and perhaps even take him to an untimely grave. Common sense, human wisdom, perhaps even sanctified prudence would have said, 'Stay, David, stay! You cannot endure the life you have chosen.'

As he looked at his present situation and pondered the course before him he used some interesting expressions. He referred to the attractions of having 'a stated home of my own', 'some agreeable society' and 'a certain place of abode'. Also he spoke of the 'tender friendship' which he most probably would be able to enjoy were he to have a homestead at Cranberry and of 'dear friends' who would surround him. Who were these 'friends'? He no doubt included among them associates in the ministry such as Charles McKnight and William Tennent who were both working in nearby fields of service, or his brother John who had been in correspondence with him and was soon to pay him a visit. However, a number of readers have been convinced that the 'tender friendship' meant much more than these colleagues in the ministry and point to his hope of enjoying the tenderest and dearest of all relationships, a wife.

We have already discussed the possibility that Brainerd may have met Jerusha when Edwards was at Yale in 1743. The tantalizing possibility that the woman who would care for him during his final illness was on his mind at this point inevitably emerges here. 'Houses' he had built both at Kaunaumeek and at the Forks, but now he speaks of a 'stated home'. A house does not make a home. If Jerusha Edwards had ignited a flame in his heart there are plausible reasons why Edwards should make no specific mention of her as an object of Brainerd's affection, or vice versa. There was a strong reticence on the part of the Puritans to speak directly about love of a sexual and romantic nature. When the mystical theologian-philosopher of Northampton spoke of his own wife, with whom he shared a profound affection, he spoke of her in the third person:

> They say there is a lady in [New Haven] who is beloved of that Great Being, who made and rules the world and that there are certain seasons in which this Great Being, in some way or another invisible, comes to her and fills her mind with exceeding sweet delight, and that she hardly cares for anything, except to meditate on him — that she expects after a while to be received up where he is, to be raised up out of the world and caught up into heaven; being assured that he loves her too well to let her remain at a distance from him always. There she is to dwell with him, and to be ravished with his love and delight forever. Therefore, if you present all the world before her, with the richest of its treasures, she disregards it and cares not for it, and is unmindful of any pain or affliction. She has a strange sweetness in her mind, and singular purity in her affections; is most just

and conscientious in all her conduct; and you could not persuade her to do wrong or sinful if you would give her all the world, lest she offend this Great Being. She is of a wonderful sweetness, calmness, and universal benevolence of mind; especially after this Great God has manifested himself to her mind.

She will sometimes go about from place to place, singing sweetly and seems to be always full of joy and pleasure; and no one knows for what. She loves to be alone, walking in the fields and groves, and seems to have someone invisible always conversing with her.[1]

Jerusha seemed to all who knew the family to be almost a carbon copy of her mother. Jerusha's father, who knew Brainerd intimately, said of his daughter that she was 'a person of much the same spirit' as he.[2] He also said of her that 'She had a heart uncommonly devoted to God, in the course of her life.'[3] There is nothing unnatural, though absolute proof is wanting, in the supposition that the Edwards family wanted to provide a context which might lead to an eventual marital union between their daughter and the young preacher they so much admired. Indeed they invited him into their home some time shortly after this point at which he was contemplating a permanent settlement. At this stage in his life his health was in serious jeopardy — more about that to come.

Brainerd's thoughts would have been encouraged to turn in the direction of domestic tranquillity from the example of his friends in the ministry nearby. William Tennent at Freehold was happily married and had three sons. Charles Beatty, who lived at Neshaminy north of Philadelphia, had proposed marriage to Anne Reading in March of that year and the wedding date had been set for 24 June. Anne was the daughter of John Reading, president of the Council and acting governor of New Jersey. Charles McKnight, who was pastor of the English congregation at Cranberry, was to marry Elisabeth Stevens on

19 August. Surely such events must have set the bachelor at
Bethel thinking in this direction. It would only have been
human for him to do so.

There will no doubt be an ongoing debate on the relationship between David Brainerd and Jerusha Edwards. The
circumstantial evidence that they would have been married
had he lived seems to me to be significant but not conclusive.
After their death Edwards had remarked that David had said of
his daughter that she was a Christian and a saint who 'by the
temper of her mind, was fitted to deny herself for God and to
do good, beyond any young woman whatsoever whom he
knew'.[4]

A final piece of evidence is the fact that David and Jerusha
were buried a few feet apart in the old Northampton cemetery.
Why this final symbolic act if their relationship were no more
than a Christian friendship?

The marriage question aside, in May 1746, after almost a
year of ministry among the Indians of New Jersey, David
Brainerd had to make a decision. Would he settle at Cranberry
among his beloved flock, or abandon such a hope? Would he
consider his suicidal missionary labours a thing of the past and
settle into the pastoral rôle, or would he press on in the life of
toil and sacrifice in distant fields?

He reached the fateful conclusion on 22 May. Deep down
in his heart he simply could not feel comfortable with the idea
of abandoning his missionary calling. It was not that he had
anything essentially against the idea of permanent settlement
considered in itself, or that he had a sort of martyr complex
which drove him to risky personal behaviour. It was simply a
matter of his own commission: 'For I never since I began to
preach, could feel any freedom to enter into other men's
labors, and settle down in the ministry where the gospel was
preached before. I never could make that appear to be my
province. When I felt any disposition to consult my worldly

ease and comfort, God has never given me any liberty in this respect, either since, or for some years before, I began to preach.'

He confesses that for a time the vision of a quiet, comfortable life as a pastor passed, as it were, with a certain pleasing appeal before his mind. Briefly this natural desire, so normal and so human, seemed to have given solace to his tired body and oft-troubled mind. But then, as if by a start sent directly from the Great Being who had summoned him from his college ambitions and led him through his former trials, he awoke from this dream. 'These thoughts', he said, 'seemed to be wholly dashed to pieces.'

The Christian life is inherently one of bearing the cross of Jesus Christ, which means dying to selfish interests and pursuits. It is not unusual in the annals of missionary history to find noble examples of sacrifice and commitment. But the self-effacing attitude of David Brainerd must be recorded as one of the noblest and most sincere examples of placing God's glory above self-interest in the history of the church. Facing as he was the choice between establishing a home and settling into a quiet pastorate or giving himself to a kind of martyrdom for the sake of the gospel, he chose the latter: 'It appeared to me that God's dealings toward me had fitted me for a life of solitariness and hardship, and that I had nothing to lose, nothing to do with earth, and consequently nothing to lose by a total renunciation of it. It appeared to me just right that I should be destitute of house and home, and many of the comforts of life, which I rejoiced to see others of God's people enjoy. At the same time, I saw so much of the excellency of Christ's kingdom and infinite desirableness of its advancement in the world, that it swallowed up all my other thoughts and made me willing, yea, even rejoice, to be made a *pilgrim* or *hermit* in the wilderness to my dying moment; if I might thereby promote the blessed interest of the great Redeemer. If ever my soul presented itself to God for his service, *without any reserve of any kind*, it do so now.'

Thus in Brainerd's own mind the comforts of a normal life represented — in his own case — an unacceptable challenge to his calling for missionary work. Whatever God had in mind for others, it was definitely not God's will for himself. The time had come now for a prayer of dedication, a kind of voluntary vow to renounce not only the evils of the world, but also its legitimate and normal comforts for the sake of the Redeemer of his soul. 'The language of my thoughts and dispositions now was, "Here I am, Lord send me; send me to the ends of the earth; send me to the rough, the savage pagans of the wilderness; send me from all that is called comfort in earth, or earthly comfort; send me even to death itself, if it be but in thy service, and to promote thy kingdom."'

Such a resolve, taken voluntarily and without any semblance of self-righteousness or conceit, was in effect a contract of perpetual abandonment to Christ. It was a vow of poverty, pain and perhaps celibacy.

He was not unaware of the value of human comforts, considered absolutely, in themselves: 'The quiet settlement, the certain place of abode, the tender friendship, which I thought I might be likely to enjoy in consequence of such circumstances appeared as valuable to me considered absolutely and *in themselves*, as ever before but considered *comparatively*, they appeared nothing. Compared with the value and preciousness of an enlargement of Christ's kingdom, they vanished as stars before the rising sun.'

The time had now come for David Brainerd, led as he believed by the inward promptings of the Holy Spirit and dispositions of God's providence, to say a final 'goodbye' to all that men in this world count as important. Charged as he was with the love of the Saviour and carried away with the vision of God's glory and the spread of the gospel, it did not really seem that hard: 'I was constrained and yet chose, to say, "Farewell friends and earthly comforts, the dearest of them all, the *very dearest*, if the Lord calls for it; adieu, adieu; I will spend my life, to the latest moments, *in caves and dens of the earth*, if the kingdom of Christ may thereby be advanced."'

And so it was that on 22 May 1746 David Brainerd in effect wrote the script for the final act in the drama of his life. He would continue to press forward in his labours as a pioneer missionary, with all the sacrifices and hardships that calling entailed. He had crossed a sort of personal Rubicon. There was no turning back. Come what may, only one thing would consume his soul now: striving for the conversion of the Native Americans. Such a course, given the state of his health, must inevitably lead to an untimely death.

28.
The trail of blood and tears

The Old Tennent Church of Freehold, New Jersey, is one of those enduring monuments to the pioneer revivalists who laboured during the turbulent days prior to the American Revolution. It was established in 1682-85 by New England settlers and by refugee Scots as the first regularly constituted Presbyterian Church in America. Its first pastor was Walter Ker, who had come ashore near New Jersey's pine country from the stranded sailing-ship *Caledonia*.

In its long history only three buildings have housed this congregation. The first one was a log church built in 1692, some seven miles south of Raritan Bay. Thirty-eight years later the congregation moved seven miles south and built a church on White (Oak) Hill. David Brainerd preached in this church on several occasions during the pastorate of William Tennent Jr, brother of the more famous Gilbert. Its close proximity to the scenes of the Indian mission afforded an excellent opportunity for the missionary and his Indian flock to receive encouragement and Christian fellowship.

The present church building was built in 1751. The most cherished article of furniture in this historic church is a time-worn communion table which for many years has occupied the front of the sanctuary. Why is it so valuable? For one reason: it was from this simple table that David Brainerd served communion to his Indian church.

Old Tennent Church, Freehold

Brainerd gives details of at least one occasion when he shared in the communion with the church at Freehold. Tennent invited Brainerd to come and assist him in the administration of the Lord's Supper in June 1746. On 7 June Brainerd, accompanied by his flock, travelled by horseback to this appointment, a distance of some thirteen miles as the crow flies. The opportunity of sharing for the first time in a communion service with a white congregation was an exciting experience for the Indians. A special service for preparation was conducted the day before the ordinance at which the missionary preached. His text was Psalm 73:28: 'But it is good for me to draw near to God.' He enjoyed 'freedom and warmth in his discourse' and God seemed to be present.

On the Sabbath day William Tennent preached just before the time of sharing the elements of communion. He had an eager and attentive audience. Walter Ker, who had founded the church and was now ninety years old, was undoubtedly present. None listened more intently than the pioneer preacher from Cranberry and his flock of converted Indians. Many of them 'sat by themselves', he tells us, and were 'agreeably affected' as the wine and bread were served. For many of the Europeans the sight of Indians joining in the festivities of the Christian faith was nothing short of astonishing. For many of them the Indians were just warlike, ignorant and superstitious pagans, as indeed many of them had been. And yet here they were freely and joyfully praising the true God and his Son, Jesus Christ. It was a powerful witness to the converting power of the gospel.

The next morning some of the Indians gathered in a secluded place in the woods for a time of worship and praise. Some white people were looking on as they 'prayed, sang, and conversed of divine things'. Tears streamed down their bronze faces as they thought of the wonderful things that God had done for them. Following this refreshing season the Indians made their way back home.

On 14 June Brainerd rode north-west to visit Eleazar Wales, who was pastor of the Presbyterian Church at Kingston, and assist in the administration of the Lord's Supper. Wales had preceded Brainerd in preaching at the Hunter's Settlement at the Forks of the Delaware, having worked there between 1731 and 1734. Although he was very weary Brainerd enjoyed great 'freedom, fluency and clearness' as he expounded the subject of the 'whosoever will' theme from Revelation 22:17. 'God enabled me to offer a testimony for himself, and to leave sinners inexcusable in neglecting his grace.' There were some notable people there, referred to by Brainerd as 'the great'. Whether they were eminent political figures, or high officials in the church, he does not say. Perhaps Jonathan Dickinson and Aaron Burr were there, for they came to visit David at 'Bethel' five days later.

On 19 June Brainerd celebrated his first full year of ministry among the Indians in New Jersey, an event shared by the officials of the missionary society that had sponsored him. What an eventful year it had been! Twelve months ago these Indians had been no different from those of the Susquehanna region who still worshipped the mysterious gods of darkness. 'What amazing things has God wrought in this space of time, for this poor people!' he wrote. 'What a surprising change appears in their tempers and behavior! How are morose and savage Pagans, in this short period, transformed into agreeable, affectionate, and humble Christians! and their drunken and Pagan howlings turned into devout and fervent praises to God. They "who were sometimes in darkness are now become light in the Lord".' This was a high day indeed. The missionary and those who sponsored him all joined in the celebration. 'To God only wise, be glory through Jesus Christ,' Brainerd wrote.

Following this high day at Freehold Brainerd was busy travelling back and forth from Cranberry to various centres of population such as Newark, Philadelphia and Elizabethtown, in order to confer with his sponsors about what he refers to several times as 'his intended journey to the Susquehanna'. After his final decision to abandon any plans for a permanent settlement as a pastor this mission had been constantly on his mind.

On 1 August he spent an evening in 'a sweet season of prayer', during which he pleaded with God for continual blessings on his congregation and for divine guidance for the trip west. God visited his soul mightily that evening: 'I found enough in the sweet duty of prayer to have engaged me to continue in it the whole night, would my bodily state have admitted of it. O how sweet it is, to be enabled to say, "Lord not my will, but thine be done."' There seems to be a reference here to the last stirrings of his soul for the physical rest and family life he naturally desired. But there was no intimation at all of any second thoughts about his chosen course.

It was a rapidly failing body that David Brainerd was driving into his last missionary tour, although he was most certainly not aware of just how ill he was. Jonathan Edwards, reflecting at a later time about his noble and sacrificial determinations, could see from reading his journal that his young protégé was drawing on the last vestiges of his life energies in order to take the gospel to the Indians on the Susquehanna. Edwards introduced the last section of Brainerd's *Journal*, containing the record of 'the termination of His Missionary Labours', with these matter-of-fact words: 'The hardships which Brainerd had endured, had now obviously affected his constitution; and unfitted him for a life of so much toil and exposure. Of this he appears not to have been aware, until the case had become hopeless; and unfortunately, the circumstances, in which he was placed, were calculated instead of retarding, to hasten the ravages of disease. He lived alone, in the midst of a wilderness; in a miserable hut, built by Indians; with few of the necessaries, and none of the comforts of life; at a distance from civilized society; without even a nurse or a physician. His labours, also, were sufficient to have impaired a vigorous constitution. It is not surprising, therefore, that his health was gradually, but fatally undermined.'

Many conflicting emotions must have stirred the soul of the Northampton pastor as he penned these lines. On the one hand, he admired the young minister's devotion to his calling and his willingness to press forward without regard to his own personal safety and health. But one can also detect that he felt some frustration that a life so bright and so promising was being sacrificed unnecessarily. The man who could have been around to gladden his family circle for many decades, and perhaps even raise up a godly family to help populate the growing nation, was about to fall a victim to his own sense of duty.

Brainerd knew that his strength was not what it had been during his previous trips west and he does appear to have taken some precautionary measures. This time he would select several of his congregation, including his interpreter, to ride with him. Their greater physical stamina and knowledge of the Indian trails west would be a great asset to him. Also they would give powerful supportive testimony to the gospel he would again preach to the Susquehanna Indians.

He would also take a different route to central Pennsylvania this time. Instead of crossing what Edwards referred to as the 'huge mountains and hideous wilderness' (expressions he borrowed from Brainerd himself) he would go through Philadelphia. His intentions were to leave the City of Brotherly Love, go up the Schuylkill river, and travel overland through the Lancaster area and up the Susquehanna from Harrisburg.

Before the trip could be taken, however, Brainerd felt that some special seasons of devotional exercise should be shared by the Bethel church. On 11 August the congregation joined together in earnest prayer that God would bless this trip and make it successful. Specifically they prayed that God would 'send forth his blessed Spirit with his word, and set up his kingdom among the Indians in the wilderness'. He expounded to his flock such texts as the second Psalm, where God promised to give to Jesus the heathen for his inheritance, and Psalm 110, where the sovereign Saviour, sitting as he is at the right hand of God, would 'judge among the nations'. He also spoke from Acts 4:31, which says, 'And when they had prayed, the place was shaken.'

The theme for the whole day had been God's promise that all nations would be blessed in the Redeemer. It was a glorious day. God helped the preacher and his interpreter, as is seen by the fact there was a 'shaking and melting' among the believers. 'My soul was refreshed to think, that this day, this blessed glorious season, should surely come; and, I trust, numbers of my dear people were also refreshed.' After expending such energy in prayer and preaching he went aside for a while to rest. The Indians stayed behind and continued to pray and sing. 'Blessed be God,' he said, 'this has been a day of grace.'

The next day, Tuesday, 12 August, Brainerd, accompanied by six selected Indian companions, set out on his fourth and final trip to the Susquehanna. His pace was apparently slowed by the walking Indians and some delaying visits, for he covered less than eighty miles in four days. He travelled from Cranberry to Philadelphia up the Schuylkill and on the Great Road to Norriton Mills and Charlestown, which he reached on Friday. The old township of Charlestown in Great Valley was located on the south side of the Schuylkill River, between present Phoenixville and Valley Forge.

David Wynbeek suggests that Brainerd and his party may have stopped at the home of Rev. Richard Treat, who lived at Abington. We know that he did go to Charlestown where the two ministers conducted services on Saturday and Sunday. Treat served as the pastor of Presbyterian congregations at both Abington and Charlestown, both of which supported Brainerd's missionary enterprises. Together they had collected

ten pounds and five shillings for Brainerd's work in New
Jersey.

On Monday morning Brainerd bid farewell to Treat and set
off on the final leg of his trip to the Susquehanna River, his
destination being 'Paxton'. He passed through the vicinity of
Derry (now known as Hershey) where there was a Presbyterian church. In the area east of Harrisburg at this time lived
the Irish minister John Elder. Eight years later a terrible war
against the Indians was to break out in which every Indian at
Conestoga and Lancaster would be massacred by the 'Pextony
boys', in spite of the protestations of Elder.

On Tuesday Brainerd and his companions reached the river
and lodged on the bank. He met no Christians in the settlement
there, which 'damped' his spirit. Also he was 'weak and
disordered' in body, an ominous sign in the light of the
difficult days ahead.

20 August was a very hard day. He had lain all the previous
night in what he calls a 'cold sweat'. He woke up the next
morning coughing up blood and suffering from 'not a little
melancholy'. After riding several miles up-river he lodged at
the home of a Mr Chambers. That night he was in the company
of 'an ungodly crew' who were drinking and swearing, which
added to his present miserable feelings. 'O what a hell would
it be,' he wrote, 'to be numbered with the ungodly!' But he had
a source of encouragement that he kept entirely to himself that
evening: 'I had a secret hope that I might speedily get a
dismission from earth, and all its toils and sorrows.'

On the next day he travelled fifteen miles further, where he
lodged with a family who 'appeared quite destitute of God'.
He sought to discuss spiritual subjects with them, but found
them to be very skilful in evading such conversations. 'O what
a death it is to some' he said 'to hear of the things of God!' The
next night, after a few more miles of progress, he slept in the
open woods 'among an ungodly company of white people'.

On Saturday, 23 August, after eleven days of travel, he finally reached the Indian capital of Shamokin. The next day he visited some of the Delaware Indians and bore witness to them about the claims of Christ. He had an audience with the Delaware king, evidently Sassoonan, on Sunday afternoon. He sent his Indian companions out on Monday to discuss Christianity with the Shamokin residents while he spent most of the day in writing.

The new believers from New Jersey were able to give public testimony to a group of the Shamokin Indians who had gathered for a service on Tuesday. These people seemed very serious, which encouraged Brainerd to hope that the Cross-weeksung awakening might be duplicated here. He 'pressed things' with all his might and then later in the evening prayed that God would set up his kingdom in this place.

Some aspects of the difficult living conditions he had to endure on this trip are highlighted in his diary entry for 27 August. The uncomfortable place where he stayed is graphically described: 'There having been a thick smoke in the house where I lodged all night before, whereby I was almost choked, I was this morning distressed with pains in my head and neck, and could have no rest. In the morning, the smoke was still the same; and a cold easterly storm gathering, I would neither live within doors, nor without, a long time together. I was pierced with the rawness of the air abroad, and in the house distressed with the smoke, I was this day very vapory, and lived in great distress, and had not health enough to do any thing to any purpose.'

On 28 August he had sufficiently recovered to be able to get out and visit some of the Indians in their town. He preached with great earnestness to them in the afternoon, persuading them to 'turn to God'. Dared he hope that the awakening at Crossweeksung would be repeated? His message was the same. He had just as much concern for the Shamokin Indians as for the others. The needs here were just as great. But alas, in spite of his faithful preaching and earnest appeals, he had to be reminded again that, apart from the sovereign work of God among them, nothing effectual could be accomplished. Here at Shamokin he wrote down a conviction, long held, often expressed, that only God could open the blinded eyes of lost sinners: 'Scarce ever saw more clearly, than this day, that it is God's *work* to convert souls, and especially poor *Heathens*. I knew, I could not *touch* them; I saw I could only speak to *dry bones,* but could give them no *sense* of what I said. My eyes were up to God for help: I could say the *work* was his; and if done, the *glory* would be *his.*'

And so the weary evangelist pressed on in proclaiming the good news of salvation, but with a renewed appreciation of the fact that all his labours to build the house of God were in vain unless the Great Builder himself intervened.

An interesting sidelight to his missionary travels appears in his diary entries during these days. It is clear that a special bonding was taking place between him and half a dozen companions from Bethel who were with him on this trip. He refers to them as 'his people', as he had often done before. But now he seemed to give to them a special endearing name, which shows how much they meant to him. He speaks of praying in secret and 'in my family' (28 August). On 31 August he wrote that he had spent some time reading and expounding the Bible and singing hymns with his 'dear family' which was with him. This shows that, in one sense, David Brainerd did have a family. Not, to be sure, a wife and children, living with him in a comfortable manse, but the Indian people who had come to God under his ministry. He was, after all, their spiritual father, and they were taking the place of the natural domestic circle.

After several days of ministry at Shamokin, without any visible result in terms of conversions, Brainerd decided to set his sights on the only other significant Indian settlement on the west branch of the Susquehanna, one he had not visited before. Some fifty miles north-west of Shamokin there were some Shawanese Indians living at the Big or 'Great Island', at the present site of Lock Haven. In between Shamokin and the Great Island was Ostonwackin (modern Montoursville), the village of the famous Madame Montour and her son Andrew. To go there was a hazardous and difficult goal. For one thing this was 'wild mountain country' which would take at least a five-day trip to complete. Also this tribe was considered especially dangerous because many of them were sympathetic to the French Canadians. The half-breed Peter Chartiers had actually led a group of them recently to join with these militant enemies of the colonial government. Such difficulties, if Brainerd knew about them, were cast aside, however, as he made his way onward.

On 1 September he slept in the woods and complained of feebleness and sweating at night. David Brainerd was by now clearly beginning to fight for his very life, even while seeking to save the lives of others. On 2 September he was so weak that he could ride only as fast as the Indians beside him walked. That night he felt that he simply could not sleep again in the open air: 'I was so feeble and faint that I feared it would kill me to lie out in the open air; and some of our company being parted from us, so that we had now no axe with us, I had no way but to climb into a young pine tree, and with my knife to lop the branches and so made a shelter from the dew.' He was wringing wet all night and woke up weak and weary. Trying as this situation was, he took comfort in the thought that he could have been in even worse circumstances. He could have been in the company of his enemies.

The missionary managed, in spite of his physical condition, to summon all his mental powers and preach to a couple of Indian towns in the Great Island area. It seemed to be a fruitless effort. 'My spirits were so low, and my bodily strength so wasted,' he said, 'that I could do nothing at all.' On 3 September he collapsed on a buffalo-skin and once again spent a night soaked in his own sweat.

He spent as much of his last day at the Great Island in preaching as his strength would allow and then he turned the matter over to his interpreter. That evening he was alone, since his Indian companions had gone somewhere else, and he had to go to bed without even a fire to cook with or 'keep off wild beasts'. The next day he rode back towards Shamokin so depleted of strength that he could only with the greatest effort stay on his horse.

Brainerd was practically an invalid during the last days he spent at Shamokin before heading back towards New Jersey. His appetite was gone and the discharge of blood was getting worse. Still he tried to speak to his own Indian party, 'through feebleness of body and flatness of spirits'.

It occurred to him, as he wrote about the trials he endured on this trip that some might conclude from these experiences that he was eminently zealous and fervent in his spirit as he engaged in his final missionary mission. He disagreed: 'O methought if God's people knew me, as God knows, they would not think so highly of my zeal and resolution for God, as perhaps now they do! I could not but desire they should see how heartless and irresolute I was, that they might be undeceived, and "not think of me above what they ought to think". And yet I thought, if they saw the uttermost of my flatness and unfaithfulness, the smallness of my courage and resolution for God, they would be ready to shut me out of their doors, unworthy of the company or friendship of Christians.' This pitiable confession leads us to conclude that Brainerd's frame of mind had descended once again to the depths of melancholy which had dogged him early in his ministry. His natural tendency to depression, the acute sense of his own unworthiness and his apparent lack of success in winning the Susquehanna Indians to Christ — these things in combination with his very sick physical condition warped his mental state and made him very miserable.

Brainerd had hoped to stay much longer in the Susquehanna region working for the conversion of the Indians there, but it was evident that he was unable to do so. The strains of this trip were beginning to show even upon his Indian companions, who were naturally inured to the inconveniences of the wilderness. He refers to the 'weakly circumstances of his own people' as one of the problems precipitating a need for a speedy return to their own community. Almost the entire trip he had endured nocturnal sweats and coughing of blood, the tell-tale signs of tuberculosis.

He spent his final Sunday (7 September) at Shamokin when he made some efforts at encouraging 'his own dear family' and discoursing to the 'Pagans'. It was not a good day. The following day he bid farewell to the old sachem Sassoonan and the noble and resourceful Shikellamy (who would later profess faith under the Moravians) and began his trek south along the river, retracing the route he had taken two weeks earlier.

29.
Falling shadows

During late August and early September the first signs of autumn are already beginning to show in central Pennsylvania. The nights are often cool and some of the shrubs and trees display the tinges of colour that will before long burst into the full glory of October.

As David Brainerd and his contingent of Indian associates rode down the Susquehanna River on their way back to Bethel they were certainly aware that the summer of life for the godly missionary was slipping away like the seasonal change they observed around them. This is seen by a comment he made on 8 September: 'I was a great part of the time so feeble and faint, that it seemed as though I never should be able to reach home; and at the same time very destitute of the comforts, and even the necessaries of life; at least, what was necessary for one in so weak a state.'

But his mind was not solely on his own physical condition. As his horse plodded along the well-beaten path which had taken so many traders and Indian warriors up and down the river, he pondered the meaning of this most recent visit to Shamokin, the Great Island and other points of the missionary endeavour. He was grateful for the positive things that had happened. He was aware that he had often been 'enabled to speak the word of God with some power' and that there had definitely been some impressions made on the hearers. Quite a number of the Indians had obviously been attracted to him and some seemed open to the gospel.

But the negatives were just as apparent. He could still picture in his mind how some of the Susquehanna Indians had mocked and shouted while he tried to speak, and how they had sought to dissuade those who were warming to the claims of Christ. No one had professed faith in the Saviour he had lifted up so faithfully.

All in all, he was not discouraged with the results of the visit and he certainly was not sorry he had taken the time once again to share the good news with these Indians. After all, the seed of the gospel does not always germinate and sprout quickly. Who could tell whether a foundation had been laid which could result in the establishment of the kingdom of God in the midst of the Delawares, Shawnees and Nanticokes? 'I was persuaded,' he wrote, 'the journey would not be lost. *Blessed be God, that I had any encouragement and hope.*'

On 9 September, the day after he left Shamokin, he rode through a thunderstorm, 'extremely weak and much fatigued'. He had an opportunity to preach to 'some ignorant souls'. Whoever they were, perhaps some white settlers, they were astonished to see his Indians ask a blessing and give thanks at the dinner. Afterwards he wrote in his diary, 'O the ignorance of the world! How are some empty outward *forms*, that may all be entirely selfish, mistaken for true religion, infallible evidences of it. The Lord pity a deluded world!'

On the 11th he passed by a meeting-house and was invited to preach, but he simply could not because of extreme weakness. The next day he rode fifty more miles and found rest in the home of an unnamed 'christian friend'. Here he was cordially entertained, a much-needed refreshment from his long and wearisome travels. On the 13th he was once again with Richard Treat, on whose preaching ministry he attended. The next day was Sunday and, at the insistence of the congregation, he mustered enough energy to occupy the pulpit twice.

His text for both services was Luke 14:23, 'Go out into the highways and hedges, and compel them to come in, that my house may be filled,' a passage that had now become one of his favourites.

On 17 September he rode to Philadelphia, coughing and spitting blood all the while. He gives no details about what took place here but one can make some assumptions, based on historical data from other sources. Two of the most important figures in the Great Awakening were here at this time. Gilbert Tennent lived in Philadelphia and also George Whitefield had arrived on the 11th to preach in 'Whitefield's Tabernacle', a new building which would soon become the 'Academy' and later the University of Pennsylvania.

If, as is possible, Brainerd, Tennent and Whitefield dined together at Philadelphia, what an interesting meeting it must have been! Tennent was the fiery orator who had inspired Brainerd at college, but was now becoming more subdued and pastoral in his approach. Whitefield, now thirty-two, was at the height of his success, enlisting people from all denominations in evangelistic efforts and preaching to huge crowds. Though not as notable at the time, the sickly Presbyterian missionary had also distinguished himself in obvious ways. What a blessed time they must have had sharing in the toils, trials and triumphs of God's work here in these dawning days of America!

After a day and night in Philadelphia Brainerd went to Treat's home in Abington. This had been a place where leaders such as Whitefield had stayed on many occasions. On Friday he rode eastward past William Penn's Manor and into New Jersey, to visit 'Mr Stockston' at Princeton. Wynbeek's research yields the following information: 'Stockton's home in "Prince-town" was beautiful Morven, now the official residence of the Governor of New Jersey, which stands on Stockton Street, a few minutes walk from Princeton University. It received its name after Brainerd's day, but the house was then already some forty years old. His host, a son of the purchaser of the original five-hundred-acre estate, was a gentleman of wealth and influence and the presiding judge in the Court of Common Pleas of Somerset County. He was the father of Richard Stockton, the persecuted and imprisoned signer of the Declaration of Independence, whose wife Annis Boudinot gave their little "kingdom" its mythical Gaelic-Norse name. Richard was sixteen years old when Brainerd visited Morven.'[1]

The next day, Friday, 20 September, the weary missionary arrived back at Cranberry where he found his Indians 'praying together'. He reported to them the experiences he and his companions had on their forty-day trip. Tears streamed down their faces as their leader and their brothers told about their labours on the Susquehanna. Thoroughly exhausted, Brainerd went to his lodging and collapsed. 'Many hardships and distresses I endured in this journey,' he wrote, 'but the Lord supported me under them all.'

Brainerd's life and work up until this time had been carefully chronicled in his journal which, as has already been noted, fell into the hands of Jonathan Edwards, who edited and published it. The Northampton pastor inserts a comment at this point in Brainerd's life, significant because of its poignancy. He notes that after his fourth trip to the Susquehanna Brainerd's daily diary is interrupted because of his declining health. In the coming days his personal comments are less frequent and detailed.

On Sunday, 21 September, he was unable to ride to the meeting-place in the morning, but he sat in his chair and spoke from Romans 14:7-8. It was, of course, disappointing to him and his people alike that he could not assume his usual place in the pulpit, but still he was grateful that at least he could minister to them. 'I returned to my lodge extremely tired but thankful, that I had been enabled to speak a word to my poor people, from whom I had been so long absent.'

He recorded on 27 September that he had no appetite, and when he did try to eat he could not keep his food down. There was, however, an important task that had to be attended to on this very day. Since moving his congregation from Crossweeksung to Cranberry he had not had a permanent place to live. At each of his previous preaching points—Kaunaumeek, the Forks of the Delaware and Crossweeksung — he had erected a small house for his own habitation. So this project had to be undertaken again, and the work was done under his supervision.

By now Brainerd knew from the all-too-evident signs that his days on this earth were numbered. 'Whether I should ever recover or no, seemed very doubtful,' he wrote on the 27th, 'but this was many times a comfort to me, that *life* and *death* did not depend upon *my* choice.' As far as he was concerned, this was a matter which was entirely in the hands of the Lord. He was content to leave the matter there, and as a result he was able to look death in the face. 'I had little strength to pray, none to write or read, and scarce any to meditate; but through divine goodness, I would with great composure look *death* in the face, and frequently with sensible joy. O how blessed it is, to be *habitually prepared* for death! The Lord grant, that I may be *actually ready also*.'

In the next few days he tried to gather his strength in order to preach to the Indians, but with limited success. On Sunday, 28 September, he spoke for a while but had to stop because of faintness.

Brainerd announced to his congregation that on Sunday, October, he would be administering the sacrament of communion to them. In preparation for this special service he preached on the previous Friday from 2 Corinthians 13:5 on the subject of self-examination. While he was speaking a surprising energy came over him and he was able to carry his message through, though he had to repair immediately afterwards to his house to recuperate. He was encouraged by the results of the message: 'The sermon was blessed of God to the stirring up religious affection, and a spirit of devotion, in the people of God; and to greatly affecting one who had *backslidden* from God, which caused him to judge and condemn himself.'

On Saturday his Indians were together again as he discoursed to them from Zechariah 12:10, a favourite text of the Puritans, which explains what happens when the Spirit of God comes in convicting power on sinners.

David Brainerd was first and foremost a preacher. His training in college was for preaching, his rôle models, such as Whitefield and Tennent, were great preachers and his own life had been devoted to the business of the public proclamation of the gospel. Without a doubt the difficulties he was having in public ministry were a great trial to him. But he pressed on. Though weak, tired and rapidly declining in general health, he sought to carry out his commission faithfully.

For the Puritan congregation the Sabbath was a high day, and the days on which the sacrament of the Lord's Supper was observed were especially meaningful. Brainerd had carefully prepared his people for the communion service on 5 October, sensing no doubt that his own participation in such times was probably drawing to a conclusion. He rose on the day feeling very weak and afraid that he would not be able to go through with the work. But God helped him and he delivered his message before the elements were served. Although he normally mentions in his diary simply the text and the general theme of his sermons, he chose to record the outline of his message. It gives an interesting insight, not only into his preaching method, but also his theology.

The text was John 1:29: 'Behold the Lamb of God, that taketh away the sins of the world.' He outlined his subject as follows:

I. In what respects Christ is called the Lamb of God

1. From the purity and innocence of his nature.
2. From his being that atonement which was pointed out in the sacrifice of the lambs, and in particular by the paschal lamb.

II. How and in what sense he 'takes away the sin of the world'

The means and manner in and by which he takes away the sins of men, was his 'giving himself for them', doing and suffering in their room and stead. He is said to take away the sin of the world, not because all the world shall actually be redeemed from sin by Him, but because,

1. He has done and suffered sufficient to answer for the sins of the world, and so to redeem all mankind.
2. He actually does take away the sins of the elect world.

III. How we are to behold him, in order to have our sins taken away

1. Not with our bodily eyes.
2. Not by imagining him on the cross, etc.
3. But by a spiritual view of his glory and goodness, engaging the soul to rely on him, etc.

Following the message Brainerd wrote down that the assembly was 'considerably melted with divine truths'. After this he baptized two and administered the elements of the sacrament to about forty Indian communicants.

This sermon is worthy of careful study, for it is typical of Brainerd's approach to the gospel. The essential content can be summed up as follows: Jesus Christ is the antitype of the paschal lamb and is qualified in every way to be the Redeemer of mankind. The atonement is *substitutionary* as it relates to man and *satisfactory* as it relates to God. Christ's sufferings are inherently adequate for all, but designed especially for the elect. Faith is not a literal view of Jesus, nor an 'imaging' exercise of the mere mind, but a view of Christ from the eye of the soul, which depends, of course, on the special illumination of the Holy Spirit. The last point was a special emphasis of the theologians influenced by Edwards and especially designed to combat the mysticism of the Quakers and the carnal literalism of the Moravians, who were obsessed with the physical pain of Jesus.

Although Brainerd was severely ill physically, the diary he managed to keep in the weeks following his return to Cranberry shows little change in his emotional sensitivities and reactions. He had the same profound sense of unworthiness and ill-deserving. Early in October he went to a meeting of the New York Synod and obviously was treated very graciously by his host, Jonathan Dickinson (who was a physician). He commented that he 'was ashamed to see so much concern about so an unworthy a creature, as I knew myself to be'. Two weeks later, while he was staying at Princeton, Richard Treat and Charles Beatty rode forty miles to see him. Afterward he commented, 'My spirits were refreshed to see them; but I was surprised, and even ashamed, that they had taken so much pains as to ride thirty or forty miles to see me.'

His great concern for his flock never changed in the least. On 24 October, though scarcely able to get about himself, he managed to find strength to supervise a project of mending the fence surrounding a wheat-field. 'Found that all their concerns of a secular nature depended upon me.' Obviously they were beginning to be anxious because of the decline of their pastor.

On 26 October he wrote, 'In the morning was exceedingly weak: spent the day, till near night, in pain, to see my people wandering *as sheep not having a shepherd*, waiting and hoping to see me able to preach to them before night.'

Amazingly he felt keenly a great compunction about what he perceived to be a waste of time, a concern he had expressed many times before. He knew that he was ill, really ill, and yet at times he was tormented about whether he was using this as an excuse. 'At other times my mind was perplexed with fears, that I was a misimprover of time, by conceiting I was sick, and when I was not in reality so. O how precious is time! And how guilty it makes me feel, when I think that I have trilled away and improved it, or neglected to fill up each part of it with duty, to the utmost of my ability and capacity.'

Early in November he was conscious that he was 'utterly incapable' of performing his work and 'having little hope of recovery, unless by much riding'. With this in mind he decided to ride into New England and spend some time with friends. After visiting each of his flock in their own homes and seeking to encourage them in the things of God, he rode to Woodbridge and from there to Elizabethtown, hoping soon to proceed further north. But his health did not permit him to leave Jonathan Dickinson's home at Elizabethtown, for shortly after arriving there he became much worse. He ended up spending the winter there.

Though his body had lost its vigour Brainerd was able while convalescing to ponder the meaning of the kingdom of God and his relationship to it. He praised God as he recalled his abundant mercies to the Indians, realizing that God had done a great work through him, even if he should never preach again. David Brainerd loved God and adored him as the most excellent and glorious of beings. 'My soul blessed God for what he is in himself, and adored him, that he ever would display himself to creatures. I rejoiced that he was God, and longed that all should know it, and feel it, and rejoice in it.

"Lord glorify thyself," was the desire and cry of my soul. O that *all people* might love and praise the blessed God; that he might have all possible honor and glory from the intelligent world!' This quotation probably summarizes as succinctly as any in his diary what Brainerd's devotion was all about. The adoration of God was everything.

While wintering at Elizabethtown he wrote a letter to his brother Israel, now a student at Yale, in which he revealed that he was in preparation for death:

> My disorder has been attended with several symptoms of *consumption*; and I have been at times apprehensive, that my great *change* was at hand; yet blessed be God, I have never been *affrighted*; but, on the contrary, at times much delighted with a view of its approach. O the blessedness of being delivered from the clogs of flesh and sense, from a *body of sin* and spiritual *death*! O the unspeakable sweetness of being translated into a state of complete purity and perfection! Believe me, my brother, a lively view and hope of these things, will make the king of terrors himself appear agreeable. Dear brother, let me entreat you, to keep *eternity* in your view, and behave yourself as becomes one that must shortly 'give an account of things done in the body'. That God may be *your* God, and prepare you for his service here, and his kingdom of glory hereafter, is the desire and daily prayer of
> > Your affectionate loving brother,
> > David Brainerd.'

In his own view at least, he was coming to the end of his earthly pilgrimage. As it turned out, he was not wrong.

30.
Passing the torch

Few ministers in the American colonies were held in higher esteem than Jonathan Dickinson, who was pastor of the Presbyterian Church of Elizabethtown, New Jersey (now called Elizabeth). A 1706 Yale graduate, he was a man of wisdom, moderation and general culture. Along with his many interests in the pastoral ministry and denominational concerns he found time not only to work his glebe, or farm, with profit, but also studied and practised the medical arts.

Sereno Dwight, who edited the 1830 works of Edwards and the diary of Brainerd, refers to him as 'the late learned and very excellent.'[1] In the view of the historian Robert Ellis Thompson he was 'the best scholar, the most effective writer, and the soundest judgment' in his church.[2] In many ways he reminds one of Jonathan Edwards, the only Christian leader who had a greater impact on David Brainerd than Dickinson. He had a reputation and influence in the middle colonies much like that of Edwards in New England.

Even in his physical appearance he bore a striking resemblance to Edwards. An extant portrait shows him with a 'white-powdered wig framed in a fine-featured face. He had large eyes and heavy black eyebrows and a strong chin, and his mouth was slightly larger and not quite as prim as Edwards.'[3]

In his relationships Dickinson was always moderate and tolerant. He took a middle ground between the Scottish high churchmen who insisted on a strict subscription to the *West-minster Confession* and the 'low-church' revivalists who were decidedly less credal. He wrote a book on the Five Points of Calvinism called *True Christian Doctrine*, but his most popular book was entitled *The Reasonableness of Christianity*. Throughout his writings he emphasized that love was the greatest of the Christian virtues.

Dickinson was involved from the very beginning in the controversy that arose over the Awakening preachers such as Whitefield and Tennent, and when the time came for him to take sides he aligned himself with the New Lights. He totally sympathized with David Brainerd at the time of his expulsion fromYale and opened his home to him as a place of refuge. It is not surprising that as Brainerd's health began to fail he turned to his preacher-physican for help. At the time Brainerd moved in with him in November 1746 Dickinson was fifty-eight years old. He was assisted in caring for Brainerd by his godly daughter Martha, then twenty-one, who was described by her contemporaries as serious, religious and very intelligent.

Brainerd was so weak during that winter that he made very few entries in his diary. At the end of January1747, he complains of a violent cough, fever, asthmatic symptoms, lack of appetite and inability to digest food. 'I was reduced to so low a state, that my friends, I believe, generally despaired of my life, and some of them, for some time together, thought I could scarce live a day.'

At the beginning of February, however, his condition began to improve. On the first day of the month he wrote that he enjoyed 'comfort and sweetness' in divine things. He meditated on the text, 'If ye, being evil, know how to give good gifts to your children, how much more will your heavenly Father give the Holy Spirit to them that ask him?' He claimed the promise of this text and his soul was encouraged and reassured.

On 24 February he managed to ride to Newark, home of Aaron Burr, returning the next day to the Dickinson residence. On 28 February an Indian came from his congregation and gave good news about the continued good behaviour of these Christians. He was able to attend a public worship service on 11 March, the first such opportunity since 21 December.

As spring approached he decided that he had recovered sufficiently to return to Cranberry, so he made the trip back, arriving on Thursday, 19 March. The next day he rose early and walked round the village 'enquiring into their state and concerns'. Not everything he heard was encouraging, a fact that made him 'gloomy'. At ten o'clock he called them together, expounded a psalm and prayed with them. This was his last public exercise as pastor of the Indian church.

After this meeting with his beloved flock Brainerd mounted his horse, left the Indian camp and headed north-east for the twenty-mile ride back to Elizabethtown. There was, so far as we know, no final 'farewell' from 'his people' for they would not have known for certain that this was to be the end of his relationship with them. Still, one can imagine these dusky sons and daughters of the wilderness watching with sadness, and even tears, as their faithful preacher passed out of sight on the road in the distance. They were, as it turned out, not destined to meet again in this world.

His strength had improved sufficiently in April for him to be able to carry out some fairly important functions. Not only was he able to attend church services, but he officiated at the wedding of Dickinson to Mary Crane on 7 April. The bride was only twenty-seven at the time, younger than Brainerd himself. This was an exciting period for Dickinson for in this very month he would become the first President of the College of New Jersey, an institution for which he had worked so long and hard.

On 9 April Brainerd attended the ordination of a Mr Tucker, of whom we know little except that he studied at Harvard

College and died within a year of his ordination. On 10 April David's brother John came to see him and plans were formulated for John to take his place as pastor of the Indian congregation.

John Brainerd was two years younger than David and had long been close to him not only in natural ties but spiritual as well. John's personality was remarkably similar to that of his more famous brother. Both of them were subject to bouts of mental depression, a problem that seemed to plague the entire Brainerd family for two hundred years. John was a freshman at Yale at the time of the Whittelsey affair, and certainly must have been hurt by the way his brother was treated. But David encouraged John to continue his education, which he did, graduating in 1746, just as David was concluding his ministry at Cranberry.

The two brothers stayed in close contact during the time that one was studying at Yale and the other was doing evangelism among the Indians. John became a confidant of David, who was able to unburden his heart about his problems and share with his brother his vision for extension of Christ's kingdom in general, and the Indian mission in particular. It was to John that he had written on 27 December 1743, 'The whole world appears to me like a huge vacuum, a vast empty space, whence nothing desirable, or at least satisfactory, can possibly be derived.' His brother would have sympathized with that statement, at times at least.

Now that David's work among the Indians was clearly over a replacement had to be found. But who would it be? From one point of view it is not surprising that John was his choice. His interests, his theology and his temperament matched those of his older brother. Of course, from another perspective one could question this move. John had no experience in ministry, either in a white congregation or on the mission field. He had no exposure to Indian life and knew none of the tribal languages.

All such problems would have been insignificant to David. He wanted someone to go and care for his flock who would have the same vision and motives as he had. He knew that John would fill this requirement. He could rest at ease, knowing that one of like faith with himself was teaching and leading his congregation. On 13 April he wrote that he 'examined' his brother. Even though it was a foregone conclusion that John would be approved, still he had to go through the trial process. The next day David records laconically, 'This day my brother went to my people.' Bethel had a new pastor.

In contrast to the silence of his diary during the winter there are several entries in the spring of 1747, though there is nothing especially unusual about his reflections. He continued to complain of bitterness and anxiety over his sin and guilt and express overwhelming gratitude for God's sovereign grace to him. 'Sometimes I could not but admire the divine goodness, that the Lord had not let me fall into all the grossest, vilest acts of sins and open scandal, that could be thought of; and felt so much necessitated to praise God, that this was ready for a little while to swallow up my shame and pressure of spirit on account of my sins' (17 April).

On 21 April he departed for New England, leaving behind for ever New Jersey, the place where the remarkable scenes of divine visitation had occurred. As he rode north he also left behind his 'dear friends', the pastors with whom he had worked, such as Byram, McKnight, Beatty, Tennent and Dickinson; his brother John, the green but eager replacement at Cranberry; and, even more significantly, 'his people', the dear flock who had been gathered from paganism into a Christian community.

His purpose was, he stated, to 'recover his health by riding'. He had many friends whose homes were along the way, so he was able to find lodging at appropriate intervals. By early May he was back at East Haddam. He was making an honest effort to regain his health which was in such a perilous state. He sought 'diversions' for his health (which had no doubt been recommended by his friends). After all, he certainly knew that a bow that has been constantly bent will eventually break. He had taken little time off for relaxation and recreation since going to Kaunaumeek to preach to the Indians. The last four years had been spent in incessant riding, preaching and writing, not to mention the supervision of his Indian community in all their physical and cultural needs.

And yet his restless introspection would not let him fully enjoy the respite from spiritual labour. Perhaps we could call it an 'overweaning conscience' that tormented his soul as he searched and probed into the motive for every endeavour. He was concerned that the 'diversions' he sought were not for the glory of God but were for 'merely selfish' reasons. This caused him to give great 'care and watchfulness' lest he 'lose that spiritual temper of mind in his diversions' (Edwards' words of commentary on his journal, the text of which he does not supply).

Back at Haddam on 10 May, he reflected on the great themes he had dwelt upon during his public ministry. He praised God that he had disposed him to 'insist on the great doctrines of regeneration, the new creature, faith in Christ, progressive sanctification, supreme love to God, living entirely to the glory of God, being not our own, and the like'. The reader might well pause and examine these expressions which embodied what was, by his own confession, the substance of his ministry. For Brainerd these were not peripheral matters, but the very essence of true religion, the absolute essentials of what true Christianity is all about: 'God thus helped me to see, in the surest manner, from time to time, that these, and the like doctrines necessarily connected with them, are the only *foundation* of safety and salvation for perishing sinners; and that those divine dispositions, which are consonant hereto, are that *holiness* "without which no man shall see the Lord". The exercise of these godlike tempers — wherein the soul acts in a kind of concert with God, and would be and do every thing that is pleasing to him — I saw, would stand by the soul in a dying hour; for God must, I think deny himself, if he cast away his own image, even the soul that is one in desires with himself' (10 May).

Brainerd was a doctrinal preacher and was especially interested in all the great themes which relate to God's redemptive plan for mankind. But the *emphasis* of his preaching was on the truths that relate to the experience of the soul in coming to know God. He studied carefully from Scripture and from the experiences of other Christians he knew, as well as from his own life, what regeneration and sanctification really were. He was deeply interested in how God's grace awakens, convicts, changes and leads his chosen people. The convictions he held on these themes were strong.

For Brainerd a knowledge of God was to be sought, not primarily in order to obtain personal satisfaction and happiness, but because of God's intrinsic holiness and worthiness. Heaven was his goal, not in order to escape from trouble but because here he would attain ultimate communion with the Almighty. At Millington, a parish of East Haddam, Connecticut, he wrote, 'I also saw, that God is the supreme good, that in his presence is life; and I began to long to die, that I might *be with him*, in a state of freedom from all sin.'

The heavenly state is desirable not so much because it will afford personal pleasure, but because God is glorified by sinlessness: 'I seemed to long for this perfect holiness, not so much for the sake of my own happiness, although I saw clearly that this was the greatest, yea, the only happiness of the soul, as that I might please God, live entirely to him, and glorify him to the utmost stretch of my rational powers and capacities' (17 May).

Brainerd's diary entries in May 1747 clearly indicate that he was making his way directly up the Connecticut River towards Northampton, Massachusetts, where his last days would be spent. Along this river are many places significant in the lives of the Great Awakening preachers. Haddam, his own birthplace, is close to Long Island Sound. Not far north is Hartford where the Second Great Awakening evangelist, Asahel Nettleton, laboured so successfully. Twenty miles above the Connecticut border is Northampton, Massachusetts, the home of Edwards.

On Sunday, 24 May, he had crossed the Massachusetts line and was in Longmeadow, which is a suburb of modern Springfield. Here he reflected and wrote, as he had done so often before, about God-centred and authentic religion, as opposed to what he considered selfish and spurious: 'Could not but think, as I have often remarked to others, that much more of *true religion* consists in *deep humility, brokenness of heart, and an abasing sense of barrenness and want of grace and holiness*, than most who are called *Christians*, imagine; especially those who have been esteemed the converts of the *late* day. Many seem to know of no other religion but elevated *joys* and *affections*, arising only from some flights of *imagination*, or some *suggestion* made to their mind, of *Christ* being *theirs,* God *loving them*, and the like.'

Brainerd is not denigrating the assurance of salvation or minimizing its importance in the Christian life. But he definitely is criticizing the confidence that is based merely on mental images or communications from some external source. For Brainerd, and those of his school of thought, visions and flights of fancy in which a person is assured of being saved are no substitute for a consciousness that he or she possesses the basic traits of spiritual renewal, such as an abhorrence of sin, complete trust in the cross of Christ, and the adoration of God. For example, if someone had heard a voice speaking in a dream stating, 'You are loved by God,' this could possibly be an encounter with a spirit other than God. But a sense of unworthiness based on a spiritual view of God's own inherent excellence cannot be counterfeited. In the one case the subject is focusing solely on self-interest; in the other he or she is entering into the very scheme of the triune God himself, who is seeking above all else to bring honour to his own name.

31.
The coming chariot

When did David Brainerd decide to come to Northampton and stay with the Edwards family, and what were the circumstances surrounding that decision? Any information on that subject in his diary must have been deleted by Edwards for we can find nothing relevant. It is clear, however, that some time prior to the spring of 1747 David had been invited to use the Edwards home as a place of rest, and if possible, recuperation. Sereno Dwight, in his *Memoir,* mentions that Mr Edwards himself had invited Brainerd to take up his abode in his house.

The remarks of Jonathan Edwards on Brainerd's diary, faith and demeanour, written while he was a house guest, are very interesting. He mentions as an editorial comment in the diary how he had first met Brainerd four years earlier at the Yale Commencement. It was on that occasion that Brainerd had apologized to the rector for his critical remarks about Whittelsey. His handling of this problem, without question, won the heart of Edwards and singled him out for attention.

The Edwards family now had an opportunity to get to know David Brainerd on a more intimate basis. Jonathan now observed at close range the traits of his personality and his general demeanour. He was profoundly impressed: 'I found him remarkably sociable, pleasant and entertaining in his conversation; yet solid, savoury, spiritual, and very profitable. He appeared meek, modest, and humble; far from any stiff-

ness, moroseness, superstitious demureness, or affected sin-
gularity in speech or behavior, and seeming to dislike all such
things.'

This commentary on David's social graces is significant for
it helps to dispel a false impression which could otherwise be
created. Brainerd's frequent entries in his diary about his own
discouragements and feelings of unworthiness might leave the
impression that he was taciturn and morose in his relationships
with others. But on the basis of Edwards' comments we must
conclude that this was not the case at all. Obviously he did not
allow his private struggles and conflicts to make him un-
friendly and inhospitable. He was, as Edwards affirms, a
delightful person to have as a personal acquaintance. This
explains in part why he had so many friends.

He often prayed in the family circle, always to the edification and encouragement of all who heard him: 'We enjoyed
not only the benefit of his conversation, but had the comfort
and advantage of hearing him pray in the family, from time to
time. His manner of praying was very agreeable; most becoming a worm of the dust, and a disciple of Christ, addressing an
infinitely great and holy God, the Father of mercies; not with
florid expressions, or a studied eloquence; not with any
intemperate vehemence or indecent boldness.'

On 31 May he consulted a physician, Dr Mather, and
received very bad, but not wholly unexpected, news. He was
diagnosed as having a confirmed case of 'consumption' (the
current word for tuberculosis) and there was no reason to think
he would ever recover. According to Edwards this information
'seemed not to occasion the least discomposure in him, nor to
make any manner of alteration as to the cheerfulness and
serenity of his mind, or the freedom or pleasantness of his
conversation'.

The prescribed treatment for his condition, one designed
not necessarily to cure him permanently but at least to prolong
his life, was to ride. After considering the matter for a while he

decided to go to Boston. His companion for this three-day journey directly across the middle of Massachusetts was to be the seventeen-year-old Jerusha Edwards. And so David and Jerusha, 'together at last',[1] set out for Boston, visiting various ministerial friends along the way.

On 18 June ulcers broke out in his lungs, bringing him 'to the gates of death'. For several weeks he was so weak that he was unable to speak, or even so much as whisper. In a few weeks he had recuperated sufficiently to walk occasionally about the house where he was staying, but even then he still could not even so much as say 'yes' or 'no'. Remarkably he felt considerable serenity of mind and 'clearness of thought', sufficient for him to make some entries in his diary.

Standing at death's door did not diminish his relish for, and appreciation of, the great truths he had proclaimed to the Indians: 'As I saw clearly the truth of those great doctrines which are justly styled *the doctrines of grace* so I saw with no less clearness, that the essence of religion consisted in the soul's *conformity to God*, and acting above all selfish views, for his *glory*, longing to be for him, to live to him, and please and honor him in all things...'

He also confessed a great longing for heaven, a state in which he could 'glorify God perfectly'. He expressed his abhorrence of the 'delusions of Satan', namely that one becomes a Christian through 'empty suggestions' of the mind that one is saved while having no 'discovery of the divine glory'.

On 30 June he wrote to his brother Israel, explaining what it was like to stand on 'the verge of Eternity': '*Eternity* is another thing than we ordinarily take it to be in a healthful state. O, how vast and boundless! O, how fixed and unalterable! O, of what infinite importance is it, that we be prepared for *Eternity*. I have been just a dying, now for more than a week; and all around me have thought me so.'

Evidently his brother had not made a profession of faith, or at least his spiritual condition was in doubt, for David admonished him rather directly to attend with great seriousness to the issue of his own salvation: 'And for you, my dear brother, I have been particularly concerned; and have wondered I so much neglected conversation with you about your spiritual state at our last meeting. O, my brother, let me then beseech you now to examine, whether you are indeed a *new creature*? whether you have ever acted above *self*, whether the glory of God has ever been the sweetest and highest concern with you? ... If you cannot answer positively, consider seriously the frequent breathings of your soul; but do not, however, put yourself off with a slight answer. If you have reason to think you are *graceless*, O give yourself and the throne of grace no rest, till God arise and save.'

He assures Israel that he does not consider his life misspent in the service of Jesus Christ: 'I declare, now I am dying, I would not have spent my life otherwise for the whole world. But I must leave this with God.'

He wrote to his brother John at Bethel encouraging him in his ministry there. Among his recommendations was that he study Edwards' treatise on *The Affections*, 'where the essence and soul of religion is clearly distinguished from false affections'. Edwards seems almost embarrassed at having included this statement in the diary, feeling perhaps that it was self-serving. He justifies the decision with the thought that the recommendation of such an eminent Christian as Brainerd would help to promote the book, particularly among some who had criticized it as being too legalistic.

Brainerd revealed in this letter how much his heart was still attached to the Indians, and how concerned he was for their welfare. They must beware of emotional religion that is not built upon solid gospel concepts. They must be careful that they do not fall back into their pagan ways and personal vice, for this will be a bad influence on the other Indians: 'Always insist,' he admonishes, 'that their experiences are *rotten*, that their joys are *delusive*, although they may have been rapt up into the *third heavens* in their own conceit by them, unless the main tenor of their lives be spiritual, watchful and holy.' Such a bold caution was based on Brainerd's own awareness of the tendency of the Indians to mystical experiences.

While in Boston he studied some papers of 'old Mr Shepherd' with great relish. He is referring to the Puritan Thomas Shepherd who was notorious for drawing a fine line between the true believer and deceived people who have made a profession of religion but have no corresponding fruit.

At this point Brainerd, for whatever good it may have done him, had attained something of a celebrity status, primarily no doubt because the news of the great revival at Crossweeksung had spread abroad. While in Boston he was visited by a large number of unnamed people, some of whom evidently had important positions in the colonial government and in the church.

All during his time in Boston, where he was staying in the home of Joseph Bromfield, he was faithfully attended by Jerusha. She kept the family fully informed as to his condition. On 23 June she gave a clinical report stating that 'He was very ill with a violent fever, and extreme pain in his head and breast, and, at turns, delirious.' He remained for two days 'in the agonies of death'. She also passed on the discouraging news that his doctor, Joseph Pynchon, 'has no hopes of his life'. In another letter on 29 June she quotes him as saying that it is impossible for him to live 'for he has hardly vigor enough to draw his breath'. The cause for this immediate danger was the continued and increasing bursting of ulcers in his lung, which was first reported on 18 June.

For some inexplicable reason he then made an 'astonishing recovery' and showed signs of improvement. He was delighted to see his brother Israel, who came to see him, but was saddened to hear that his sister Spenser, who lived at Haddam, had unexpectedly died. This was especially distressing to him for he and his sister had enjoyed 'much intimacy in spiritual matters'. Israel stayed with him till he left Boston and accompanied him and Jerusha on the trip back to Northampton. They left 'in the cool of the afternoon' on 20 July and arrived back at the Edwards' manse on the 25th, travelling about sixteen miles a day.

From time to time during the summer Brainerd was able to enter into conversation with the Edwards family about personal, theological and spiritual matters. Edwards commented specially on his opposition to 'principles in religion which tended to "antinomianism", "separationism", meaning those who dissented from the "standing ministry"' (Baptists and Quakers would have been included in this, no doubt) and 'noise and show in religion'. He lamented the lack of response to the recent proposal from Scottish ministers that there be 'united extraordinary prayer' for a great revival of religion.

On Saturday, 5 September, his brother John came to see him from Cranberry and shared with him how things were going with the Indian congregation. It was on this occasion that John brought from New Jersey some of David's private writings, and especially the diary which he had kept for several years. These papers came under the supervision of Jonathan Edwards and formed the basis of the later publication of Brainerd's life.

Brainerd had been consulted earlier in the summer by the commissioners of a London missionary society about the possibility of their appointing two missionaries to take the gospel to the Six Nation Indian confederation. This enterprise had been made possible by the legacy of Rev. Daniel Williams of London. After much deliberation Brainerd wrote a letter in which he recommended Elihu Spenser of East Haddam and Job Strong of Northampton for these posts. Unfortunately neither of these young men was able to stay long in these jobs.

His brother Israel returned to see him on Thursday, 17 September, and never left, for David had now been reduced to such a weak state that he could never again leave his room. But he wrote exultantly of his anticipated release from a world of sin and suffering and entrance into eternal glory: 'O I was *made* — for eternity — if God might be glorified! *Bodily pains* I cared not for; though I was then in extremity, I never felt easier. I felt willing to *glorify God* in that state of bodily distress, as long as he pleased I should continue in it. The *grave* appeared really sweet, and I longed to lodge my weary bones in it...'

The Edwards family recorded some of the things he said at this time, which were very similar to those he had written earlier in his diary. He is quoted as saying, 'My *heaven* is to *please* God, and to *glorify* him, and to give all to him, and to be wholly devoted to his glory... Had I a *thousand souls*, if they were worthy anything, I would give them all to God. It is no matter where I shall be stationed in heaven, whether I have a high or a low seat there; but to live, and to please, and glorify God is all.'

He ended his message to those about him on this touching occasion with these words: 'When you see my grave, then remember what I said to you while I was alive; then think with yourself, how the man who lies in that grave, counselled and warned me to prepare for death.'

His brother Israel listened to this searching admonition and became a candidate for the ministry, no doubt moved by the witness of his brother. Unfortunately Israel died that very winter, on 6 January 1748 after an illness of two weeks. He had become by then, in the view of Edwards, 'an ingenious, serious, studious and hopefully pious person'. He was no doubt the last person David Brainerd won to the Lord.

For the last two weeks of his life David suffered greatly with severe bodily pains, vomiting and near strangulation. On

25 September he wrote with his own hands the prayer, 'O, blessed God, I am speedily coming to thee, I hope.' After these remarks, all his comments were written down by his brother Israel, who served as a sort of secretary. On 27 September he said, 'I was born on a *Sabbath-day*, and I have reason to think I was newborn on a *Sabbath-day*; and I hope I shall die on this *Sabbath-day*.' Then he cried out, with apparent great expectation and desire for an end to his life, 'O, why is his chariot so long in coming? Why tarry the wheels of his chariot?'

Jerusha attended him constantly during his last days. Of her Jonathan Edwards said, 'She was a person of much the same spirit with Brainerd.' In one of the most revealing of Edwards' footnotes he mentions that Jerusha and David conversed much about spiritual matters, sharing of their common faith in Christ and desire to honour him. She had, according to her father, 'a heart uncommonly devoted to God'. Brainerd saw her sterling character and often expressed to her parents 'his great satisfaction concerning her true piety, and his confidence that he should meet her in heaven'. He considered her not only a true Christian but 'a very eminent saint, one whose soul was uncommonly fed and entertained with things which appertain to the most spiritual, experimental, and distinguishing parts of religion'. She, according to Brainerd, was one 'who by the temper of her mind, was fitted to deny herself for God and to do good, beyond any woman whatsoever, whom he knew'. She was, no doubt, also eminently 'fitted' to be his wife, had he lived.

On Sunday, 4 October, Jerusha walked into his room in order to care for him in the usual way. Edwards himself recorded what he said to her on this occasion: 'He looked at her very pleasantly, and said, "Dear Jerusha, are you willing to part with me? — I am willing to part with you: I am willing to part with all my friends, I am willing to part with my dear brother John, although I love him the best of any creature living; I have committed him and all friends to God, and can leave them with God. Though if I thought I should not see you, and be happy with you in another world, I could not bear to part with you. But we shall spend an happy eternity together.'"[2]

On 7 October his brother John came to see him for the last time, having been delayed by a serious outbreak of illness among the Christian Indians. David had enough strength that night to discuss at length the situation among the Indians.

In the latter part of this evening he let it be known that the pain he was undergoing was extreme beyond description. 'It is another thing to die, than people imagine,' he said, referring to the bodily pain and anguish that preceded death.

Towards morning, at about six o'clock on 9 October, as he was lying immovable, with eyes fixed, his soul, in the words of his host Edwards, 'was received by his dear Lord and Master, as an eminently faithful servant, into that state of perfection of holiness, and fruition of God for which he had so ardently longed'. David Brainerd was dead. The chariot, in God's own due time, had come.

32.
One among a thousand

Brainerd's funeral was held in the Northampton church on the Monday following his death. There came to this service 'a great concourse of people', which included eight ministers and many distinguished citizens. Edwards preached the funeral message, using as his text 2 Corinthians 5:8: 'We are confident, I say, and willing rather to be absent from the body, and to be present with the Lord.' It was printed in its entirety in Sereno Dwight's edition of Edwards' works and runs to twenty-six pages. It must have taken approximately two hours to deliver. The message explains in clear and precise terms, and under five major heads, the hope the believer has of entering immediately into the presence of God upon death. At the end of the sermon several references are made to Brainerd's life and character, in which he is held up as an example of self-denial, meekness, peace, assurance, zeal for God and submission in times of great privation and suffering.

Shortly after Brainerd's own passing, two of those closest to him also passed through the portals of death to their eternal home. Israel, David's brother, died on 6 January and was buried in New Haven. The 'flower of the family', as Jerusha was called, was prematurely cut down by disease in February 1748, and was buried on Valentine's Day next to David in the town lot. There is no definite record of the cause of her death,

Brainerd's tomb

although some have assumed that she contracted his disease. In a footnote to Brainerd's diary, Edward makes this remark: 'It has pleased a holy and sovereign God to take away this my dear child by death ... following, after a short illness of five days, in the eighteenth year of her life.' As Pettit observes, the two deaths were 'linked in Edwards' mind'.[1] On her headstone are chiselled these words from Psalm 17: 'I shall be satisfied, when I awake, with Thy likeness.'

John Brainerd perpetuated to the best of his abilities the missionary enterprise at Cranberry which his brother had left to his supervision. Leaders such as Dickinson, Burr and Edwards had great faith in John, who in temperament, training and theological perception was so much like his brother. He was described by the missionary agency as 'a pious and ingenious youth' who carried out his task with 'diligence and success'.

But the Indian missionary station at Cranberry was not long to endure. White settlers continued to push across western New Jersey and take away the land claims of the Indians. A scheme was initiated by Edwards to secure new lands in New York, but this effort came to naught. Seven years after John bid farewell to David the Indian community of Bethel was dissolved. After years of lawsuits and pressure from the whites, John deeded the land at Wigwam Brook to Peter Deremer in July 1754.

John lived to be sixty-three years old and served as an army chaplain in the Indian wars. He was a pastor-missionary for fifteen years at the only Indian reservation ever founded in New Jersey, located at Brotherton. Early in the nineteenth century the remaining Indians moved from the reservation to New York, and in 1822 the last surviving remnants of this settlement went to Green Bay, Wisconsin. Here along Lake Michigan, far from the rolling countryside of New Jersey where God's Spirit had worked so mightily among Brainerd's

Indian tribes, their descendants, for many generations, told and retold the story of the young Yankee and his brother who had preached to them the gospel of God's grace. How different these two men were from so many other whites who cheated them, lied to them and corrupted them with their 'demon rum'!

The history of David Brainerd's witness and influence did not end on 9 October 1747 when he died. The reason for this relates to his persistent habit, formed early in life, of writing down his ideas and experiences, for some time on almost a daily basis. These papers, which were brought by John from New Jersey and left in the custody of the Edwards family, have become a treasure for the Christian church. In addition to his personal diary he composed a journal in which he chronicled the history of his ministry among the Indians. In this he explained in detail the manners and customs of the Indians, the doctrines he preached among them and the difficulties and successes he had.

The *Journal* was prepared at the insistence of the leaders of the missionary society which had hired him. It was readily published by the society, which introduced it by a preface. This account of the great revival became an important instrument in stirring up interest in the missionary work among Indians and an encouragement for the raising of funds to support other missionaries to these people. It was eagerly read not only in America but in Great Britain as well. Edwards remarked in his reflections on Brainerd's ministry that it was a remarkable providence of God that his life was preserved long enough for him to finish this for publication. 'If Brainerd had taken ill but a little sooner he had not been able to complete his Journal, and prepare a copy for the press.'[2]

At the time of Brainerd's death Edwards was already a well-known writer. His first publication in 1731 was *God Glorified in Man's Dependence*, a sermon on 1 Corinthians 1:29-31. Others followed, such as the *Narrative of Surprising*

Conversions (1736) dealing with the Great Awakening, *Sinners in the Hands of an Angry God* (1742) and *Religious Affections* (1746). This last volume was the one in which Edwards sought to explain 'the nature of true religion', as he put it, meaning the characteristics of a genuine work of divine grace in the human heart. Edwards' treatise on the affections was inclined to be technical and abstract, and was by no means universally acclaimed.

When Edwards secured the diary of his young friend, David Brainerd, whom he had nurtured and counselled during his difficult times with the college and while he was preaching among the Indians, he realized that he had found a perfect example and illustration of the qualities he had extolled in his book. Edwards decided immediately to prepare the memoir for publication. Brainerd has been spoken of as the 'phantom figure' in Edwards' work on the *Affections*. Pettit says, 'If it is true that his treatises were too abstruse to make an impact on the spiritual life of the ordinary person, then his *Life of Brainerd* represents an effort to reach a larger audience and to teach by example.'[3] Edwards agreed with the comment of the Scotsman 'Mr Willison' who, after reading Brainerd's *Journal* wrote to Edwards in March of 1749, 'Worthy Mr Brainerd was one among a thousand.'[4]

Edwards' *Life of Brainerd*, which was published in 1749, was not the first collection of gleanings from the diary to appear in print. William Bradford of Philadelphia published portions of it in 1746 under the title *Mirabilia Dei inter Indicos*, or *The Rise and Progress of a Remarkable Work of Grace Amongst a Number of the Indians in the Provinces of New Jersey and Pennsylvania*. In 1748 Philip Doddridge edited *An Abridgement of Mr David Brainerd's Journal Among the Indians*. It was Edwards' own personal edition, however, which included his comments and notations, that became the standard biography. A complete edition appeared in 1765 in

Edinburgh and an abridged American edition was published at
Worcester in 1793. In 1843 the Presbyterian Board of Publi-
cation printed an abridgement entitled *The Missionary in the
Wilderness, or Grace Displayed among the Heathen.*

Throughout the years Brainerd's life has been published
numerous times with various editorial notes and alterations.
John Wesley included it in a reduced form in volume 12 of his
collected works (Bristol, 1771-1774). A complete London
edition was printed in London in 1858 with a preface by
Horatius Bonar. Among more recent publishers have been
Moody Press, Zondervan, Intervarsity, and Marshall, Morgan
and Scott. Modern biographers include Richard Ellsworth
Day, David Wynbeek and Norman Pettit.[5]

We can well calculate that the life of David Brainerd, one
which exemplified such spiritual intensity and zeal for the
salvation of souls, would have a profound impact on all who
read it. Such has indeed proved to be the case. Only eternity
will reveal how many fires of evangelistic zeal have been lit by
the perusal of the account of this short but powerful ministry.
W. W. Sweet remarked in his *Story of Religion in America*:
'Indeed, David Brainerd dead was a more potent influence for
Indian missions and the missionary cause in general than was
David Brainerd alive.' A few examples are in order.

No name ranks higher in the annals of missionary endeavour than that of the Baptist William Carey (1761-1834) who
laid the groundwork for Christian witness in India. His three
beloved heroes were Paul the apostle, John Eliot and David
Brainerd. Early in his life he read about how Brainerd 'in three
seraphic years had burned himself out for these Indians and
God'.[6] Whenever he found his heart growing cold, he never
failed to rekindle it by turning to Brainerd's memoir. One of
the rules of the mission group of which he was a part was to
read Brainerd's life three times a year: 'Let us often look at
Brainerd in the woods of America, pouring out his very soul

before God. Prayer, secret, fervent, expectant, lies at the root of all personal godliness.'[7]

Henry Martyn (1781-1812) was a brilliant scholar at Cambridge and intended to pursue a legal career. He studied the life of Brainerd in his early twenties and was deeply stirred. His original intentions were to go to India, but when this door closed he was eventually sent to Persia where he devoted himself to the study of Arabic and Persian, as well as Hindustani and Sanskrit. His missionary career was one of bitter hardships, physical weakness and suffering and loneliness of spirit. Like Brainerd the power of his life was to be found not so much in multitudes of converts as in its exemplary faithfulness. Of Brainerd he wrote, 'I long to be like him; let me forget the world and be swallowed up in a desire to glorify God.'[8]

Robert Murray M'Cheyne (1813-1843) was a Scottish preacher whose saintly life and ministry made an impact on thousands. He was deeply moved and influenced by studying the lives and teachings of Jonathan Edwards and David Brainerd. In January 1832 he wrote, 'Life of David Brainerd. Most wonderful man! What conflicts, what depressions, desertions, strength, advancement, victories within thy torn bosom! I cannot express what I think when I think of thee. Tonight, more set upon missionary enterprise than ever.'[9] M'Cheyne spent several months as a missionary in Israel to the Jews.

Jim Elliot went to the Auca Indians of South America with the gospel of Jesus Christ in the 1950s. He, along with his flying missionary companions, was martyred in 1956. In his diary he recorded how the life of Brainerd inspired him: 'Confession of pride — suggested by David Brainerd's Diary yesterday — must become an hourly thing to me.'[10] He wrote a prayer in which he said, 'Oh, that I might receive the apostle's passion, caught from vision of Thyself, Lord Jesus.'

He then commented, 'David Brainerd's diary stirs me on to such in prayer.'[11]

Oswald J. Smith was the pastor of The People's Church, a large evangelical congregation in Toronto, Canada. Early in his life he was a missionary to Indian tribes. He says, 'So greatly was I influenced by the life of David Brainerd in the early years of my ministry that I named my youngest son after him. When I feel myself growing cold I turn to Brainerd and he always warms my heart. No man ever had a greater passion for souls. To live wholly for God was his one great aim and ambition.'[12]

Even some who did not sympathize with Brainerd's Calvinistic theology admired him. John Wesley (1703-1791) held him in the highest esteem and recommended his life to all his followers. He once said, 'Find Preachers of David Brainerd's spirit, and nothing can stand before them, but without this what will gold or silver do?'[13] In the instructions to the members of the Methodist discipline he said, 'Let every Preacher read carefully over the "Life of David Brainerd". Let us be followers of him, as he was of Christ, in absolute self-devotion, in total deadness to the world, and in fervent love to God and man.'[14] In a letter to a correspondent he commended the same qualities, although he added, 'But how much of his sorrow and pain had been prevented, if he had understood the doctrine of Christian perfection.'[15]

Brainerd's life and ministry provide a marvellous confirmation of the fact that the gospel of God's sovereign grace, when proclaimed from the lips of holy men, and with earnestness and compassion, can be a mighty force for good. It is sometimes argued that such theological concepts as man's innate depravity and inability to save himself, the vicarious atonement of Jesus Christ and the necessity of a sovereign and effectual work of the Holy Spirit to convert sinners are doctrines which chill missionary and evangelistic fervour.

The ministry of David Brainerd provided irrefutable proof that
this is not true. He was a Calvinist through and through and
found that these truths, because they are the teachings of Holy
Scripture, are eminently blessed of God. They did not dissuade
him from going forth in faith to win souls; they inspired and
encouraged him. He did not find that they hardened the hearts
of the lost; he found instead that when accompanied by the
Spirit's power, they opened up the glories of God to those who
were brought to faith.

It should be stressed, however, that the *central theme of
Brainerd's preaching was the cross of Jesus Christ.* He
emphasized over and over again in his diary and journal that
whenever he sought to change the hearts of the savage Indians
by public ministry he relied on the truth concerning the person
and work of Jesus Christ as the most effective message. He
gloried in this fact, and in an appendix to his *Narrative* entitled
'The Doctrines preached to the Indians' he says:

> I have oftentimes remarked with admiration, that
> whatever subject I have been treating upon, after having
> spent time sufficient to explain and illustrate the truths
> contained therein, I have been *naturally* and *easily* led to
> Christ as the *substance* of every subject. If I treated on
> the being and glorious perfections of God, I was thence
> *naturally* led to discourse of Christ as the only 'way to
> the Father'.
>
> If I attempted to open the deplorable misery of our
> fallen state, it was natural from thence to show the
> necessity of Christ to undertake for us, to atone for our
> sins, and to redeem us from the power of them.
>
> If I taught the commands of God, and showed our
> violation of them; this brought me in the most *easy* and
> natural way to speak of, and recommend the Lord Jesus
> Christ, as one who had 'magnified the law', which we

had broken, and who was 'become the end of it for righteousness, to every one that believes'. Never did I find so much freedom and assistance in making all the various lines of my discourses meet together and centre in Christ, as I have frequently done among these Indians.

There is more to be learned from Brainerd's life, however, than the fact that the gospel minister must have the right message. This life, so full of love to God and man, so devoted to the pursuit of holiness, so willing to sacrifice fame, fortune and even legitimate earthly comforts, shows that *the truth of God is much more effective when it is backed up by a life without moral blemish.* Like every true believer who lives close to the throne of God, Brainerd lamented and groaned over the corruptions of his mind and heart. But such confessions only show how profound was his commitment to godliness. He walked in the light as God is in the light, and the glow of his ministry has shown the way for many pilgrims who are seeking the way to heaven.

Brainerd's life sets a wonderful pattern for *faithfulness in prayer and fasting.* He not only often spent days in earnest intercession for lost souls, but he reinforced such concern by fasting. When Jesus returned from the Mount of Transfiguration and found the disciples discouraged because they were unable to cast out a demon from a child, he reminded them that such power comes only by 'prayer and fasting' (Matt. 17:21). Brainerd exemplified that standard and God chose to commit to him, as he did to Jacob of old, an abundant measure of 'power with God and man' (Gen. 32:28).

David Brainerd's life demonstrates, as few of the worthies of history have done, *what it means to live solely for the glory of God.* He intensely loved the souls of men; there is no doubt about that. He especially loved the Indians to whom he dedicated his life. But for Brainerd evangelism is more, much more, than simply seeking to do good to others. The primary motive for living and preaching is to advance Christ's kingdom, and thus honour and glorify him. In 1743 he said, 'My soul was concerned, not so much for souls as such, but rather for Christ's Kingdom, that it might appear in the world, that God might be known to be God, in the whole earth.' He entered fully into the vision of the Hebrew prophets and New Testament apostles that God's kingdom should come in glory and power among men.

In our own day 'self-love' in some religious circles is given paramount consideration as the motivation for striving for excellence in this life. Some Christian psychologists place great emphasis on the need for 'self-esteem' and 'feelings of self-worth' in the life of the believer. What a rebuke the testimony of David Brainerd is to this neo-narcissism! Not only did he strive to put his own selfish interests behind him in the pursuit of honouring his Redeemer, but he even regarded *faith itself* as consisting primarily of a perception of the inherent beauty, power and glory of the Saviour, rather than an appropriation of personal benefit. It is absolutely true that he frowned on 'selfish conversions'. Perhaps he went too far in that direction. But how refreshing, how uplifting it is to be reminded by Brainerd that the chief end of the believer is to 'glorify God and to enjoy him for ever'!

Like many great people of history Brainerd suffered frequently from mental depression. In this respect he takes his place along with such giants as Job, King David, Jonah, Martin Luther, Abraham Lincoln, Charles Haddon Spurgeon and Winston Churchill. In itself, of course, depression is neither virtuous nor healthy. But for a certain order of minds mental and emotional conflicts become a sort of school in which Jesus Christ develops the qualities that make these servants of his eminently useful. This tendency does, in fact, often accompany that poverty of spirit, meekness and brokenness that cause the truly regenerated person to turn upwards towards heaven.

Spurgeon, whose bouts with depression are well known, said, 'Before any great achievement, some measure of the same depression is very usual. Surveying the difficulties before us, our hearts sink within us... This depression comes over me whenever the Lord is preparing a larger blessing for my ministry.'[16]

On another occasion he testified that in the depths of grief God spoke powerfully to him: 'In heaviness we often learn lessons that we could never attain elsewhere ... there are views to be seen from the tops of the Alps that you could never see elsewhere. Aye, but there are beauties to be seen in the depths of the dell that ye could never see on the tops of the mountain... Men will never become great in divinity until they become great in suffering.'[17]

History demonstrates clearly that the great saints have been great sufferers. Calvin studied, preached and wrote for the edification of the church while suffering from many diseases. Madame Guyon bore her sweet testimonies out of a life of domestic tyranny. Issac Watts was plagued for many years with insomnia. Fanny Crosby composed her beautiful hymns in the darkness of physical blindness. The great orator Robert Hall carried on a dynamic ministry while suffering excruciating pain. But we do not need to look outside the Bible to learn how God uses affliction in the lives of his people. Joseph suffered rejection, Job knew great personal loss as well as physical suffering and, of course, Paul had his 'thorn in the flesh'.

The followers of Freud, Jung and Maslow can and will, no doubt, give their clinical names to the personal valleys of the Puritan mystic, David Brainerd. Even some Christians, whose temperamental inclinations make them strangers to Brainerd's struggles, will judge harshly his often confessed lack of joy. But like the rose petal which yields the sweetest fragrance when crushed, the beauty of David Brainerd's life cannot be separated from the crucible of physical pain and spiritual trauma which he experienced. This is a life that sets a high standard for the pursuit of a devout walk with God. It calls people away from a world which tempts with its charms and enticements. It beckons the Christian pilgrim to leave his own selfish pursuits and go out into the highways and byways to compel people to turn to God. It illustrates the standard set by the Saviour of men who said, 'Seek first the kingdom of God and his righteousness.'

Notes

Introduction
1. Norman Pettit, *The Life of David Brainerd* (Yale University Press, New Haven and London, 1985), p.3.

Chapter 2 — Puritanism
1. Iain H. Murray, *D. Martyn Lloyd-Jones* (The Banner of Truth, Edinburgh,1990), vol. 2, p.460.
2. Samuel Eliot Morison, *Oxford History of American People* (Oxford University Press, New York,1965) p.74.
3. J. I. Packer, *A Quest for Godliness, The Puritan Vision of the Christian Life* (Crossway Books, Wheaton, Ill., 1990), p.24.

Chapter 3 — Native Americans
1. Bill Crouse in 'Native American Religion' (*C.I.M. Outline No. 37,* n.d.), p.1.
2. Cited by A. Hyatt Verrill, *The American Indian, North, South, and Central America* (D. Appleton and Co., New York, 1927), p.59.

Chapter 4 — The Great Awakening
1. Arthur Dallimore, *George Whitefield* (Banner of Truth Trust, London, 1970) vol. 1, p.413.
2. Joseph Tracy, *The Great Awakening* (Banner of Truth Trust, Edinburgh, reprint edition 1989) p.39.
3. Dallimore, *George Whitefield,* p.ix.
4. Edwin C. Dargan, *A History of Preaching* (Baker Book House, Grand Rapids, 1974), vol. 2, p.307.
5. Benjamin Franklin, *The Autobiography of Benjamin Franklin* (Spenser Press, n.d.), p.137.
6. *Ibid.,* p.133.
7. Jonathan Edwards, *The Works of President Edwards* (Leavitt, Trow and Co., New York, 1818),vol. 3, pp.234-5.
8. *Ibid.,* p.135

Chapter 5 — Growing up in Haddam
1. A quotation from Thomas Brainerd, the biographer of David's brother John, cited by Pettit, *Life of David Brainerd*, p.33.
2. For a detailed description of Puritan worship see 'The Cure of Souls' in Allen Johnson, ed., *Fathers of New England* (Yale University Press, New Haven, 1919), vol. 2, pp.161-77.

Chapter 6 — The pilgrimage begins
1. *Memoirs of the Rev. David Brainerd*, vol. X of *The Works of President Edwards in Ten Volumes* (Leavitt, Trow and Co., New York, 1830), pp.43-4.

Chapter 7 — Yale scholar
1. David Wynbeek, *David Brainerd, Beloved Yankee* (Wm B. Eerdmans Publishing Co., Grand Rapids, 2nd ed., 1964), p.21.
2. *Ibid.*, p.21.
3. Pettit, *Life of David Brainerd*, p.38.
4. Wynbeek, *Beloved Yankee*, p.23.
5. From Dexter's *A Documentary History of Yale, 1701-1745* (New Haven, 1916) cited by Pettit, *Life of David Brainerd*, p.41.
6. Wynbeek, *Beloved Yankee*, pp.32-3.

Chapter 8 — Dealing with disgrace
1. *Memoirs of David Brainerd*, p.55.
2. *Ibid.*, p.117.
3. From Thomas Brainerd's *Life of John Brainerd*, cited by Pettit, *Life of David Brainerd*, p.44.
4. Pettit, *Life of David Brainerd*, p.45
5. *Memoirs of David Brainerd*, p.99.
6. *Ibid.*, pp.106-7.

Chapter 9 — Sanctuary
1. Pettit, *Life of David Brainerd*, p.55.
2. From David Duley Field's *The Genealogy of the Brainerd Family in the United States* (John F. Trow, New York, 1857), cited by Pettit, *Life of David Brainerd*, p.55.
3. From Archibald Alexander, *Biographical Sketches of the Log College* (Presbyterian Board of Publication, 1851), cited by Pettit, *Life of David Brainerd*, p.56.
4. Pettit, *Life of David Brainerd*, p.56.

Chapter 10 — Ingathering of the heathen
1. Pettit, *Life of David Brainerd*, p.25.

Chapter 12 — Indian mission boot camp
1. There are two spellings of this family name: 'Brainerd' and 'Brainard'. According to Lucy Abigail Brainard in *The Genealogy of the Brainerd-Brainard Family America, 1649-1908*, the former is the French spelling and the latter the German (p.13).

2. Wynbeek, *Beloved Yankee,* p.65.

3. Among the historians who attribute a romantic relationship to David and Jerusha are Alexander V. G. Allen, Henry Bamford Parkes, Ola Elizabeth Winslow, Alfred Owen Aldridge, Elizabeth Dodds and Perry Miller.

Rev. David D. Field, author of *The Genealogy of the Brainerd Family in the United States,* says, 'They had anticipated great happiness in married life in this world…' (p.283).

Thomas Brainerd, who was in possession of the original diaries of David and John Brainerd, seemed to have no doubt that they were betrothed. 'The relationship of David Brainerd to this young lady,' he writes, 'constitutes one of the most romantic incidents of his personal diary' (*Life of John Brainerd,* p.121).

Modern biographers Richard Ellsworth Day (*Flagellant on Horseback*) and David Wynbeek are of the same mind.

On the other side of the issue it should be mentioned that Samuel Hopkins, the first biographer of Edwards and a personal friend of Brainerd, ignores this relationship altogether. Also in a privately written essay 'The Romance of David Brainerd and Jerusha Edwards' by Patricia J. Tracy, the engagement theory is debunked, based on the fact that in Edwards' original publication there is no mention of it. This essay, printed privately in 1985, is a part of a booklet *Three Essays in Honor of the Publication of 'The Life of David Brainerd'* (Yale University Press) by Rev. Winthrop Brainerd, Norman Pettit and Patricia Tracy.

Chapter 13 — Developing a theology
1. Joseph A. Conforti, *Samuel Hopkins and the New Divinity Movement* (Christian University Press, Grand Rapids, 1981), p.27.
2. An interesting discussion of the ecstatic experiences of Sarah Edwards is found in 'To the Breaking Point and Back,' chapter VIII in Elizabeth D. Dodds' book, *Marriage to a Difficult Man* (Westminster Press, Philadelphia, 1979), pp.99-106.
3. Samuel Hopkins, D.D., *Works* (Boston: Doctrinal Tract and Book Society, 1852), vol. 1, p.34.

Chapter 14 — Into the wilderness
1. This quotation is from Wynbeek (*Beloved Yankee,* p.86). It is not in the *Memoirs* which are vol. 10 of Edwards' *Works.*
2. Wynbeek, *Beloved Yankee,* p.87.
3. *Ibid.,* p.88

Chapter 15 — Passion for the lost
1. Elsie Singmaster, *Pennsylvania's Susquehanna* (J. Horace McFarland Company, Harrisburg, Penn., 1950), p.1.
2. Wynbeek, *Beloved Yankee,* p.116.

Chapter 16 — The winter of the soul
1. Wynbeek, *Beloved Yankee,* p.124.

Chapter 17 — Harbingers of revival
1. Wynbeek, *Beloved Yankee,* p.126.

Chapter 18 — Springs in the desert
1. Wynbeek, *Beloved Yankee,* pp.148-9.

Chapter 19 — The windows of heaven open
1. This information is found in Wynbeek, *Beloved Yankee,* pp.155-8.

Chapter 21 — Region of the shadow of death
1. Wynbeek, *Beloved Yankee,* p.136.
2. C. Hale Sipe, *The Indian Chiefs of Pennsylvania* (The Ziegler Printing Co., Butler, Pa, 1927), p.95.
3. Wynbeek, *Beloved Yankee,* p.137.

Chapter 24 — Bethel, the house of God
1. Wynbeek, *Beloved Yankee,* p.177
2. *Ibid.*
3. *Ibid.,* pp.177-8.
4. *Ibid.,* p.203.

Chapter 27 — A fateful choice
1. *Memoirs of Edwards,* vol 1. of *Works* (G. & C. & H. Carville, New York, 1830), pp 114-15.
2. *Memoirs of David Brainerd,* p.412.
3. *Ibid.*
4. *Ibid.*

Chapter 29 — Falling shadows
1. Wynbeek, *Beloved Yankee,* p.232.

Chapter 30 — Passing the torch
1. *Memoirs of David Brainerd,* p.379.
2. Robert Ellis Thompson, D.D., *A History of the Presbyterian Churches in the United States* (The Christian Literature Co., New York, 1895), p.35.
3. Wynbeek, *Beloved Yankee,* p.91.

Chapter 31 — The coming chariot
1. Wynbeek, *Beloved Yankee,* p.239. This respected Brainerd scholar affirms anew his conviction that they were intending to marry, had it been possible.
2. *Memoirs of David Brainerd,* p.412. The dying missionary's statement of his greater love for his brother John than all others, including Jerusha, seems to militate against any intention on his part to make her his wife. But considering the fact that he had no prospect of living, such a candid remark is not really inconsistent with a profound attachment to her which in other circumstances would have been sufficient to make the basis of a marriage.

Chapter 32 — One among a thousand
1. Pettit, *Life of David Brainerd,* p.70
2. *Memoirs of David Brainerd,* p.444.

3. Pettit, *Life of David Brainerd,* p.74.
4. Dwight's *Memoir of Edwards,* p.271.
5. A more complete list may be found in Pettit, *Life of David Brainerd,* pp.77-9.
6. S. Pearce Carey, *William Carey* (Hodder and Stoughton, London, n.d.), p.51.
7. *Ibid.,* p.249.
8. Wynbeek, *Beloved Yankee,* p.236.
9. *The Works of Rev. Robert Murray M'Cheyne* (Robert Carter and Brothers, New York, 1853), vol. 1, p.20.
10. Elisabeth Elliot, ed., *The Journals of Jim Elliot* (Fleming H. Revell, Grand Rapids, 1994), p.143.
11. *Ibid.,* p.166
12. Oswald J. Smith, *David Brainerd, His Message for Today* (Marshall, Morgan and Scott, Ltd, London, 1949), p.vii.
13. *The Works of John Wesley* (Zondervan, Grand Rapids, n.d.), vol. 3, p.294.
14. *Ibid.,* vol. 8, p.328.
15. *Ibid.,* vol. 12, p.284.
16. Elisabeth Scoglund, 'Spurgeon's Private Battle,' *Eternity,* May 1979, p.56.
17. Elisabeth Scoglund, 'The Gold of Depression,' *Eternity,* June 1959, p.50.

Index